Into the Mother Tongue

A Case Study in Early Language
Development

Clare Painter

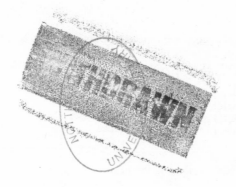

Frances Pinter (Publishers)
London and Dover, N.H.

First edition published in Great Britain in 1984 by
Frances Pinter (Publishers) Limited
5 Dryden Street, London WC2E 9NW

Published in the United States of America in 1984 by
Frances Pinter (Publishers), 51 Washington Street,
Dover, New Hampshire

British Library Cataloguing in Publication Data

Painter, Clare
 Into the mother tongue—(Open linguistics series)

 1. Children—Language
 I. Title   II. Series
  401'.9   B1139.L3
ISBN 0-36187-463-3

Library of Congress Cataloging in Publication Data

Painter, Clare, 1947-
 Into the mother tongue.

 (Open linguistics series)
 Bibliography: p.
 Includes index.
 1. Language acquisition. 2. Halliday, M. A. K.
(Michael Alexander Kirkwood), 1925-   ; I. Title.
II. Series.
P118.P26 1984   401'.9   84-7630
ISBN 0-86187-463-3

Typeset by Joshua Associates, Oxford
Printed in Great Britain by SRP, Ltd, Exeter

Into the Mother Tongue

Open Linguistics Series

The *Open Linguistics Series*, to which this book makes a welcome contribution, is 'open' in two senses. First, it provides an open forum for works associated with any school of linguistics or with none. Linguistics has now emerged from a period in which many (but never all) of the most lively minds in the subject seemed to assume that transformational generative grammar—or at least something fairly closely derived from it—would provide the main theoretical framework for linguistics for the forseeable future. In Kuhn's terms, linguistics had appeared to some to have reached the 'paradigm' stage. Reality today is very different. More and more scholars are examining approaches to language that were formerly scorned for not accepting as central the particular set of concerns highlighted in the Chomskyan approach—such as Halliday's systemic theory, Lamb's stratificational model and Pike's tagmemics—while others are developing new or partly new theories. The series is open to all approaches, then—including work in the generativist–formalist tradition.

The second sense in which the series is 'open' is that it encourages works that open out 'core' linguistics in various ways: to encompass discourse and the description of natural texts; to explore the relationships between linguistics and its neighbouring disciplines such as psychology, sociology, philosophy, artificial intelligence, and cultural and literary studies; and to apply it in fields such as education and language pathology.

This book is 'open' in various of these ways. But above all it contributes significantly to the field of child language studies—both in that it supplies additional empirical support for the pioneering concepts developed in Halliday's *Learning How to Mean* (1975), and in that it takes those proposals further in a number of significant ways.

Open Linguistics Series Editor
Robin P. Fawcett, The Polytechnic of Wales

Modal Expressions in English, Michael R. Perkins
Text and Tagmeme, Kenneth L. Pike and Evelyn G. Pike
The Semiotics of Culture and Language, eds: Robin P. Fawcett,
   M. A. K. Halliday, Sydney M. Lamb and Adam Makkai
Functional Approaches to Writing, Barbara Cauture
Language of the Nuclear Arms Debate, Paul Chilton

Contents

List of Figures

Foreword

This book is an account of an important phase—perhaps the most important phase—in the development of a human child. It is an account of the transition from child tongue to mother tongue.

Clare Painter has documented in great detail the language learning experience of her son Hal during the first few years of his life, observing how he communicated and how he responded to the communications of others. She shows how, long before he begins using words and structures, he is already 'meaning' in a clear and consistent way, using symbols he has created for himself. These symbols express the things he wants to say at the time, like *ma* 'I want that, give it to me', and *ga* 'that's interesting; what's going on?'

Early vocalizations like these are not unsuccessful attempts at English; they are expressions in their own right. It is not just that they are not English words; what is significant about them is that they are not words at all. The child tongue, or 'protolanguage', is not constructed the way the mother tongue is. It is a code of a different kind, without either words or structures. It is related to the adult language in much the same way as is the language of other species, such as chimpanzees and dolphins, as far as we can tell.

When the time comes for Hal to move into the mother tongue, early in his second year, he starts creating a new language that is much more than a simple inventory of signs. He has to take the giant step—taken in the course of evolution by our ancestors hundreds of thousands or perhaps millions of years ago, and no doubt over a long period of time—of inventing a grammar: a purely abstract network of relations that will enable him to code highly complex meanings into relatively simple sequences of sounds. The meanings are too rich to be encoded directly into speech; there has to be an intermediate stage. This mediating code consists of words in structures —a lexicogrammar, in the terminology of linguistics.

Hal, of course, has a model, the language that is spoken around him. Reading Clare Painter's account we can follow how Hal made this critical transition, from the simple (but no less functional) two-level system of the protolanguage to the distinctively human three-level system that we call language, in one of its many varieties. She takes the story through to the point where the mother tongue is firmly established, showing what meanings Hal has construed by this time and what structures he had for expressing them.

What emerges very clearly is the way Hal builds up his language on a functional foundation, as a mode of action and as a mode of thought. These are the twin pillars on which every human language is supported, and it is important for us to understand its developmental origins. Hal is developing a resource, which is at one and the same time a resource for doing—a way of interacting with the people around him and of getting them to organize his world for him; and a resource for learning—a way of representing to himself and others the patterns of his experience, of making sense out of what happens in the world. To do this he constructs the network that is at the centre of the adult grammar, the network of options that we call a clause. The clause is the abstract coding process by which these two motifs are brought together and combined into a unified message.

We are shown how Hal achieved this. But Clare Painter's book is more than a detailed record of one child's progress towards maturity. She offers a theoretically rich interpretation of the developmental processes involved. The systematic expansion of the child's meaning potential is explained step by step by reference to the functions he is making language serve for him at the time, and the functional, or rather 'metafunctional', organization of the adult language to which he is gradually approximating. Grammatical structures like Process-Medium-Agent or Subject-Finite-Predicator-Adjunct are shown to arise as symbolic instruments which make it possible for the child to reflect on and to act on his environment. With her insights into developmental linguistics Clare Painter is able to provide both a dynamic representation of a child's emergent language and an interpretation of how it develops into a language of the adult kind.

The study of child language, and of how children build up a semantic system, is now recognized to be fundamental to our understanding both of the nature and functions of language and of human learning and human development. Those concerned with the tasks and problems of early childhood education, or with developmental disorders and learning disabilities, are well aware of the central place that language takes in all human learning and experience; but they can justifiably point out that no adequate picture of the early years has yet been given. Such a picture will not of course emerge from any one piece of research. But Clare Painter's work shows the rich results that can be obtained from the intensive study of a single child, in spontaneous interaction in natural contexts, and provides a point of departure for further explorations of this complex but rewarding field.

University of Sydney   M. A. K. Halliday
March, 1984

Introduction

The major part of this book comprises a case study of one child's development of language from the age of nine months to two years. The data are interpreted from a systemic theoretical viewpoint, based on M. A. K. Halliday's account of language development, reported in his book *Learning How to Mean* (1975a) and elsewhere (e.g. Halliday 1978b, 1979, 1984a).

Halliday has made a number of claims about the nature of language and the process of developing it, based heavily on a single case study, that of his own son, Nigel. In outline, Halliday postulates that from a very early age—about nine months—the infant creates a vocal communication system which in certain respects may be deemed to be language. This 'child tongue' or 'protolanguage', as it has been termed, is eventually abandoned in favour of the mother tongue language. But there is a certain continuity between the two systems, such that for a time (perhaps six to eight months) the linguistic system is in transition between the two. This is not to say that the language oscillates between the earlier and later systems in some way, but that the child adopts an interim strategy for organizing his linguistic resources on the way to developing an essentially adult system. This interim mode of organization, which Halliday calls the 'transition', has links with the earlier protolanguage and provides a way into the adult language.

Since Halliday's work first appeared, there has been a wealth of research into language development, particularly into the origins of first words, and the prelinguistic antecedents of linguistic communication. While some of this can be related to Halliday's work at various points, there has been no subsequent research carried out within the same theoretical framework, partly perhaps because it has not been very well understood. Thus, the systemic theory of language development is still based on a detailed study of only one child. One important aim of the present research is therefore to take the first steps towards extending the data base on which the theory rests. This is clearly vital if we are to begin to build up a picture of which aspects of Nigel's development were idiosyncratic to himself, and which may prove to be common ground. The present study follows Halliday's in being again a case study of a single child, since the orientation of the theory suggests that a set of comparable longitudinal studies constitutes the ideal data base for language development research. It will be seen that the case study of the current subject, Hal, largely serves to support Halliday's claims as outlined above.

A second goal of this book has been to provide a more detailed step-by-step linguistic description of development, particularly of the transition period, than was done for Nigel. This is in order to present the data as explicitly as possible and to provide as clearly empirical a base as possible for claims about the changing nature of the language. In this way Halliday's ideas should be made more accessible, and the detailed descriptions should also point up issues arising from an attempt to adapt to a developmental study the theoretical apparatus and formalism created for a synchronic description of adult language.

In this book, the evolution of Hal's language is described in Chapters 4 to 9, following an account of the nature of the data and methods of collection and analysis given in Chapter 3. Before coming to this, a brief sketch will be given in the opening chapter of earlier language development work which has provided the context for current studies. Then the systemic theory of language will be discussed, in both general and developmental terms, in Chapter 2, so that it will be made clear how systemic theory differs from other approaches, and in what respects it has advantages as the basis for a study of early language development.

1 Developmental research since the 1960s: non-systemic approaches

Any discussion of language acquisition, any description of an individual child's development of language, has to take as its starting point some view as to the phenomenon being 'acquired'. What counts as development will depend on the researcher's view of the nature of language, even if he or she is primarily exploring the psychological factors involved. A theory of language development is thus never separable from a theory of language, and the shifts in emphasis in child language studies over the past twenty years reflect very clearly the changes in the preoccupations of linguists. In order to explain why this study uses a systemic-functional framework rather than one more popular with recent child language researchers, I would like to give some preliminary account of the state of the art in language development research, pointing up its relation to considerations of linguistic theory. This will involve a brief review of earlier work which has provided the intellectual context for current research, as well as an outline of the principles of systemic theory which inform the approach to language development to be explored in this book.

Language as syntactic structure

With the advent of the 'Chomskyan revolution' in linguistics, language was redefined as 'a set of sentences' (Chomsky 1957: 13), grammar as 'a system of rules that . . . assigns structural descriptions to sentences' (Chomsky 1965: 8), and the goal of linguistic theory as accounting for the knowledge that native speakers have of their language. Chomsky's work led to a wealth of language acquisition studies and kindled a number of lively controversies, but I will not be concerned here with tracing the history of transformational studies in child language in any detail. My interest is rather in the way that developments of the late 1960s and of the 1970s in child language studies grew out of a dissatisfaction with the received transformational view in linguistic theory generally, and among child language researchers in particular. Although some of this more recent work appears more compatible with the systemic approach which I shall be adopting, it has evolved from the same American structuralist tradition and does in fact share some of the same preconceptions about the nature of language as the earlier work it is repudiating. I hope to illustrate this in outlining the course of language development research over recent years, and thus to clarify the distinctiveness of the systemic theoretical approach.

David MacNeill may be taken as a typical and influential exemplar of the classic transformational line on language acquisition. In his paper 'The capacity for the ontogenesis of grammar' he says:

Every language contains the same basic syntactic categories. Sentences, Noun Phrases, Predicate Phrases and so forth. Every language adheres to the same basic grammatical relations among these categories—subject and predicate, verb and object, modifier and head, and others. All such syntactic universals are aspects of the deep structure of sentences. [MacNeill 1971: 21.]

He further claims that knowledge of deep structure is innate, since:

In acquiring the transformations that define language children learn to relate deep and surface structures, but the deep structures of sentences are never displayed in the form of examples, stimuli, responses or anything else. They are abstract and, for one who does not already know the language, inaccessible. [MacNeill 1971: 18.]

Various longitudinal studies of the 1960s (Braine 1963; Brown and Bellugi 1964; Miller and Ervin 1964), taking a traditional distributional approach to analysis, had all come up with a description in terms of two word classes—Pivot + Open (and variations on this). MacNeill in this paper goes on to discuss such data as evidence that the child has knowledge of deep structure from the time of 'earliest patterned speech'.

The following interrelated points may be said to characterize the transformational view of language development:

  (i) Universal deep grammar is innate.
 (ii) Following from this, external stimuli, whether situational or linguistic, are not of primary importance to the child, or therefore a primary focus for the researcher.
(iii) Also following from (i) and from Chomsky's competence/ performance distinction, language is viewed as the 'property' of an individual.
 (iv) Language is in essence syntactic structure—a set of sentences defined by structural rules.

(v) Following from this, the production of the first syntagms—the 'two-word stage'—is the crucial milestone to be explored in acquisition studies and mean length of utterance (MLU) is an appropriate measure of development.

Even before the hegemony of the T.G. view of language foundered on disagreements over the treatment of semantics, views such as Mac-Neill's were being challenged at various points. On the fourth point listed above, Lois Bloom's 1968 thesis was a landmark in its insistence on the importance of taking situational context into consideration in interpreting early syntactic forms. In her view, the very requirements of an explicit generative grammar necessitated this. For example, one of her subjects produced both:

no dirty soap (rejecting a used piece of soap in favour of a new bar), and
no pocket (when unable to find a pocket in M's skirt). [Bloom 1970: 172]

This clear difference in meaning between the two surface forms should determine that the two Ss do not receive the same structural description—as Pivot + Open or anything else. But to appreciate that they have distinct deep structures requires close attention to situational context by the analyst.

Language as semantic structure

Bloom was raising methodological issues which came to the fore when using a generative grammar for a specific corpus, rather than challenging the theory itself. But soon there was a more radical move from a psychologist, I. M. Schlesinger, who again stressed the importance of environmental factors, this time from the child's rather than the analyst's point of view. He outlined a case (Schlesinger 1971) for a 'performance model' which he felt avoided the necessity of assuming innate knowledge of linguistic structure, and in effect challenged most of the transformational tenets listed above. In his theory the child moves not from deep to surface structure, but from intention or 'I-marker' to expressed utterance. An I-marker is a formal representation of those of the speaker's intentions which get verbal expression, and comprises concepts (which appear to be words in base morphological form) and certain relations holding between them, such as Agent-Action or Action–Object. These relations are: 'given in the situation and not imposed by language. I-markers are determined by the innate *cognitive* capacity of the child. There is nothing specifically linguistic about this capacity.' [Schlesinger 1971: 70.] As he stresses in a later paper, 'cognitive structures'— the child's mental representation of the here-and-now situation— are 'infinitely richer and more variegated than the I-markers which function in language' (Schlesinger 1974: 144). Although in this last paper Schlesinger seems prepared to consider that language may come to influence cognitive structures, his position is basically that I-markers represent a selection of cognitive structures operative at the moment of utterance, and that the same elements are present in both, i.e. words/concepts and relations of the Agent–Action type. Thus the material ongoing situation is composed of elements some of which are selected for mental representation. Some of these mentally represented elements are then further selected for verbal expression. Clearly in this theory linguistic elements and structures are very closely identified with the extralinguistic reality they are seen as representing.

The publication in 1968 by Charles Fillmore of his paper 'A case for case' was to provide a possible linguistic underpinning for Schlesinger's approach. Fillmore (1968: 17) suggested that since 'no semantically constant value is associated with the notion of "Subject of"', the Subject should be recognized as an exclusively surface structure phenomenon, and not necessarily even a universal one. This clearly challenges the view of MacNeill quoted earlier. Fillmore proposed that the basic phrase structure rule should be expressed in relational terms, i.e.:

$$S \longrightarrow M(\text{modality}) + P(\text{proposition})$$
$$P \longrightarrow \text{Verb} + \text{Agent}$$
$$\text{Verb} + \text{Object} (+ \text{Instrument})$$
$$\text{Verb} + \text{Dative etc.}$$

rather than in the traditional class terms $(S \rightarrow NP + VP)$ from which the 'Subject of' relation can be derived. These 'deep' cases of Agent, Object, etc., were to be converted into surface elements such as Subject by various rules.

A universal deep structure element such as Agent is much more readily approachable as part of Schlesinger's linguistically translated cognitive structure than a supposedly purely formal element like Subject, and child language researchers in the 1970s found this a very congenial viewpoint. Melissa Bowerman was one of the first to make use of it (Bowerman 1973), and in the title of a later paper derived from her book she redefines the key question of language acquisition research as: 'Structural relationships in children's utterances: syntactic or semantic?' (Bowerman 1978).

She finds that children do not appear at first to

understand basic grammatical relations [i.e. 'surface syntactic' relations] or the constituent structure they entail . . . [but] learn simple order rules for combining words which in their understanding perform semantic functions such as agent, action and object acted upon. [Bowerman 1978: 230.]

The child's task is then redefined as learning to code 'semantic relations' such as Agent–Action into 'syntactic' structures such as Subject–Predicate, in an ontogenetic move which parallels Fillmore's derivational path from semantics to syntax. Bowerman concludes that the notion of *subject* emerges when the child eventually realizes that nouns in various semantic roles (such as *John* in *John likes food* and *John breaks the window*) are 'treated identically'. It is at this point that the child is seen as making a *linguistic* generalization. This view that the child gradually learns the syntactic encoding of semantic relations would still seem an appropriate one for theories which view syntax as an arbitrary formal device for expressing a certain kind of meaning, and is still current, as we shall see.

At about this time several researchers began to question the assumption that language begins with two-word speech and turned their attention to the period of the 'holophrase' or 'single word at a time'. This stage obviously presents a challenge to the view of language as structure, whether semantic or syntactic. One of the best-known studies is that of Greenfield and Smith (1976), which is explicitly based on a modified version of Fillmore's case grammar, and their thesis is that language can still be viewed in structural terms even at this early period.

They accept that two elements are required for a semantic relation, but suggest that in the early stages of language, verbal elements may combine with non-verbal situational elements to produce semantic, though not syntactic, structure. In distinguishing the two they remark: 'To call an isolated word an agent is reasonable, provided that an action has occurred; to call it a subject is ludicrous.' [Greenfield and Smith 1976: 16.] It is clear here that 'Agent' is seen as part of a situation, while 'Subject' is part of a sentence. Their claim is that 'situations are structured like sentences on a cognitive level' (Greenfield and Smith 1976: 54), and language development is viewed as the process of making more and more elements of the situation verbally explicit. As they put it:

Children might use the context of real world events as a structured framework which could be gradually filled in with verbal forms. [Greenfield and Smith 1976: 30.]

Base structure is a purely cognitive or conceptual one gradually filled in with words at the surface level of expression. [Greenfield and Smith 1976: 201.]

Thus, like Schlesinger they assume that the situation contains inherent semantic structure and that there is an isomorphism between situation/cognitive structure and deep linguistic structure. They are supported in this view by the tendency of case grammatical theorists to use 'real world' rather than linguistic criteria to define cases (see discussion pp. 21–2), and by the linguist's assumption that all languages embody the same case grammar—since deep grammar is regarded as universal.

When it comes to interpreting language data which do not fit into the main case categories defined for adult language, the inadequacy of postulating such categories unconstrained by a consideration of linguistic oppositions becomes apparent. One such example would be Greenfield and Smith's 'Modification of an event' role, of which the following are examples cited:

(i) *too* in *too hot* (as M wipes child's face with hot flannel).
(ii) *wait* in the sequence *pull, wait* (as the child verbalizes a decision/self-instruction to pause before pulling a handle).
(iii) *more* in *more round* (when M picks up toy child has been spinning. (Greenfield and Smith 1976: 154–5.)

Too could certainly be classed as a Modifier in the structure *too hot*, and perhaps *more round* could be argued as a comparable structure. But on the grounds they offer for 'Modification of an event', Greenfield and Smith would be led to treat nominal group Sub-modifiers as clause functions in adult language too. Then both of these are classed with the verb *wait* which appears to be included simply because of its specific lexical meaning, and it would be equally true of adult speech that any instruction to *wait* would 'modify' the event that was going to have taken place. Setting up linguistic categories on such *ad hoc* grounds is no more satisfactory for analysis of child language than for any other kind of language.

An alternative view to that of Greenfield and Smith is to be found in Lois Bloom's study of the single-word period which was published before theirs, but worked on concurrently (Bloom 1973). She emphatically rejects the approach of assigning semantic functions to single-word utterances, and questions Schlesinger's treatment of semantic roles as identical with cognitive structures, pointing out that case roles are linguistic categories.

Bloom asserts that children have not learnt case relations at the single-word stage. In her view they can do two things: they can name objects and they can talk about 'the relations in experience among persons, objects and events' (Bloom 1973: 45). An example given of the latter is the child uttering *chair* on going towards it at mealtime. In Bloom's view, when children know enough words, they can talk about more than one aspect of an event or relation in successive single-word utterances, but she finds no evidence for a match with any underlying linguistic (structural) representation. Before mastering syntax the child is viewed as learning words to encode different aspects of experience or behaviour, that is to say different aspects of 'cognitive representations' such as 'locating events', 'persons-moving events', or 'persons-affecting-objects events'. By hearing adults talk about such events, the child comes to 'discover the semantic relations that exist between words' (Bloom 1973: 119–20). It is not until words have been designated into linguistic classes that the child can learn to sequence them in semantically appropriate ways.

Bloom does not enter the semantics vs. syntax debate. Her account instead draws a sharp distinction between lexis and grammar (i.e. structure), since she distinguishes between lexical representations of 'cognitive categories' and the 'semantic-syntactic' relations embodied in sentences (Bloom 1973: 55). Her work is perhaps most important for its emphasis on the distinction between extra-linguistic experience and linguistic coding, which leads her to regard the assignment of structural functions where there is no linguistic structure as a meaningless task. She also gives explicit recognition to the fact that the child's environment is a linguistic as well as a material one, something which is easily lost sight of by others. On the other hand she has no adequate framework within which to provide any explicit description of the child's linguistic system at the one-word stage. Indeed she suggests he has not got one—just a developing cognitive system and a repertoire of words he will in due course learn to stick together into sentences.

Under the influence of Chomsky, the development of language was seen as the acquisition of a specific set of rules defining sentence structures, rather than in terms of developing ways of interacting with others, developing self awareness, learning to act on the environment, create imaginary worlds, etc., by means of language. Common preoccupations during this time, then, were with such matters as whether the child learnt order rules or grammatical category rules first, and the focus tended to be on the difference between the child's utterances and 'equivalent' adult speech.

Moreover, one important characteristic of all these researchers taking some kind of post T.G. 'semantic' approach to child language, is what may be termed their 'experiential bias'. By this I mean the heavy concentration on the role of language in encoding informational or representational content.

Schlesinger, for example, interprets a vocative *Mummy* as having the following underlying structure: 'Agent (I) Action (demand) Animate Object (Mummy)' (Schlesinger 1974: 139). Here, what he is treating in terms of case roles clearly relates to the status of the utterance as a call or summoning of some sort. In his model, where illocutionary aspects of the utterance have no recognition, and everything has to be interpreted in case terms, he is forced to posit such 'underlying' elements which will never get a 'surface' realization.

Since they are explicitly following Fillmore's model, Greenfield and Smith do recognize both 'modality' and 'propositional' elements to their structure, but like Fillmore they concentrate on the latter. Their treatment of modality is at worst confusing and at best imprecise. They allow for early utterances which have no representational content, such as *bye-bye*, or non-specific demanding or rejecting terms, or pointing while uttering a nonsense syllable, and describe these as 'performatives', in a rather curious adaptation of Austin's (1962) notion. These are regarded as pure modality elements, but they claim that after learning names: 'The expression of mode is relegated to intonation and non-linguistic means, and aspects of the event are encoded' (Greenfield and Smith 1976: 52). Despite this, the word *want*, among others, is categorized by them as a volition modality element.

While they take the step of recognizing that utterances simultaneously express both case and illocutionary aspects of meaning, only with the case category of 'Object' do they cross-classify in terms of the two different modalities they recognize—the indicative and the volitional. Furthermore, there is no systematic analysis of intonation, the chief carrier of modality, except to mention in passing that the child tends to whine when he wants something, or that one child requested names 'in a way that was intonationally distinct' (Greenfield and Smith 1976: 157). Case roles on the other hand are analysed in very explicit detail.

Even the way they talk about mode being 'relegated' to intonational expression, and as 'not encoded' because not expressed lexically, suggests both that modality becomes less important as the child develops, and that the kinds of linguistic resources that typically realize it are somehow less worthy of consideration.

Bloom for her part observes that her subject used *more* to request additional food and then to request a repetition of being tickled.

This to her is 'the same word [being] ascribed to referents with different figurative properties' (Bloom 1974: 289), and she wonders what could 'lead a child to extend the meaning of a word like *more* to refer to aspects of objects and events that in themselves differ both perceptually and functionally' (Bloom 1978: 164). Obviously the common factor is not to be sought in the nature of the world in terms of food and tickling as such, but in the nature of the utterances as requests or demands of a parallel kind.

Language as communication

Perhaps the most striking characteristic of the latest round of child language studies (Bates 1976; Bates *et al.* 1979a,b; Bruner 1975a,b; Dore 1973, 1975, 1978; Moerk 1977; Ochs and Schieffelin 1979) has been a counterbalancing focus on 'communicative function', 'pragmatics' or 'speech acts', rather than grammatical structure. And this shift in orientation has led to an interest in earlier stages in the language development process. Clearly if early language is viewed in terms of communicative acts of one sort or another, it becomes feasible to seek its antecedents in prelinguistic communicative (or other) behaviour. To quote Waterson and Snow on this point:

Recognition that what and how the child communicates is the true object of language acquisiton research has greatly expanded the age range studied. Behaviours of infants as young as 9–10 months can be identified as truly communicative. [Waterson and Snow 1978: xxiii.]

Despite this different stance, a number of these studies are nonetheless compatible with the work of Schlesinger and Greenfield and Smith. Bruner, for example, is interested in 'the possible isomorphism between grammatical structure and the structure of action' (Bruner 1975b: 5). This is something very much in tune with their approaches. But Bruner's concern is largely with the manner in which the child initially develops concepts such as 'agent'. His conclusion is that the repetitive behaviours of caretakers and infants in joint interactions consist of sequences of substitutable acts, claiming that: 'At the outset, in this process, the mother is almost always the agent of the action, the child the recipient or "experiencer".' (Bruner 1975b: 13.) Later the roles may be reversed and interchanged. Bruner sums up his position on the structure of action as follows:

the infant first learns prelinguistically to make the conceptual distinctions embodied in case grammar, and having mastered privileges of occurrence in action sequences in which these distinctions are present, begins to insert non-standard signals that mark the distinctions . . . In time . . . the signalling becomes more conventional. [Bruner 1975b: 5.]

Thus what characterizes Bruner's approach to the ontogeny of case relations is both an interest in the move from prelinguistic to linguistic behaviour, and also his notion, derived from careful observations of infant behaviour, of 'joint action formats' from which the child may learn to understand such role relations as: 'referencer and recipient, demander and complier, seeker and finder, task initiator and accomplisher, actor and prohibitor.' (Bruner 1975a: 261.)

This is therefore a specifically interactive view of the nature of concept development, and one may compare Bruner's account of the development of the 'agent concept' from role-shifting in games and other formats with a more orthodox approach from Moerk. The latter talks of the child producing effects on objects and concludes simply:

He has to become aware, therefore, of the concept of ± agent from his own activity as well as from observing the acts of other persons. [Moerk 1977: 88.]

As an account of infant experience Bruner's certainly seems more revealing, though the roles that Bruner suggests as arising from these formats could probably be viewed equally well in terms of the development of dialogue roles (speaker—respondent, requester—acceder to request, etc.) as in terms of case roles as he does.

Although Bruner does not make this suggestion, it is not because he only recognizes case structures in language. His work is also distinctive in its recognition of the non-experiential area of language. In this regard he suggests a corresponding isomorphism between 'attention structures' and the Subject–Predicate structure of sentences, which he regards as corresponding to a Topic–Comment distinction.

He describes attention as:

A feature extracting routine in which there is a steady movement back and forth between selected features and wholes . . . . A process of positing wholes (topics) to which parts or features may be related. [Bruner 1975b: 4.]

He then claims that: 'Topic-comment structure in language permits an easy passage from feature to its context and back.' (Bruner 1975b: 4.) It is not obvious to me how a typical Subject–Predicate child sentence such as *mummy cut bread* illustrates this process, and the linguistic process of topicalization which is cited as evidence for the parallelism between Topic–Comment structure and 'visual inspection' is not one very prominent in early language. In any case, those linguists who have explored the notion of Topic are united, if in nothing else, in agreement that 'Topic' cannot simply be equated with surface Subject in English. And of course in some languages, such as Japanese, it is not even encoded by word order, although Bruner's thesis seems to imply this as a universal norm.

In sum, Bruner's view of case relations makes the now familiar assumption that these are situational, not linguistic, categories, though the fact that 'recipient' and 'experiencer', which he uses as synonyms, are quite distinct case roles in all linguistic analyses should perhaps have hinted that making such direct correspondences between adult grammar and specific situation types, such as give-and-take games, is not a valid undertaking. And his view of early mother tongue utterances as a conventional form of what baby vocalizations already encode is one that this case study will show cannot be supported.

Where non-experiential structure is concerned, Bruner fails to distinguish two quite distinct kinds of structure—the 'interpersonal' and the 'textual' in systemic terms (see p. 24). In equating the Subject–Predicate structure with a Topic–Comment one, he manages, in a paper entitled 'The ontogenesis of speech acts', to ignore any consideration of illocutionary force and its relation to the grammatical system of MOOD which one would expect to be the focus of interest.[1]

For a genuine exploration of the ontogenesis of speech acts we must turn to the work of John Dore. Dore (1973) defines a speech act as a linguistic message communicating both information or conceptual content (via the proposition) and illocutionary force. The latter conveys how the utterance is to be taken, expressing the speaker's attitude to self, hearer and proposition. At times Dore appears to equate 'speech act' with illocutionary force, for example when the child's task is defined as one of acquiring a 'repertoire of speech act types', which are then defined in illocutionary terms only. At any event it is clearly with the forces rather than propositions of utterances that he is chiefly concerned.

Like Greenfield and Smith, Dore regards prosodic features as the most significant carriers of proto-illocutionary force or 'primitive force', as he calls it. He explores this aspect more seriously than they do, observing that four tone contours appear to carry such meaning

---

[1] Bruner states in his introduction: 'The relation between the instrumental or illocutionary function of an utterance and its grammatical structure is crucial to language acquisition . . . we shall examine this matter in more concrete detail later'. However, what in fact get examined are 'action structures' and case grammar, 'attention structures' and topic-comment.

in his corpus of pre-school data. He outlines how such recognizable prosodies become systematically associated over time with identifiable contexts, and where Greenfield and Smith concentrate their analysis on case roles, he focuses on primitive forces.

Dore's work is very valuable in its foregrounding of the communicative aspect of the linguistic system and in its careful distinction between the force of an utterance (e.g. *Can you pass the salt?* as a command) and its grammatical form (e.g. *Can you pass the salt?* as an interrogative). This is of course a very well recognized distinction, and there is an extensive body of literature on indirect speech acts, but child language researchers tend to be very casual in their use of technical linguistic terms—for example, Bates *et al.* in a recent work blithely use the traditional MOOD terms 'imperative' and 'declarative' as categories of 'general performatives', identifying them entirely in non-formal terms (Bates *et al.* 1979a: 114).

In discussing the various approaches to the holophrase Dore claims:

There is no need to postulate underlying syntax, nor underlying semantic transitivity, nor underlying case relations. That is, what has prompted other approaches to posit underlying semantic or syntactic structure in the one word is revealed by a speech act analysis to be the child's pragmatic intention in using a rudimentary referring expression. [Dore 1975: 32.]

This then is much the same criticism I applied to Schlesinger's treatment of vocatives (see p. 10) and a perspective Bloom appears to need in her explication of *more* (see p. 11).

Dore's work is based on linguistic developments of the work of the philosopher Austin (1962). 'Speech act theory' developed as an adjunct to a linguistic tradition which treated knowledge of decontextualized syntax as the proper object of study, and was one attempt to approach language in context by formulating rules for the use of syntax (see Wells 1978 for a discussion of other closely related attempts which make use of the sociolinguistic notion of 'communicative competence' or knowledge of rules of use).

According to Dore:

a speech act theory cannot be solely a semantic theory . . . many of the conditions which apply to the successful performance of speech acts (such as the context . . .) are not semantic. In fact they are entirely non-linguistic factors, and are more appropriately part of a pragmatic theory of human communication as distinct from a semantic theory of structural meaning. [Dore 1973: 11.]

If the language system is viewed as structure defined by rules, then the manifestation of language in discourse can probably only be approached in this way. And the difficulties of formalizing the intentions, beliefs, expectations, etc., of the speaker–hearer as a preliminary to explicating the illocutionary force of an utterance are apparent, and readily admitted by Dore. In effect, even when the focus has switched to language occurring in conversational inter-actions, speech act theorists are still looking at individual utterances as distinct isolable entities to be explored in terms of the individual speaker's mental processes.

When examining Dore's work on language development, there are some general difficulties. One is that the course of development is taken to be the gradual encoding of 'proto-illocutionary force' by conventional means such as the MOOD system, but no details of this are offered, beyond the outline of stages of utterance forms given in Figure 1.1. Dore recognizes that it is necessary to have

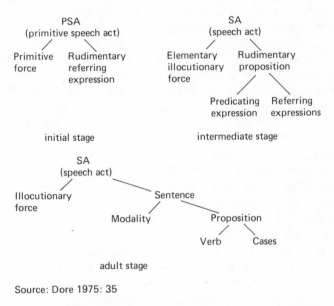

Source: Dore 1975: 35

Fig. 1.1 Dore's representation of speech act development

a means of integrating the formal and functional aspects of language behaviour, and he suggests some unspecified kind of conditioning of linguistic realizations by higher level elements, as indicated by the arrows in Figure 1.2.

In effect he is seeking a technique of 'pre-selection' which is built into the paradigmatic approach of systemic theory (see p. 19) but which appears less easily adaptable to the syntagmatically based descriptions he is working with.

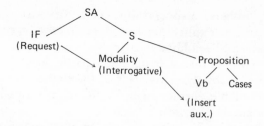

Source: Dore 1975: 36

Fig. 1.2 Dore's method of relating speech acts and grammatical forms

One criticism of Dore's work made by Wells is that Dore simply presents primitive forces as an 'open-ended list without any internal structure' (Wells 1978: 9). One could add that this list is offered with no psychological or sociological developmental framework to explain its members, although he carefully notes the linguistic and contextual factors which characterize them. In his (1973) thesis, Dore does give some consideration to the purposes of speech acts specifically in relation to child development, quoting Reeves' work on non-communicative functions of language. This seems to be a necessary. part of the picture, though one which is not built into Dore's theory and certainly is not used to organize the presentation of the speech act repertoire.

At least Dore does better here than Griffiths (1979) who chooses simply to ignore linguistic behaviour identified by Dore as 'labelling' and 'practising' on the grounds that these acts are not intentionally communicative (and philosophers have defined speech acts in terms of communicative intentions); as though the fact that such non-communicative acts are distinctive to children in the early stages of language development required no explanation.

In a more recent paper, Dore has addressed himself to the problem of motivating a categorization of speech acts or IFs, and does in fact adopt the network formation of systemic grammar to display relationships among them, avoiding the list presentation of earlier work (Dore 1979: 354). However, the only oppositional relations described are those of the IFs themselves (designated 'conversational functions' at the most general level and 'particular conversational acts' at the most delicate). Grammatical realizations of these in terms of MOOD forms, etc. are given but not presented as a system at all. Perhaps this may be considered fair enough if all Dore is interested in at this point is the taxonomy of speech acts. However, grammatical form is one of the criteria given by him for motivating his analysis and some kind of description of the lexico-grammatical level is surely a prerequisite for this. Yet as Martin (1981a) has pointed out, Dore's grammatical criteria are a mix of different kinds of linguistic features applied in an *ad hoc* way. For example, the speech act of *identification* is realized according to Dore by the class of processes which share the feature [intensive] in a systemic grammar, whether also [identifying], e.g. *I'm Robin* or [attributive], e.g. *that's a car*; *we have a boat.* Yet certain [attributive] clauses, e.g. *the car is red* are implicitly distinguished by Dore since these are said to express the different speech act of *description*, and these clauses are grouped with quite different processes such as *we did it*; *it fell on the floor.*

Of course Dore is not bound to adhere to the systemic classification of process types, but he does need to offer some account of grammar to support what otherwise appear to be idiosyncratic groupings. Again, as Martin points out, there is no explanation of why just one of the four principal conjunctive relations of English —that of cause—should be singled out by Dore to justify the recognition of a specific conversational act—that of *explanation*. That is to say, if any conjunction is to be a definer of a speech act category, then one should attempt to show a general correspondence between the system of conjunction and that of speech acts— similarly with process types and speech acts.

The reason that the causal relation is given special status (also by Wells *et al.* 1978: 14) is doubtless the intuition that in educational contexts *explanations* are especially valued. But this is nowhere stated, and no educational or other extra-linguistic theoretical framework is used even loosely to provide a non-linguistic motivation, either for the speech acts proposed or for the relationships between them, despite the doubtfulness of the motivation from 'below' (i.e. from grammar).

Summary

I have been critical of theories used by most language development research on a number of related grounds.

1. One-sidedness in the view of language adopted. This may be defensible in linguistic theory generally as a necessary narrowing of focus, but it is a clear drawback in developmental studies. It will lead either to a mis- (or non-) interpretation of what is going on (experiential bias), or to an account which lacks the means to be explicit in an area where ambiguities and multiple interpretations abound (speech act bias).

2. Lack of linguistic criteria to motivate analyses.
3. The acceptance by all the major studies that language proper is to be equated with syntactic/semantic constituent structure. This has a number of other related consequences:

   (i) It creates obvious difficulties if we wish to see language development as a continuum as suggested by Watson and Snow.

  (ii) It sets up an opposition between function and form which is difficult to bridge.

 (iii) It provides no way of taking the context of speech into account other than by viewing case relational categories as derivable from the situation where not verbally expressed.

In the following chapter, I would like to explore the rather different perspective on language and language development which has been offered by systemic theory, which at least avoids the particular problems outlined above.

2 Systemic theory

The general theory: paradigmatic and functional

Systemic theory is distinctive in being functional and paradigmatic in orientation, and this aspect should perhaps be explicated first. Saussure long ago made the point that the meaning of a linguistic item was its position in a network of paradigmatic and syntagmatic relations. The system–structure theory of Firth, out of which systemic theory evolved, elaborated the view that the significance of a linguistic unit was determined by its location in a paradigm operative at a particular place in structure (see Firth 1957).

Halliday developed Firth's theory by recognizing that a set of paradigmatic choices—technically known as a 'system'—may occur in the context of another paradigm. Thus, for example, the context for a paradigmatic gender choice for an English pronoun is a certain choice from the person and number paradigms. (See Hudson 1971: 44 for a detailed explication of the paradigmatic axis in systemic linguistics; also Halliday 1976, Chap. 8; Halliday and Martin 1981: 18–20.) Structure, in systemic linguistics, is seen as the manifestation or realization of underlying paradigmatic choices. This is illustrated in the simplified fragment of an English MOOD network given in Figure 2.1.

Thus, according to Figure 2.1, the manifestation of major clause is the presence of the structural element Predicator. If the mood of the clause is indicative, the structure will also have Subject and Finite elements. Then the sequential ordering of these structural functions depends on a further selection of options in the network, or 'features' as they are called. The selection of [declarative] is expressed by Subject preceding Finite, while the features [interrogative: polar] determine a Finite before Subject sequence.

At the lexico-grammatical level, networks are set up for each of the three 'ranks' of clause, group/phrase and word, but most if not all the features of the lower rank networks will be 'preselected' by features at the highest rank. (As, for example, the clause feature [imperative] selects the form of the verb, an option of the verbal group in the rank below.) Similarly, features at a lower stratum

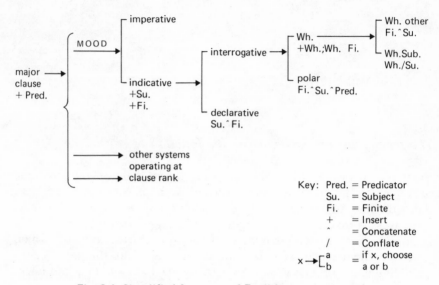

Key: Pred. = Predicator
      Su.   = Subject
      Fi.   = Finite
      +   = Insert
      ˆ   = Concatenate
      /   = Conflate
      x→⌈a = if x, choose
        ⌊b   a or b

Fig. 2.1 Simplified fragment of English MOOD network

(phonology) will be largely predetermined by lexico-grammatical choices, and lexico-grammatical choices themselves may be pre-selected by choices at the higher stratum of semantics. System networks are open-ended and the most delicate choices at the lexico-grammatical level will tend to be realized by lexis rather than structure. Thus, the relation between the two is one of general to specific rather than the 'mortar and bricks' approach typical of child language studies. Detailed accounts of the terminology, formalism and/or history of the theory can be found in Hudson 1971; Halliday 1976; Halliday and Martin 1981 and elsewhere.

Undertaking analysis and description of English in terms of paradigmatic relations led Halliday to observe that the clause 'options' cluster into three relatively independent sets of highly interrelated choices (Halliday 1968, 1973, 1978a, etc.). The three clusters of options define the systems of TRANSITIVITY (which largely corresponds to case relations), MOOD (choice of imperative of indicative, etc.) and THEME (related to the Topic–Comment notion). Because surface structure is manifestation of underlying system (paradigm) rather than of underlying structure, there is no requirement that one kind of structure be derived from another, or that one be treated as semantic or meaningful and another as purely formal. Systems may occur simultaneously, and the structural functions which realize systemic choice may be mapped on to one another in the resulting syntagm. Thus, for example, a major clause has not only the indicative/imperative MOOD choice illustrated in Figure 2.1, but at the same time a choice of PROCESS TYPE, as shown in Figure 2.2. A MOOD choice such as [indicative] may result in the

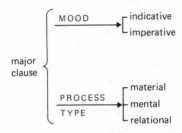

Fig. 2.2 Illustration of simultaneous systems

presence of a Subject element, and a PROCESS TYPE option such as [material] may result in another function, that of Actor. Two (or more of) such functions may be conflated together in the syntagmatic structure. This conflation may occur as an additional realization of one of the features which produced the elements ([indicative] or [material] in this example), or may occur as the realization of a choice from yet another system, such as VOICE or THEME. Any structural element in the syntagm may therefore be multiply determined, and all structural functions are equally a matter of grammar, and equally meaningful.

The question of meaning, semantics and grammar will be pursued further a little later. For the moment, the point is that the theory takes account of all three aspects of language which the other theories used in developmental research have recognized as requiring analysis. Moreover, it can certainly be argued that the analysis resulting from a paradigmatic functional approach is more satisfactory than that offered by more traditional ones.

For example, if we compare the TRANSITIVITY analysis of systemic grammar with that of case grammar, it can be seen that the latter tends to identify linguistic categories on extra-linguistic criteria, whereas a theory based on the notion of linguistic oppositions is less tempted to do so. Chafe, for example, analyses the clauses *he ran* and *it dried* as Agent–Action and Patient–Process respectively (Chafe 1970: 98). These are thus seen as two different kinds of process (the element expressed by the verb) in relation to two different kinds of participant (the element expressed by the noun). This may appear intuitively satisfying; after all running is in actual fact a very different matter from becoming dry. But we cannot assume that every language is going to encode structurally all such 'real world' distinctions, and it is not clear on what grounds Chafe is claiming that English interprets the two differently. On purely linguistic grounds one can say that the two are in fact interpreted alike. Both *he ran* and *it dried* are equally opposed to a different process type such as in *he saw*, since, unlike them, this latter 'mental' process may take a Fact Complement (e.g., *he saw that it was hopeless*), and also requires a conscious participant, which they do not. Alternatively, *he ran* and *it dried* may be jointly opposed as 'middle' clauses to those differing in voice potential such as *he dried it*, which have a passive form not shared by them.

Fillmore, although he seeks and at times offers syntactic justifications for his classifications, tends none the less to define the cases in real-world rather than linguistic terms (see Fillmore 1968: 64-5). For example, he treats the Subject of *he received a gift* as a Beneficiary (Fillmore 1968: 6) or Dative (p. 24), because the lexical meaning of the verb determines that 'in reality' *he* is a recipient of something. But it is not clear what linguistic justification there is for suggesting that the participant in this clause behaves differently—i.e. enters into different linguistic oppositions—from *he* in *he gives*. Again, while there may be linguistic grounds for distinguishing *the wind* in *the wind opened the door* from Subjects functioning as Agent or Instrument, the discussion by Fillmore (1977) is couched entirely in terms of the actual nature of the event, and not at all in terms of its encoding as a clause.

When comparing analyses, one can also see that by concentrating on linguistic oppositions Halliday has produced a much richer interpretation of 'relational' clauses than any case grammar. He unpicks two sets of variables to allow the disambiguation of deceptively simple clauses of 'being' (see Halliday 1984b). Further than this, Halliday recognizes that the one-participant (Medium only) vs. two-participant (Medium + Agent) choice is relevant also for relational clauses, which share the voice potential of other clause types. The difference between approaches is clear here, since if using extra-linguistic criteria to define cases, it would probably be absurd to come up with a category of Agent here, but Halliday makes out a convincing case for his analysis based on the symmetries of the language itself. By contrast, case grammar has always concentrated heavily on 'material' processes, almost to the exclusion of the relational type (see, e.g., Fillmore 1968, 1970, 1977).

I have drawn illustrations from the area of TRANSITIVITY because this is the one most worked over by the kind of mainstream linguistics which has been influential in child language studies. On other aspects of language, Martin's (1981a) account of SPEECH

FUNCTION in English (discussed also on p. 28 of this book) may be favourably compared with that of Dore (1975, 1978) or Wells (1978). Elsewhere (Martin, forthcoming) he has also compared a standard Phrase Structure approach to grammatical MOOD with a systemic one. He points out that instead of fulfilling the original goal of displaying relationships between sentences, the post-*Syntactic Structures* approach to deep structure simply offers a list of MOOD forms with no relationships between them specified, rather as Speech Act theory tends to do for SPEECH FUNCTION. The same charge cannot be laid against systemic descriptions of MOOD (see, e.g. Hudson 1971; Halliday 1976; Huddleston 1981; Martin, forthcoming).

Finally, Fries (1983) has presented the arguments in favour of Halliday's approach to the Topic–Comment axis of the clause. Halliday distinguishes the system of INFORMATION (distribution of Given and New elements), which is realized by tonic placement within the tone group, from that concerning THEME—'the point of departure for the message'. This is done on the demonstrable grounds that the two can be shown to vary independently, even though there is an unmarked association of the elements Theme and Given, just as there is of Theme and Subject.

The advantages of a systemic approach to language can therefore be argued on the grounds that a more comprehensive, better motivated and better integrated interpretation of grammatical structure is provided. But the importance of systemic theory for language development studies does not rest simply on its account of the lexico-grammar of English. So far the theory has been discussed as 'functional' in its paradigmatic approach to analysis. This approach has led to descriptive insights, but has far wider implications. It ultimately permits the linguistic system to be related to the social context, allowing us to take account of the fact that actually occurring speech is text in context, without setting up either an artificial distinction between form and use, or a concept of situational context which cannot be related to a quite distinct notion of linguistic code.

Before taking up these points, it will be necessary to explore the notion of a functional theory of language a little more fully. As well as being concerned with the functional oppositions, systemic theory is a functional theory in the sense intended by Bruner when he claims that 'the structure of language is non-arbitrary' (Bruner 1975b: 1). However, whereas Bruner means that syntagmatic structures in language rather directly mirror the structure of 'action' or 'attention', Halliday would interpret the 'structure of language' in such a claim as meaning its internal, paradigmatic organization. Thus the tripartite paradigmatic organization of the clause (as listed below) is not seen as a matter of chance, but as reflecting 'the demands we make on language, the functions it has to serve' (Halliday 1970: 141).

Since at the highest grammatical rank systemic options cluster into three simultaneous sets, and each of these relates to a distinct kind of meaning, Halliday has proposed three basic general functions of language. These are termed 'metafunctions' to distinguish them from the unlimited number of extrinsically defined uses to which language may be put. The three metafunctions are described as follows:

1. The *experiential*: language serving for the expression of content, the representation and structuring of our experience of the outer and inner world. This function is encoded principally by the lexico-grammatical system of TRANSITIVITY'.
2. The *interpersonal*: language serving for the establishment and maintenance of social relations, the expression of social roles, including speech roles, and the expression of the individual self. This function is encoded principally by the semantic system of SPEECH FUNCTION and the lexico-grammatical systems of MOOD, MODALITY and POLARITY.
3. The *textual*: language 'making links with itself and with features of the situation in which it is used' (Halliday 1970: 143). It is that which makes an instance of language relevant rather than random, and is encoded principally by the semantic systems of LEXICAL COHESION and REFERENCE and the lexico-grammatical systems of THEME and INFORMATION.

Because all three clusterings of grammatical options—TRANSITIVITY, MOOD and THEME—are given a functional interpretation in this sense, Halliday has also been able to suggest a meaningful interpretation of the so-called 'syntactic' or 'surface' Subject role in English. This particular role, required in the specification of different MOOD Structures, is viewed by Halliday as the modally 'responsible' element in the clause (Halliday, in press). That is to say, in imperative clauses it is the addressee who is responsible for the success of the clause on an interactive level. For indicative clauses the notion is more abstract. Halliday proposes that by being made finite, an English clause is set up as an arguable proposition. The speaker further has to make clear the entity in respect of which he is arguing, and this is the Subject. It is not so much the thing one is talking about, as 'something by reference to which the proposition can be affirmed or denied' (Halliday, in press).

Thus, while no one could fail to recognize the existence of the category Subject in English, since it is involved in such concord relations as the language has, as well as being a key element in co-ordination and other processes, systemic theory is almost unique in modern linguistics in treating it as meaningful. (Chafe 1976 also assumes it must be meaningful, but working without a meta-functionally organized grammar is not directed to an interactional kind of explanation and ends up giving it a traditional textual kind of meaning—the element we are 'adding knowledge about'. He discusses only declarative sentences.)

The tendency of modern linguists to treat the Subject as an 'empty' syntactic slot may be seen when we compare the account of a 'functional theory of language' advocated by language development researchers. Bates and MacWhinney formulate a functional theory as one which recognizes that structural elements are necessarily multi-determined, as a means of 'communicating non-linear meanings onto a linear speech channel' (Bates and Mac-Whinney 1979: 169). This is clearly compatible with the systemic view, but their functional grammar still maintains the Subject as a 'surface syntactic role', even though it may encode both the 'semantic' role of Agent and the 'pragmatic' role of Topic. Theirs is a model adapted from the autonomous syntax tradition, and is thus in a sense not so far removed from that of Bowerman discussed earlier, even though two 'deep' strands are now recognized. Consequently, the hypotheses concerning language development which result are not ones which would arise from systemic theory.

To sum up then on the question of *function*. Systemic theory is a functional one in the following senses of the term:

1. Linguistic description is undertaken in terms of paradigmatic functional oppositions.
2. (i) Structural description is in terms of functions in structure (realized by classes) rather than simply category terms.
   (ii) Elements in the syntagm may be multiply determined, i.e. structural functions may be mapped on to one another.
3. The organization of language reflects the basic functions that language serves. These functions which are thus built into language are termed 'metafunctions'.
4. Pivotal structural functions, such as Subject, Actor, Theme, are interpretable as having a (meta)functionally derived meaning.

Systemic theory: language and context

It can be seen from the foregoing account that systemic theory is
a comprehensive one, both in its account of grammatical structure
and its attempt to explain the very nature of grammar in functional
terms. In fact, the framework is even broader than has been indicated,
and in order to consider fully its ramifications for developmental
linguistics, it is necessary first to explore the systemic view of the
interface between language and non-language.

I have explained that the selection of paradigmatic features at one
stratum may be determined—totally or probabilistically—by
selections of such features at a higher level. Further than this, Halliday views the relation of language and 'outside reality' in the same
terms. There are two aspects of this.

First, there is the outside world, which provides the context for
the whole linguistic system itself. This is the culture or the social
system within which the language exists. Halliday views the social
system, like language itself, as a system of meaning relations. He
says: 'These meaning relations are realized in many ways, of which
one . . . is through their encoding in language.' (Halliday 1975a: 60.)

One example of this idea is to be found in his recent work on
DIALOGUE and SPEECH FUNCTION. The network reproduced in
Figure 2.3 represents a move in DIALOGUE at the 'social-contextual'
or 'semiotic' level, and 'expresses the potential that inheres in one
move in the dynamics of personal interaction.' This social-contextual
system may then be encoded in language, and this will take the form of

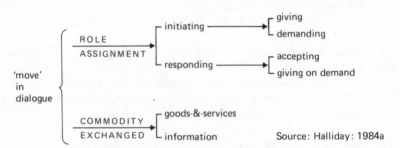

Fig. 2.3 Halliday's network for 'move' in dialogue

a selection of options in the semantic system of SPEECH FUNCTION
represented in Figure 2.4. Halliday's point is that the SPEECH
FUNCTION network is the first step in the *linguistic* realization
of a move in the system of dialogue, which may in principle be realized by any other semiotic system.

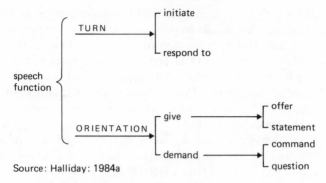

Source: Halliday: 1984a

Fig. 2.4 Halliday's SPEECH FUNCTION network

A second way of approaching the interface of language and context is from the point of view of a particular manifestation of the linguistic potential. Any particular instantiation of choices within the linguistic system will result in the creation of text. The outside world which provides the context for text (i.e. for a selection path through the linguistic potential) is the situation or social context. It is especially in work on child language that the importance of situational context has been generally recognized, usually in terms of the ongoing, observable material environment of speech. However, Halliday does not view situation in these terms, but rather as a symbolic construct, and he has suggested that in view of the functions language serves for man, the situational context for any manifestation of language is interpretable as a corresponding tripartite construct comprising *field, mode* and *tenor.*

Field is the ongoing social action and includes the 'subject-matter' of the discourse.

Tenor concerns the role relationships among the interactants.

Mode concerns the role that language plays and includes the language medium.

(See Halliday 1977b: 200-1, 1978a: 21, and elsewhere.)

Field, mode and tenor are to be understood as 'the environmental determinants of text' (Halliday 1975a: 131). This does not of course mean that any specific individual text could be predicted, given an account of field, mode and tenor, but that a text type could be. That is to say, choices made in field, mode and tenor networks will bias the selection of options in the semantics (to be discussed pp. 31-6) which in turn preselects options in the lexico-grammar, where choices at a higher rank may determine the selection of options at a lower rank, and where phonological choices are largely determined. Thus, the model in principle provides a means of relating the situation and the text in a coherent way. The relation of the linguistic system to the text is seen not as a system of structural rules to which rules of another, 'pragmatic', kind are applied, but as one of potential to actual. Furthermore, the activation of the linguistic potential is itself being probabilistically determined by features of the speech situation.

Perhaps a further example from systemic work on SPEECH FUNCTION would be helpful here. Martin's (1981a) paper sets out to motivate a SPEECH FUNCTION network on language-internal grounds—on the basis of realizations in the interpersonal area of the grammar (i.e. MOOD, on which SUBSTITUTION and ELLIPSIS depend, POLARITY and VOCATIVE systems) and on adjacency pair patterns of discourse. On these criteria a total of seventeen basic speech acts can be identified. However, Martin points out that to achieve the more delicate analysis necessary for many applied purposes, or to predict the relations between the SPEECH FUNCTION options and the grammatical ones that realize them, the particular situation type under consideration will have to be specified. Thus, we cannot in practice extend the SPEECH FUNCTION network in delicacy as Butler (1976) attempts to do (to range commands in terms of most to least polite, specifying the congruent grammatical realization) without reference to a particular context. Martin cites R. Lakoff's example of a modulated declarative: *you must try this* as either deferential, as from a hostess at a tea-party, or peremptory, depending on the context. Any such context will be interpreted in terms of field, mode and tenor networks, and it is the last of these, since it concerns the role relationships among the interactants, that will determine what more delicate SPEECH FUNCTION categories can be defended and what the grammatical realizations might be.

Field, mode and tenor networks have not yet been worked out, and the validity of the claim that these variables are the determinants of text has not yet been empirically validated, but the hypothesis is testable (see Martin 1981b), and the theory does provide at least a framework within which language can be seen as existing and developing within a context—the culture—and operating in the creation of texts within those 'instance[s] . . . of the meaning that make up the social system' that may be termed situations or social contexts (Halliday 1977b: 200).

Implications for a developmental study

The outline of systemic theory given in the previous section concerns the general theory, and it is now time to consider some of
the broad implications which follow for developmental linguistics.

1. Since the linguistic system is viewed in terms of paradigmatic
   choices, and text is viewed as an implementation of such choices,
   the exploration of the origins of language can begin at whatever point there is evidence of meaningful choice being verbally
   expressed.
2. Following from this, development will be considered not in terms
   of MLU, but rather in terms of expansion or reorganization of the
   paradigmatically defined resources for communication.
3. If purely lexical realizations are those of the most delicate choices
   in adult, the move from single to multi-word utterances may at
   some points be conceivable as a move from encoding the particular
   to something more general, rather than in terms of learning words
   first, and subsequently learning how to shuffle them together
   into sentences. We are not bound either to see every move 'into
   structure' as one from an elliptical to an explicit sentence.
4. The defining characteristic of adult language is that different
   metafunctions can, indeed must, be simultaneously expressed
   in the creation of text. Thus, one of the developmental linguist's
   chief tasks is to explore the development of this ability to 'mean'
   more than one (kind of) thing at a time.
5. Language is as it is because of the general functions it has to serve
   in man's life. These functions are reflected in the paradigmatic
   organization of language. A consideration of the ontogenesis of
   language will therefore be concerned with the initial functions
   language appears to serve for the child, and we will expect changes
   in the nature of the demands made on language by the child to
   be reflected in the organization of his linguistic system.
6. We do not have to regard language as unlearnable, and therefore
   necessarily innate, when we appreciate that every instance of
   language to which the child is exposed is systematically related
   to a social context. At the same time the child will not interpret
   the context initially in the same terms as the adult. Therefore, if
   social or psychological theory can provide an insight into the range
   or kinds of social contexts relevant for the infant, and within
   which speech may be expected or interpreted, then the linguistic
   theory can make use of this. Moreover, we will expect the child's
   changing interpretation of the context to be reflected linguistically,

given the hypothesized relation between metafunction and situation in adult language.

These are the kinds of assumptions on which a systemic account of language development will be based, and some of the questions already investigated by Halliday, and which I hope to explore further in this study. There are also fascinating questions arising from the model concerning the child's socialization into (or 'recreation' of) the social system by means of language. Halliday has also considered this angle (Halliday 1975a,b; 1978a) and although I shall here be focusing only on the linguistic system itself, it is important to recognize that the theory is one which makes such issues relevant and approachable.

Outline of Halliday's account of language development

Halliday's case study begins at the point where there is some systematic correlation between a vocalization by the child and a broadly conceived 'meaning' such as may be glossed 'I want that' or 'I like that'. These meanings are derived from a framework of functions which the language serves for the child. Initially (at about nine months) there are four of these 'microfunctions':

INSTRUMENTAL — language to obtain goods-&-services— 'I want';

REGULATORY — language to control the behaviour of others —'Do that', 'Let's do . . .';

INTERACTIONAL — language of interaction with significant others, with whom to share attention, etc. —'You and me';

PERSONAL — language to express awareness of self in contradistinction to environment—'Here I come';

and later two more are added:

HEURISTIC — language in exploration of environment— 'Tell me why';

IMAGINATIVE — language to create an environment— 'Let's pretend';

and last of all:

INFORMATIVE — language to communicate information— 'I've got something to tell you.' (Halliday 1975a: 19-20.)

In respect of each function there is a *content* which may be described in terms of a small set of systemic options, and an *expression* in sound which is quite idiosyncratic to the child. This is Phase I of language development—the *protolanguage* or child tongue.

The protolanguage evolves, with the introduction of mother-tongue lexis and the beginnings of dialogue and narrative, into a system which embodies two broader linguistically defined functions. The *mathetic* function is language as reflection, language for learning; and the *pragmatic* is language as action, language with which to impinge on the environment. Since any utterance can be linguistically assigned to one or other function, the context of any utterance can be seen as being interpreted or defined by the child as of one kind or another. This is Phase II—the *transition.*

Eventually the two kinds of meaning come to be expressed simultaneously, and this is reflected in a move to a metafunctionally organized linguistic system, with the simultaneous selection of options from two principal systems of TRANSITIVITY and MOOD. (The textual metafunction is omitted from the account for simplicity's sake.) The child can now simultaneously convey informative content—a development from the mathetic function, and can adopt and impose speech roles—a development from the pragmatic function. This is Phase III, the adult system in its basics, and by this time contexts for speech are interpreted as having a component of 'things going on' and another of 'persons taking part' (Halliday 1975a: 133), i.e. in terms of field and tenor (and also mode if we fill out the picture with the textual metafunction).

Systemic theoretical and terminological issues

In this chapter, the general nature of systemic theory has been sketched out and also its perspective on language development. However, before going on to discuss the data of the present case study, certain difficulties in interpreting Halliday's writings need to be examined.

Halliday interprets the nature of the development of the adult system in two ways:

1. During the protolanguage period (Phase I), the child is operating with only a semantics (the system of meanings) and a phonology (the vocalizations realizing the meanings). The move to adult is a move away from this bi-stratal system to a tri-stratal one of

semantics, lexico-grammar and phonology. Thus, language development may be viewed as the addition of an intermediate level of
coding between content and expression (Halliday 1975a: 67).
2. The move from protolanguage to adult is one of functional reorganization. The language is initially organized in terms of
extrinsically defined functions equivalent to distinct social contexts for the child. During the transition, a particular kind of
functional generalization is built into the language itself, and
by Phase III the language is metafunctionally organized, and
social contexts are interpretable in terms of field, mode and
tenor components.

Thus, language development is characterized by Halliday in
terms of the development of a lexico-grammatical stratum and of
a metafunctional organization of paradigmatic resources. Since it is
the lexico-grammar which is most obviously metafunctionally
organized, this seems a perfectly consistent way to look at development.

However, Halliday in his language development writings and
elsewhere consistently refers to the metafunctions as 'the functional components of the (adult) *semantic* system' (e.g. Halliday
1975a: 88, 128; Halliday 1977b: 176-9). He says also: 'The linguistic system is in fact essentially tri-modal at the semantic level.'
(Halliday 1975b: 856.)

There seem to be several ways this can be (and has been) taken.
If we consider Halliday's (1984a) account of the system of
DIALOGUE discussed earlier (see p. 26), we see him arguing very
explicitly for a stratified approach to language involving three non-
phonological networks: those of social context, semantics and
lexico-grammar. This approach seems consistent with the view of
the lexico-grammatical level as a system-structure cycle as I outlined on p. 19. That is to say, this level comprises networks of
lexico-grammatical features operating at each rank with lexico-
grammatical realizations of selections of 'bundles' of these. The
SPEECH FUNCTION network is here described as a higher, semantic
one, whose features are realized not in structure but by selections
of features in the lexico-grammatical network. From this account
it looks as though the SPEECH FUNCTION network therefore
constitutes the interpersonal component of the semantic system—
or part of it at least.

However, a difficulty arises when we consider the lexico-grammatical system of TRANSITIVITY. The experiential metafunction is
always given equal status with the interpersonal as a component

of the semantic system, and Halliday talks of field, mode and tenor as 'calling forth a network of options from the corresponding semantic component' (Halliday 1978a: 36), as though there were semantic networks for each metafunctional component. But no network has ever been put forward as mediating between social context and the lexico-grammatical system of TRANSITIVITY in the way that the SPEECH FUNCTION one mediates between social context and the system of MOOD for the interpersonal component.

One could simply assume that experiential networks at the semantic level will be required in the long run but are as yet to be worked on, or at least published. In this case, when Halliday says: 'It is the paradigmatic environment, the innumerable subsystems that make up the semantic system, that must provide the basis of the description.' (Halliday 1977b: 195), we must understand him to be outlining the most comprehensive framework for the theory while aware that gaps remain to be filled.

However, given the way Halliday has written about semantics, there remain at least two other possible interpretations. One is that 'semantic system' could be meant as a kind of gloss on the meaningful nature of the linguistic code as a whole, rather than referring to a specific stratum. All the main grammatical systems *and* their structural realizations have a meaningful interpretation in terms of metafunctions and are thus all equally 'semantic'. If this is the case, then an alternative term for the stratum above the lexico-grammar would be helpful. In support of this view we may note that on p. 158 of *Learning How to Mean* the metafunctions are described both as 'abstract components of the grammar' and as 'abstract functional components of the linguistic system'.

Alternatively, it might be that all non-phonological system networks are to be taken together as the semantics, with realizations in the form of words and structures as grammar. This leads to the picture given in Figure 2.5.

This approach could have a certain attraction. For if we take seriously a *narrower* view of semantics as a level of system networks mediating between social context and lexico-grammatical networks, then we are surely faced with the daunting task of describing the adult experiential semantic system before we can explore the child's route towards it, in order to follow up claims such as the following: 'A child learning his mother-tongue is constructing a semantic system.' (Halliday 1975b: 861.)

However, although this view of semantics as equivalent to system networks does allow the notion of the 'experiential component of the semantic system' to be interpretable in the light of systemic

Semantics (= system networks)			Grammar
Interpersonal Component	DIALOGUE MOVE network	SPEECH FUNCTION network	MOOD POLARITY., etc. networks	Structures (Subject˙ Finite, etc.) + lexis
Experiential Component			TRANSITI- VITY, etc. networks	Structures (Process˙ Medium, etc.) + lexis
Textual Component		LEXICAL COHESION REFERENCE, etc., networks	THEME, etc., networks	Structures (Theme˙Rheme, etc.) + lexis

Fig. 2.5 One interpretation of Halliday's account of semantics and grammar

descriptions published so far, such a view cannot be reconciled with Halliday's (1984a) account of DIALOGUE, SPEECH FUNCTION and MOOD, nor with any writings which refer to lexico-grammatical *features*, since these are options in the network. Indeed, it is hard to understand what would be meant by a linguistic stratum which comprised only realizations in form.

Robin Fawcett is one systemic linguist who has adopted an approach close to this one whereby the distinction between semantics and grammar is equated with a distinction between system and structure. He provides only one level of networks, collapsing together the interpersonal SPEECH FUNCTION and MOOD systems. Fawcett claims:

Such a model reflects more sharply than any possible alternative Halliday's view of 'language as a meaning potential, a . . . range of options in meaning [that] constitute the functional components of the semantic system.' [Halliday 1975a: 17.] [Fawcett 1980: 39.]

Martin (forthcoming) disagrees with Fawcett's approach, demonstrating that different networks at the two levels of semantics and grammar are necessary to model incongruence between levels in at least the interpersonal area of meaning. This argument provides a tangible criterion for stratification, and one may then suggest that if all relationships between 'forms' and 'meanings' can be captured in a single network, as appears to be the case in the experiential area of language, then no higher semantic level need be postulated. On this account the metafunctions would be a kind of interpretative gloss on clause or other systems, not a set of networks at the semantic stratum, and this is the view to be adopted in this book.

It has been necessary to raise this thorny issue here because so much of Halliday's description of language development is couched in terms which require some interpretation of the term *semantics*. For example:

Our approach will be through semantics; the learning of language will be interpreted as the learning of a system of meanings. [Halliday 1975a: 8.]

or

With the quite startlingly sudden leap that Nigel took into Phase II, it is all the more striking to find an essential semantic continuity . . . [Halliday 1975a: 8.]

Moreover, as I have said, he explicitly defines the protolanguage as a bi-stratal linguistic system, comprising a semantics and a phonology, and adult as a tri-stratal system comprising semantics, lexico-grammar and phonology. Thus, by his account, both protolanguage and adult language systems should have semantic networks and phonological ones, with the adult system having an additional grammatical level. This is illustrated in Figure 2.6. Yet the adult system as actually described in Halliday's work

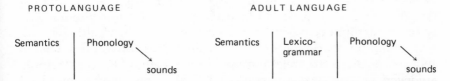

Fig. 2.6. Halliday's characterization of the proto- and adult linguistic systems

appears in the main bi-stratal (phonology and grammar), having only a single semantic network (that of SPEECH FUNCTION); while Halliday's protolanguage descriptions have no phonological networks and thus appear mono-stratal, as shown in Figure 2.7. However, the protolanguage may fairly be regarded as bi-stratal (rather than mono-stratal) on the understanding that while Halliday has only shown the

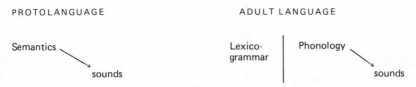

Fig. 2.7 Characterization of proto- and adult linguistic systems inferred from Halliday's formal descriptions

signs forming a system of meanings with respect to one another, an exhaustive description would take that set of signs and also represent the output as a network of phonological oppositions. Thus the protolanguage would be most comprehensively described in terms of two formal system network cycles operating on two strata.

None the less, even if the protolanguage is accepted as a bi-stratal language system, it still remains open to question whether the introduction of lexis and then structures into the realization path should necessarily be interpreted, as it is by Halliday, as the interpolation of a grammatical stratum between a semantic and a phonological one. It is this characterization of the developmental process which seems to be equating systemic features with semantics and lexical and structural realizations with grammar, on the model outlined in Figure 2.5. Yet such a model is inconsistent with most of Halliday's general formulations of the theory, and unsatisfactory with respect to the interpersonal systems of adult language, as Martin has shown.

Since in this study non-phonological features will not be regarded as necessarily semantic with structural realizations as grammar, on Fawcett's model, I shall avoid this characterization by Halliday of the developmental process. Instead, the whole non-phonological system-structure cycle will be treated as the 'grammar', although this is to imply no restriction on the meaningfulness of features. Only if and when there are relationships which cannot be satisfactorily modelled in a single network shall I stratify the description. Thus I shall not be distinguishing SPEECH FUNCTION and MOOD unless and until there is some evidence of non-bi-uniqueness between the two, and I shall not concern myself with the nature of a possible semantic system above the grammatical one of TRANSITIVITY. I should add here that nowhere will I be attempting any description of the phonological level as such.

3 Data

Data collection: the non-neutral observer

The subject of the case study reported here is my own son, Hal, a first-born child. Since the goal of the research was to explore the changing organization of his linguistic system as a whole, rather than any theoretically isolable aspect of development, the most appropriate method of data collection was a diary study. While there are clearly difficulties and limitations in such an approach, it provides unique advantages for tracking the spontaneous production of utterances and responses, and for interpreting them usefully.

Admittedly, for many purposes it will be unsatisfactory to wait for spontaneous productions of language, especially if any kind of comparative study is attempted, and it has been fashionable in psycholinguistics, as in psychology generally, to set up experimental situations in order to explore a particular hypothesis deriving from one theoretical model or other. Uncontroversial though such an approach has been, it is by no means a straightforward matter to come up with fruitful results. One simple and prosaic reason is of course that children begin to develop language in their first year or two of life when they make very unsatisfactory laboratory subjects. Examples may be drawn from two psycholinguistic studies of the 1970s: those of Rodgon (1976) and Benedict (1976).

Maris Rodgon records great difficulty in persuading her 16–21 month-olds to co-operate in various sensori-motor assessment tests, including the performance of symbolic and role play to order (Rodgon 1976: 49–53). Specifically language-orientated tests in such experimental situations invariably seem to be crude proceedings, given the number of non-linguistic factors that will affect an infant's readiness to fulfil a particular task. Rodgon, for example, was judging a toddler's preference for long vs. short command sentences by noting how often he/she carried out a command given in a particular style, noting ruefully: 'the number of commands obeyed by any subject is far fewer than the total number of commands administered' (Rodgon 1976: 56.)

Helen Benedict's (1976) dissertation attempted the ambitious task of assessing the lexical comprehension of a group of 10–16 month-old toddlers. One of her principal conclusions was that very young children are 'switched on' to language for only relatively brief periods, since after a short time her subjects apparently ceased attending to anything that was said. This must directly contradict the experience of any parent–observer, who will notice for example that in the flow of conversation between adults, or emanating from the radio, anything recognized or interpreted as a familiar word may be seized on by the child and responded to or repeated with satisfaction. And this is when the child is not even being addressed, and may appear quite preoccupied with his own thoughts and concerns. I was certainly frequently surprised to notice how Hal was constantly alert to the language environment; so much so that it seems more than probable that Benedict's infants switched off or became tired with the experimental situation itself. If this was the case then no conclusions as to how infants typically process the linguistic environment in actual (natural) learning situations can be drawn from the study.

Psychologists themselves have therefore been taking a different approach in recent years to the study of infant behaviour and development, and Colwyn Trevarthen, one of the pioneers of new observational methods, has concluded that:

> If one reviews this recent, highly fruitful period and awakening of interest in infant psychology, it may be seen that the art of the new experiments is in letting infants express themselves more naturally . . . Unfortunately, when controls and recording devices are set up to obtain quantitative data on a restricted range of questions, the findings may give a distorted view of infant intelligence. [Trevarthen 1977: 227.]

Other psychologists have recently made even stronger statements in support of a participant–observer or 'insider' approach in developmental studies. They claim that longitudinal diaries and time-consuming observations of naturally occurring behaviour are not simply a regrettably necessary substitute for the desirable ideal of rigorous, controlled data collection within a tightly structured experimental situation, but that the latter approach is fundamentally misconceived. Newson (1978: 36) argues that the traditional objective scientific paradigms are simply inappropriate for understanding or even describing 'the reality of intersubjectively shared experience', and argues strongly the necessity of looking at the communicative process from the point of view of a participant–observer. He concludes:

> We as observers, must use an effort of imagination so as to share with the baby's caretaker the general feeling of what it is to engage in an ongoing dialogue with

him, otherwise we will not be in a position to describe the evolution of those shared understandings which subsequently begin to develop through this intimate process of interpersonal involvement and negotiation. [Newson 1978: 42.]

Perhaps the most cogent formulation of the new approach is that articulated by Shotter in a discussion of what he calls the 'hermeneutical approach', one which is concerned 'not with explaining natural phenomena but with interpreting human ones.' (Shotter 1978: 53.) This means that:

Rather than the testing of theories by experimentation, it abandons the search for that kind of knowledge—objective knowledge—altogether. Instead its central activity is that of seeking . . . interpretations of the meaning of people's actions. [Shotter 1978: 50.]

He claims this is a valid, indeed necessary, approach since people (including mothers and infants) regulate their interactions in terms of the meanings they assign to each others' behaviour. And even further than this:

Our investigation of such social practices is itself a social practice with the same concern . . . Thus . . . whatever methods we may propose that mothers and children use in their attempts to make sense to one another, and develop their capabilities in their exchanges with one another, are also methods that we may use in our attempts to make sense of them. [Shotter 1978: 45.]

He gives a simple example of one consequence of the hermeneutic approach to the study of young infants: 'We must begin by taking the common sense view that mothers take of their infants at birth, that they begin life in some sense *persons*.' (Shotter 1978: 55.) Thus, any debate as to whether a newborn is 'really' more accurately seen simply as a biological organism, rather than a social being, is simply irrelevant.

My own study is not focusing on mother–infant interaction or psychological development as such, but these new orientations in developmental psychology are clearly relevant to the nature of my research as a linguist. Developmental linguistics has naturally been closely allied to the discipline of psychology, and this is reflected in the number of psycholinguistic experimental studies which have been undertaken. Since a diary study such as mine clearly has many flaws viewed from within that tradition—the issues to be explored are too open-ended, only one subject can be studied, interpretations of language and behaviour are to be made by a participant, not a detached observer, there are no control situations to validate interpretative judgements, etc.—it is worthwhile pointing out that within developmental psychology itself there is a shifting of attitude. This change constitutes a move to reformulate both objectives and techniques of observation and interpretation, all of which are sympathetic to a parental diary approach to the exploration of the development of language.

Methods of data collection

Data recorded by hand

Although Braunwald and Brislin's helpful paper 'The diary method updated' (1979) was not available to me at the time the data were being collected, I in fact followed very largely the precepts they offer concerning what to record with notebook and pencil, except that I paid greater attention to intonation than they suggest. Thus Hal's speech was taken down in broad phonetic script and where possible I noted intonation also. For any utterance of his which I collected in this way I also aimed to note any surrounding linguistic context, the situation (what the child was doing, attending to, etc.), how he was responded to—linguistically and otherwise—and where relevant, his reactions to this response, etc. In addition, I freely added any 'marginal notes' concerning interpretation, frequency or uniqueness of such utterances or dialogues. Finally, although the study is one of production, I also took note (for the early period especially) of what the child appeared to understand, and whether non-verbal cues to comprehension were available to him or not.

One great advantage of being the parent of the subject is that at any given time a new linguistic happening is immediately recognizable, and I noted carefully all new forms and usages. This meant not only first occurrences of course, since a number of instances are required to elucidate relevant patterns in the use or interpretation of the child's utterances. I also added informal notes observing when linguistic behaviour of any kind was either highly favoured or strikingly unusual, or when a previously favourite form was fading out.

The easiest things to notice and record are first occurrences of forms or kinds of responses, and my record of Hal's early language is probably complete on that score. But my interest was not just with observing milestones of this sort, but with gaining as comprehensive a picture as possible of the language at any specified time. Therefore I was in the habit of additionally taking notes of whatever linguistic interaction Hal was involved in, as it occurred, for 10–30 minutes at a time. This was done sometimes two or three times a day, sometimes only two or three times a week, depending on circumstances.

Obviously, if I was the only other interactant it was rarely possible at such times to record all utterances, or all the relevant contextual details, so frequent valuable small samples of this kind were supplemented again by tape recorded data.

Tape recordings

My initial aim was to make at least two tape recordings of 30–45 minutes per month. In the event I found that during the early proto-linguistic period tape recordings were not very helpful—vocalization was sparse and much more efficiently recorded by hand, along with all the relevant contextual factors. I therefore abandoned the collection of tape recorded data until Hal was twelve months old, after which I ran the recorder for one to three hours a month, usually spread over two or three sessions. Almost invariably I transcribed these that same evening, so that at least some contextual details could be filled in from memory, to supplement any sketchy notes that were made at the time. The taped data amount to twenty-five and a half hours, collected over forty-four separate occasions.

Constraints of a naturalistic study

It has evidently been the case in some developmental studies that the child subjects have become aware that their speech is under attention without ever being told so. Scollon, for example, recounts how on one occasion his infant subject took the microphone of the tape recorder, of whose function she was supposedly ignorant, and held it up to the observer's mouth repeating *word*, after which she handed the observer her notebook, repeating *paper; paper; paper; paper; paper; pen; pen* (Scollon 1976: 15).

Even more striking are the following instances taken from Braunwald and Brislin's paper, where the children explicitly demanded that choice utterances be written down. One subject, aged 25 months 19 days, evidently came out with the following: *Our friend 'green car Braunwald' has a motor. I said our friend 'green car Braunwald' has a motor. You writing it down. I probably like that.* They also report a slightly older child, L, aged 29 months 16 days, as engaging in the following dialogue:

L: I said 'mamma cessa'
M: I don't know what that means
L: Write it down

M: But
L: I said write it down (insisting that M do so). [Braunwald and
    Brislin 1979: 41.]

Whatever might be the effect on the child's language of his being
aware that his speech is under observation, I am quite certain that
it can be discounted as far as this study is concerned. Hal never
became aware that I was interested in his language, never connected my jottings with pen and paper with himself, and never
realized the function of the cassette recorder. He called the latter
a 'radio', doubtless because it sometimes played music, and he
was in due course given as a toy a very similar model—long since
broken, however. He enjoyed fiddling with this, pressing the
switches, etc., and seemed to accept that the other one was
my toy.

It may be the case that Hal's continuing naïvety as an informant
was a result of my initial conception of a naturalistic study. Although
I was necessarily playing the twin roles of parent–interactant and
linguist–observer, the former always took precedence in a case of
possible conflict. This was not only to avoid any such personally
awkward conflict, but was in any case required for a study of
natural language development uninfluenced in its course by being
language development under observation.

This meant that I never engaged in any linguistic interactions with
Hal in order consciously to explore, test or expand his linguistic
capacities (though doubtless various instinctive parental behaviours
did this kind of thing). Moreover, if ever it was not possible to
respond adequately to the child and simultaneously attend to/
memorize/write down the linguistic exchange we were engaged in,
then I temporarily abandoned the role of linguist. This meant too
that if I set the tape recorder going and Hal chose to bang bricks
about or disappear outside I did not attempt to prevent him purely
for the sake of data collection.

Obviously this policy led to the 'loss' of much potentially valuable
data and meant that neither hand-written nor tape recorded data
collection took place at consistent, systematically spaced intervals
for consistent regular periods of time. But I make no apology for this,
as a diary study can certainly be defended as the best way to approach
data collection for a comprehensive, naturalistic longitudinal study,
and the compromises I have outlined seem necessary to avoid affect-
ing the data under observation.

Data analysis

The data were analysed into a series of six-week stages. I wished to maintain comparability with the Nigel data which was one factor in this choice, but I also experimented for the protolanguage period and found that shorter periods were less satisfactory—the system had either not changed very noticeably or there was not time to establish with any clarity the genuinely new developments. After this, I simply maintained the six-week period somewhat arbitrarily as one that was short enough to ensure that continuity with the previous period was recognizable, but long enough in purely practical terms to space out the initial sortings and preliminary analyses of data in a way that suited me. This arose from the attempt I made to carry out a very rough investigation of each stage as it was completed, while I still retained an intuitive knowledge of that 'language', although exhaustive analyses had to wait until all data collection was finally completed.

Formal representation of the language

All the linguistic theories I have discussed as providing a basis for child language studies idealize language as a static synchronic system, and all are therefore constrained to display development as a series of synchronic stages. And systemic theory does no better in this regard. This is despite the fact that there has been a resurgence of interest in recent years in diachronic descriptions of language with the growth of variation studies of creolization and sociolinguistics. However, these have paid almost no attention to ontogenetic development, and even when they have (e.g. Bailey 1973: 110), the predictions made are purely phonological in nature.

The only child language research which has attempted to model diachrony in any other manner than by a presentation of 'frozen' synchronic stages is that conducted by W. and T. Labov (1978). However, the Labovs concern themselves only with 'Wh-Questions', and are using variation methodology within a transformational framework to ascertain at what point a T-rule is learned. Their methods, which involve collecting every single instance of a form over a two or three year period, are clearly impracticable for a more widely based study, and their 'autonomous syntax' stance, inherited from Transformational Grammar, leads them to some odd analyses. For example, the formula: *How about* + *noun* used by the child to point out an object, is treated as a precursor of the command form:

How about you + *verb*, itself seen as an earlier development of an interrogative such as *How did they get back?*, and all are given underlying Q elements. Obviously, on both methodological and theoretical grounds their work is difficult to adapt to a study such as this, which is concerned with the development of language as a whole and committed to a functional approach which attends to meaning and focuses on changes in paradigmatic systems.

Despite its limitations then, I will be following the traditional series of synchronic stages approach here. None the less, the fact of diachrony will be allowed to influence these synchronic idealizations at various points. For one thing, knowledge of later developments is a relevant factor in the validation of systemic features at an earlier stage, or in preferring one earlier-stage description over another. These considerations will be discussed as they arise in the presentation of the language descriptions.

There will also be points where Labov's interest in different ways of saying 'the same thing' will arise—e.g. *more!* vs. *more* + *noun!* This may be expressed paradigmatically as a choice between closely related features, and a preference for one or other form, which may vary over time, can be indicated by weighting features. In some cases one form will be replaced by a more mature one (e.g. *verb* by *verb* + *noun*), but normally with an intervening period when both forms are produced. The dynamics of such a change may be indicated by reweighting the probabilities of features which these forms realize, as in the hypothetical example given in Figure 3.1. The probability weightings used here are on a seven-point scale: 0 0+ ½− ½ ½+ 1− 1 first proposed by Halliday (1956: 179), and are intended to be a general guide only and certainly not to claim

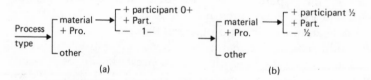

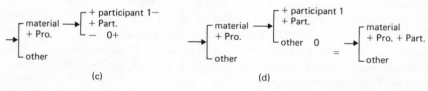

Fig. 3.1 Proposal for systemic formalization of one aspect of developmental change

any statistical validity. Where there is an equal probability of either of the features in a two-term system being chosen, this is indicated by each feature being weighted ½. A distribution of ½+ to ½— indicates a slightly stronger likelihood of the ½+ feature being selected, while a distribution of 1— to 0+ indicates a strong preference for the 1- feature. A distribution of 1 to 0 between two features indicates that there is no systemic choice in fact, the feature marked 1 is obligatory.

Although this appears to be a possible method of representing the dynamics of structural change, and is one I have used to some extent for the period 21-24 months, in fact most of the steps of a development such as that illustrated above might reach completion within one or two months. In the event then, a comparison of one synchronic stage with another 6 weeks later does not necessarily provide the opportunity to depict changes in such detail.

When Halliday first used the notion of probability weightings, it was not in the context of a developmental description at all, but in recognition of the fact that the adult linguistic system is probabilistic in nature. In any synchronic description it is therefore relevant to indicate whether the choice between features is inherently equiprobable or unbalanced, and systemic descriptions for adult language are now beginning to take this into account (see, e.g. Martin, forthcoming). For the simple systems of the protolanguage and early transition I have simply noted favourite or rare choices, but where the systems are more complex, as in the final network, I have weighted not only delicate options relating syntactically similar forms in a state of flux (as in Figure 3.1), but more general choices (e.g. interrogative vs. declarative) where these are clearly unbalanced.

In other respects I have followed traditional systemic formalism, using the generally accepted network notation (explained in Halliday 1976: 15; Fawcett 1980: 20; Halliday and Martin 1981: 10-11; and elsewhere). On networks I have used If-Then (I, T) symbols to indicate conditioning factors, and where necessary these are numbered I_1, T_1; I_2, T_2, etc. As far as possible I have provided realizations of feature bundles on the network itself using the ↘ realization arrow. Realization symbols are as follows:

+ = insert
· = unordered Functions
^ = concatenate
/ = conflate Functions
§ = order into first position
§ = order into final position

At the stage where structures are limited to two elements, a . . . convention may be used with lexical realizations to indicate sequencing thus:

⌄ + blue . . .   ⌄ + . . . shirt

Once a rank scale develops, the realization of a clause function will take something like the following form:

e.g.   ⌄ + Med.
                     Med.[nom.gp.] Head:[noun animate]
                     Med.ˆ Pro.

This reads: (i)   Insert Medium
                 (ii)   Medium to be realized by nominal group the
                        Head of which is preselected as of the class
                        animate nouns
                 (iii) Order Medium before Process
(The Process will have been inserted by the choice of another feature in the system.)

In a few cases realizations cannot be stated directly on the network figure because of conditioning factors. In these cases, feature bundles and their realizations are listed separately below the network.

Sample texts throughout have been prefaced by the child's age in months and days as follows:

21 (9) = 21 months, 9 days

4 The protolanguage

The functional framework

Language development researchers are continually pushing back the point at which the origins of linguistic behaviour can be perceived. Obviously the child makes vocal noises from birth, but these become properly the object of linguistic study only when they may be deemed symbolic rather than involuntary, reflexive utterances.

The question then arises of how to judge when an utterance is a symbolic one. Bates, following philosophical definitions, suggests that we cannot regard a communicative utterance as a symbolic one unless there are grounds for inferring that the child has 'objectified the vehicle-referent relationship' (Bates *et al.* 1979b: 38). However, as their own research shows, true *naming* of this kind is neither the beginning of the story nor the whole of it, and it is useful to have some criteria to allow consideration of the antecedents of naming which will yet exclude from the definition of language any instinctive and unsystematic cries and babblings.

Halliday has proposed two such criteria to determine what infant vocalizations should count as language, i.e. as symbolic utterances. First, there must be 'a constant relation between content and expression' (Halliday 1975a: 14). This is the requirement of systematicity —sound must be consistently correlated with meaning. Secondly, the meaning or content must be interpretable in terms of the social context. This is the requirement of functionality.

I have explained how any adult text is ultimately relatable to (or derivable from) a social context or situation, interpretable as a tripartite construct. In the first instance, however, social contexts for the infant obviously cannot be viewed in terms of field, tenor and mode components, since that interpretation of context will evolve alongside the development of a metafunctionally organized linguistic system, and this is the culmination rather than the beginning of the process under study.

Halliday has suggested that the child's limited social world can be viewed as comprising a very limited number of ways of behaving that are expressed symbolically. These ways of behaving are the uses to which the child puts his language, the latter being the set of vocal symbols he has invented. The content or meaning of any proto-linguistic expression is thus to be derived from one of the six micro-functions described earlier. In Nigel's case, four of these—the interactional, personal, instrumental and regulatory—were apparent in the first instance.

It is important to consider in what terms the validity of these functional contexts can be argued. Dore regards them as: 'Quite useful categories, descriptively adequate on a general level and motivated on sociolinguistic but non-structural grounds.' [Dore 1979: 352.] I take this to mean that although there are obviously linguistic constraints on the formulation of such a framework, the functions are not verifiable on purely language-internal grounds, in the way adult phonological or grammatical categories can be. This is not a shortcoming to be regretted, however. It would be inappropriate to seek a purely linguistic justification for the microfunctions, except in the important sense that there must be distinct content-expression pairs in the data to support a postulated relevant context. The microfunctions constitute the social contexts which instances of the language may be interpreted as realizing, and it is thus quite appropriate that they be extrinsically defined. Halliday describes his framework as influenced by Bernstein's social theory, since this is one offering some view of relevant contexts for language (Halliday 1975a: 18), and also at other times as hypothesized 'on general socio-cultural grounds' (Halliday 1975a: 63).

What matters is not whether the six microfunctions are *the* initial uses of language, but that the early systematic vocalizations be given some interpretation in terms of context, and that, if the goal of the study is to be the development of language itself, the social-contextual framework be formulated in terms that make the proto-language relatable to later language. It is clearly for this reason that Halliday has chosen to view context in terms of function (see Halliday 1975a: 18).

Since publication of the case study of Nigel there have been a number of studies by psychologists and others interested in inter-subjective approaches to neonatal and infant development, and these provide a very interesting context for studies of the proto-language (e.g. Schaffer 1977; Sylvester–Bradley and Trevarthen 1978; Lock 1978; Bullowa 1979).

On the question of whether linguistic capacities or even linguistic structures are innate or learned from the environment, which was previously such a controversial issue, a consensus seems to have emerged in the psychological literature. The common view now is not surprisingly that both biological and social structures are necessary for language development to occur. Language itself need not be viewed as innate if we recognize that the infant is preadapted to selectively attend to human faces and speech-like sounds as described by Richards (1978). Or as Trevarthen puts it:

[in] the results of rigidly structured experimental tests on visual and auditory discrimination, very young subjects have consistently exhibited preferences for physical constellations of stimuli that, in the ordinary world, are unambiguous signs of persons attempting communication. [Trevarthen 1977: 234.]

(Trevarthen's interpretation in terms of the 'ordinary world' may be related to the empathetic, common-sense, insider approach discussed earlier, pp. 38-9.)

Moreover, infants appear to have an inbuilt sensitivity to 'the timings of alternations and reciprocations of social partners.' (Richards 1978: 25.) This fact leads Shotter to observe: 'The establishment of turn-taking is not so much a matter of the mother imposing such a structure on the baby's activity as finding it within it.' (Shotter 1978: 66.) Sylvester–Bradley and Trevarthen, in considering the mother's role in early interactions, have shown how in the first few months the mother 'mirrors' her baby's vocal and gestural behaviours, later moving to more assertive forms of game playing 'which requires the mutual understanding and confidence which mirroring is adapted to foster.' (Sylvester–Bradley and Trevarthen 1978: 88.) And a number of writers have also stressed the fact that mothers persistently impute meaning to their babies' utterances. This, according to Newson (1978: 370) is crucial in bringing the child to meaningful action, and induces the infant, by means of pacing and intonation signals, to experience shared states of feeling.

Any interpretation of language development today therefore has to take account of the fact that by the time the first word is uttered, the infant has a long interactional history behind him, an experience of communicative behaviours with significant partners which is changing and adapting as he changes. Moreover, all this is built upon his ability to discriminate between social and asocial contexts, and his biological predisposition to attend and respond to communicative behaviour addressed to him.

Perhaps the most interesting aspect of this kind of research into prelinguistic communication, as far as a consideration of the proto-language is concerned, is the emerging picture of a developmental milestone occurring at about 8 to 9 months of age. Trevarthen and Hubley discuss a development of brain function at about forty weeks, which leads to a new acceptance of people by the child.

They say the infant's new reaction to persons 'is voluntary not reflexive', and involves combining his interest in the environment of objects with acts of communication addressed to persons, aspects previously expressed separately (Trevarthen and Hubley 1978: 183).

Bates *et al.* (1979b) also describe this change. Up to the age of about 9 months, their infant subjects were observed to fuss, reach and cry in the direction of a desired object, but would turn to the adult, if at all, only as a source of comfort when upset at failing to get the object. But at 9 months two new developments were observed: the children began to alternate eye-contact between desired object and adult whilst vocalizing, and also began to give or show objects to persons as a means of securing attention.

Newson also notes the development of the ability to make 'a visual checkback from object to person' (Newson 1978: 40) and further claims: 'The ability to refer from thing to person and back to thing again must be seen as a significant accomplishment in the communicative history of any child.' And he points out that distinctions between self and other and between person and thing are all involved (Newson 1978: 41).

When we turn to Halliday's account of Nigel's protolanguage we see that it is at this point, when the combination of acting on objects and communicating with persons is possible, that Nigel develops his first gestural and vocal symbols. Furthermore, when we consider the initial functions Halliday has proposed as contexts for interpreting these symbols, we find that they imply the very distinctions between self and other, person and thing that Newson cites as validated by research on neonatal development. The particular contexts of achieving objects by verbal control of the adult, and interaction with the adult mediated by objects are built into Halliday's description, as well as direct expression of interest in the environment and non-mediated address to persons. None of this of course demonstrates that interpreting early vocalizations in terms of an initial set of four functions is 'right', but it does suggest that contexts rather similar to these sociologically defined ones might also be formulated from a psychological perspective, in the light of recent research.

A final point of course is that the systemic approach to language development is a sociolinguistic one 'in which the learning of the mother tongue is interpreted as a process of interaction between the child and other human beings.' (Halliday 1975a: 5–6). It is this focus which allows the protolanguage—Phase I of language development —to be readily seen as a development of the earlier interactional behaviours which have been so minutely described over the past five or six years by psychologists exploring the notion of inter-subjectivity in relation to early communication.

Obviously there may be non-linguistic theoretical grounds for altering or realigning the functions proposed by Halliday. However, my interest in the protolangauge is as part of a linguistic continuum, and for my purposes the microfunctional framework as articulated by Halliday will be a viable one on the following two conditions:

1. If the functions proposed prove a manageable and usable way of interpreting early utterances without doing violence either to the observed data or to our understanding of the child's social and mental world.
2. If at the same time it can provide an analytic tool which allows later language development to be seen as bearing some relation to earlier infant vocalizations.

Some kind of functional framework can clearly fulfil the latter demand, if only because it relates easily to the notion of illocution-ary function or speech act in adult, which would be the only kind of (non-phonological) category within linguistic theory which is remotely applicable to the pre-mother-tongue period. With regard to the first point, I have argued that in general terms the micro-functional analysis seems compatible with the picture we have of the child's social and cognitive growth in the first year of life. The extent to which I have found it 'manageable' and applicable to my data will become clear in the following section presenting the proto-language data.

A number of writers have expressed doubts as to the practicability of applying Halliday's analytical system. Dore has complained that no decision procedure for classifying utterances according to function is given by Halliday, and continues: 'Moreover Halliday's own glosses for his data often strike some readers as bizarre, the basis for them being unclear.' (Dore 1979: 352.) Edwards believes Halliday's approach 'to be in danger of overinterpreting early utterances in terms of distinct functional classification', and feels the functions cannot be satisfactorily defined, 'whether on formal, semantic or pragmatic grounds.' (Edwards 1978: 469). Grieve and Hoogenraad for their part feel that it would be difficult to replicate the analysis even working on the same data. They say: 'We suspect that another investigator using the same classificatory system and the same words and glosses might have classified them in a different way.' (Grieve and Hoogenraad 1979: 102.) This could mean either that the grounds for assigning vocal expressions to functions are too vague to apply or that the criteria for the assignment and placement of features in the network for any one function are inexplicit—or perhaps both.

All of these writers are sympathetic in general terms to a functional and/or interactional approach to language development and their criticisms need to be taken seriously. I would agree that Halliday's analysis is insufficiently explicated, though this does not mean that it is simply unprincipled. I shall here attempt to be more explicit by discussing first the recognition criteria I employed for the determination of functions. Then, in the course of presenting the analysis, I shall discuss the grounds for the organization of features wherever there seem to be alternative possibilities. It is unavoidable that the motivation of features in child language descriptions will be less clear-cut than in adult, and perhaps the best one can do is to make clear the terms on which the analysis is to be defended. Also, in the process of presenting the protolanguage in stages, I shall provide a brief note on the specific contexts of occurrence of the utterances to justify the glosses I have provided.

As a final preliminary, then, to presenting the case study, I shall return to the two criteria of functionality and systematicity required of symbolic utterances. In considering the first, I shall define the functions and note the extent to which utterances could be reliably assigned to them, and in considering the second, I shall define the requirement itself and raise some problems associated with its application.

The microfunctions

INSTRUMENTAL. This is the use of language to obtain goods-&-services. It involves using the adult to act on the environment on the child's behalf, but it is the possession of the object or the result of the service (getting the door opened, the cardigan unbuttoned) rather than the exercise of control over some specific individual which is at stake for the child, according to Halliday. This particular distinction is clearly going to be hard to validate for a child constantly in the company of only one adult, since it requires observing whether the child is concerned about *who* provides the object or service, provided it comes. In Hal's case such a distinction was not of any great moment, since he did not create signs in a regulatory context on the whole (see below). Instrumental signs were easily recognizable in that Hal repeated them until he gained possession of the object or was provided with the service; and if he was to be denied it, he would fuss and cry unless skilfully distracted into attending to something else. Generally speaking, his attention would focus on the object to be acquired (or the door to be opened, the tap to be turned on, etc.) whilst vocalizing, and then his gaze would often switch to the person addressed and then back to the object for a subsequent vocalization.

REGULATORY. This is described by Halliday as the use of language to manipulate the addressee, and is directed at a particular person who is required to perform some action—typically 'do that again' in the first instance. The distinction between instrumental and regulatory has sometimes been misunderstood as one between obtaining goods on the one hand and services on the other (see, e.g. Edwards 1978: 469; McShane 1980: 79). In fact it is rather one of focusing on the object or environment (instrumental) as against focusing on the person (regulatory). However, as will be seen, Hal did not appear to devise consistent symbols for this function during the truly protolinguistic phase.

INTERACTIONAL. This is the use of language to gain and maintain the attention of the addressee for the sake of the interaction itself. It obviously requires the presence of an interactional partner as does the instrumental, but is not directed towards an end other than the being in interaction. Eye-contact between child and adult during the vocalization was a key recognition criterion used, especially to distinguish these from personal signs. Eye-contact is probably the most readily observed evidence of attending to another person, but doubtless many additional small signs of body language, etc. are also involved and contributed to an intuitive feeling on my part as to whether an utterance was interactional or not.

It is possible that Hal looked for a verbal response to interactional signs, and some verbal response was indeed almost invariably offered, but he did not appear to be waiting for this. Any evidence of being in contact was his success criterion; achieving eye-contact certainly, any responsive facial expression, a smile, a laugh or a hug were all accepted, and probably other less conscious responses too. Presumably on Hal's part monitoring the addressee's body language in general was important in understanding whether his utterance was successful.

PERSONAL. This is the use of language to express the self and the self's awareness of the environment. Feelings, reactions and curiosity about the world all come in here. This function is distinctive in that it does not depend on the participation or even the presence of an addressee. On those occasions when the child is not in any kind of interaction with an adult at the time of speaking, the personal function will be easily recognizable. However, these signs will also be uttered when the child is engaged in some activity with the adult. But unlike interactional utterances, personal signs in such a case will be uttered with the child's attention on the external features of the environment engaging his attention, rather than involving any preliminary establishment of eye-contact with the partner. And although the adult may well respond to the child's vocalizations just as for interactional ones, this is not looked for by the child. Given the fact that a demanding baby, especially a first one, may be in almost constant interaction with an adult partner, and that the adult is often working to achieve shared expressions of feeling and reaction, and given that interactions with the other are often mediated by objects in the environment, there is clearly quite a lot of scope for ambiguity between personal and interactional functions, even though the most clear-cut cases appear totally distinct. This potential for ambiguity would not cause great difficulties provided we can recognize the signs from the unambiguous occurrences, but it is also the case with my data, and to some extent with Halliday's, that some of the sign-expressions themselves occur in both functions. In other words, the same sign-expression occurs in contexts which meet all the interactional criteria (eye-contact, expectations of acknowledgement), and again in contexts which are manifestly personal (no adult attending child, child does not look up or round at any addressee, does not repeat utterance on failing to get a response).

While this may be interpretable in terms of the common pattern that both 'private' explorations of the outside world and interactions mediated by objects eventually provide contexts for naming, it may equally well suggest that the functional framework is imposing an untenable distinction on the data and needs reworking. It may be that 'pure' interactional utterances need to be distinguished from those mediated by objects, and that the latter should be related more directly to non-interactional utterances where attention is focused on objects. As will be seen, my data provide some support for such a view, and in any case objected-mediated vs. non-object-mediated is an important interactional option recognized by both Halliday and myself.

IMAGINATIVE. This is the use of language to create an environment and develops into a world of 'let's pretend'. There is no great difficulty in recognizing pretend play, and Halliday also treats early sound play and rhyming games as imaginative, since the child is exploring a world (of sound) that he has created himself, rather than the given material one.

HEURISTIC. This is the use of language to find out about the environment. It is the last protolanguage function to appear in Halliday's description of Nigel's language, and its appearance is probably a signal that the language is changing its functional orientation. To account for my data, it would have been superfluous to introduce this as a distinct protolinguistic function, since it is subsumed in the mathetic macrofunction of Phase II. The grounds for recognizing this reorganization will be dealt with later.

Systematicity

Not every vocalization uttered by the infant will be interpretable as a sign. A recognizably 'same' phonetic form must be used consistently in a recognizably 'same' context for a sign to be recognized. To use this criterion we must first determine how many instances of a content-expression pair are required for consistency, and how much variation in either content or expression is acceptable.

On the whole, like Halliday, I found that vocalizations were either obviously occasional or random, in which case I ignored them in writing up the description, or else they were so frequent over a particular period that they were obviously part of Hal's language. However, especially at the very beginning, there were some doubtful cases, and of course the less frequent the vocalization, the less easy to judge whether there was a common functional thread linking the specific contexts of occurrence. I used a criterion of at least four instances of a sound on distinct occasions (not, for example, all in one play session and never again) that could be functionally interpreted in the same way, for the sound to count as a sign. Only one or two signs hovered round this borderline for any six-week period under analysis.

Contexts of occurrence were usually materially similar enough to provide no problem, although it was not always easy to frame a revealing gloss for a particular sign. Occasionally a sign-expression changed its context of use over time, but six-week periods between described stages proved sufficiently long to allow this to be fairly clearly revealed.

Phonetic variation was much more of a problem, especially for personal sign-expressions in the context of the child acting on objects. I have represented the vocalization in I.P.A. symbols, but as Halliday points out, this suggests a much greater precision and consistency of articulation than was usually the case. A sign [ga] might at times be more like [gɛ], and then since consonants too appeared to be somewhat unstable, the velar might alternate with a palatal, which might alternate with a dental, so that where there is a continuum of intervening articulations one could argue for [ga] and [dɛ] being the same expression. Alternatively of course there may have been a contextual shift which was not noticed, in which case the analysis does not give the ultimate steps in delicacy. In order to avoid making any unwarranted judgements on this, I have given all the common different expressions or variants of an expression which occurred in what was judged to be the same context.

A related difficulty I encountered, which apparently Halliday did not, concerns the occurrence of apparently random one-off vocalizations which alternated with clearly recognizable symbols in a single context; again, most frequently within the personal function. It is true that the infant does not invariably use a vocal symbol where the context seems appropriate (e.g. a greetings context does not necessarily produce the sign which has been developed for this), but it seems surprising that the child should evolve a symbol for a context, and then use it only some of the time that he chooses to *vocalize* in that context. If one does not accept this, then these apparently random sounds must be seen as signs too—shortlived ones, not recognized because the record is insufficiently detailed to have recorded sufficient instances, and perhaps indicating some contextual alteration correspondingly unobserved.

But since it is again in the context of rather vaguely defined private activity by the child that this phenomenon occurred, I suspect that these sounds are not signs and only *appear* to alternate with genuine sign-expressions because the context for these latter has been conceived by me in too general terms. In other words, what I judge to be the same context, the child did not. Without a continuous audio-visual record to check on this with hindsight, I have simply discounted the random sounds on the consistency criterion, and leave the observation about their problematic appearance here for future studies to take account of.

A description of Hal's protolanguage

The rest of this chapter will be a description of Hal's protolanguage. For each stage a brief informal characterization or discussion of interesting points will be given initially. The description itself will take the form of small system networks for each function identified. Accompanying this are notes giving details of the nature of the contexts of use, to elucidate and help justify the formal analysis.

The language at 9 months

It is not until Hal is 8 or 9 months old that he can be seen to be using a few distinct signs, and these are interpretable only within two functions: the interactional and the personal. He could acknowledge the presence of another person verbally, or signal the use of an object to mediate an interaction with another. Alternatively, he could signal relaxed contentment or engagement with objects or sounds. In addition to this tiny productive language, he was able to give certain non-verbal responses (see below) which have not been included in the formal account.

The system as it stood at 9 months is presented in Figure 4.1. Features of the network are identified by number and typical contexts of use and other related factors are described below. One factor that deserves mention here is that one particular sound—[ga] —is the expression for two different signs, one interactional and one personal. Moreover, these distinct contexts are related in that both involved objects. The occasions of use within the different functions are given in the notes below, but a discussion of this aspect of Hal's protolanguage will not be taken up until later (pp. 99–101), when the language and the descriptive framework as a whole will be considered.

Notes on the language at 9 months (refer to Figure 4.1)

INTERACTIONAL
1. [Object mediated] H would hold up an object he was playing with, look at the adult and say [ga] loudly. Gaining eye-contact seemed a satisfactory completion of the interaction, although he usually got verbal acknowledgement as well.
2. [acknowledge] This was a pleased response to a new person coming into the room, or to himself coming upon someone in the house. It could therefore be seen as a greeting, but seemed in fact on the borderline of interactional and personal functions, almost being a private expression of pleasure. The sound was uttered softly, and although looking up at the adult, he only met the latter's gaze fleetingly. Moreover, he did not seem concerned on those occasions, especially with non-family members, when his sign was not noticed by the addressee.

Non-verbal responses. Although he had no symbolic responses to being addressed, Hal did look round and face the caller when his name was called. He also engaged in turn-taking games: variations of peep-bo and banging hands on the table alternately with M. Although these did not enter his language here, they are noted as

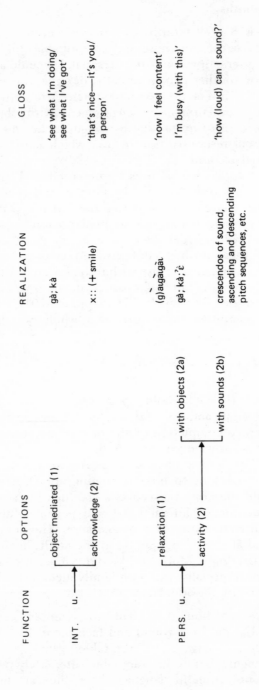

FUNCTION	OPTIONS	REALIZATION	GLOSS

INT. u.

object mediated (1) gà; kà 'see what I'm doing/ see what I've got'

acknowledge (2) x:: (+ smile) 'that's nice——it's you/ a person'

PERS. u.

relaxation (1) (g)àuàgàuà 'now I feel content'

activity (2)

with objects (2a) gà; kà; ʔɛ̀ 'I'm busy (with this)'

with sounds (2b) crescendos of sound, ascending and descending pitch sequences, etc. 'how (loud) can I sound?'

u. = utterance

Fig. 4.1 9 months——protolanguage

part of the interactional picture, since in the first case he was acknowledging a purely verbal form of address, and in the second he was engaged in an interaction which involved playing parts in turn. Both of these may be seen as primitive aspects of the mastery of dialogue.

PERSONAL

1. [relaxation] He would contentedly 'sing' this as he finished a bottle of milk (usually lying on the rug on his back).
2a. [activity: with objects] This was spoken as H manipulated objects, picked things up, touched things, etc.
2b. [activity: with sounds] It may well seem illegitimate to treat playing with sounds as an instance of using signs. However, these were unmistakable cases of H exploring his capacities *vis-à-vis* the world of sound (repeating a syllable or a squeak more and more and more loudly, or 'singing' or humming up and down the scale). As such, I am arguing that this sound-play parallels his exploration of his capacities in the world of objects. In the latter case the sign accompanies the activity, whereas in the former it constitutes the activity.

For the consistency of expression criterion to be applicable I have to see it as a style of expression rather than a particular syllable that can be identified.

The language from 9 to 10½ months

By 10½ months, the instrumental function was apparent in Hal's use of language, although there was only a single sign here. The two original uses of language—the personal and the interactional—continued with an expansion of options.

Notes on the language at 10½ months (refer to Figure 4.2)

INSTRUMENTAL

1. [demand] This was the only possibility within this function. It was predominantly a sign for demanding food while waiting for it to appear at mealtimes, or while looking at an edible object out of reach and reaching to it. There was a single occurrence with a different, more regulatory, meaning. This occurred when H was standing at F's knee, looking up at him as if to request a cuddle or some amusement.

INTERACTIONAL

1. [object mediated] This mode of exchanging attention continued.

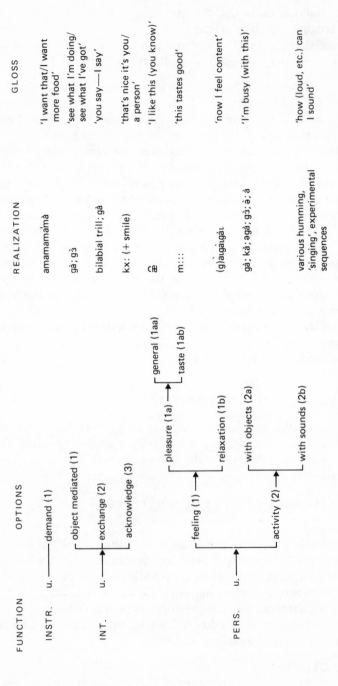

Fig. 4.2 9–10½ months—protolanguage

Usually it served to initiate an interaction, but not necessarily, as the following text shows:

9(10) H: (standing in bath, back to M) gà
(several times, fiddling with tap each time)
M: (makes remark to H)
H: (turns to address her, hand on tap) gà ::
(loudly)

(If the tap had been portable it would doubtless have been held up to M)

2. [exchange] The turn-taking games, referred to before under non-linguistic responses, now had an additional vocal form. M would mimic Hal, either his most constant utterance [ga] or his bubble-blowing trills. H recognized what she was doing and would delightedly return the sound to her.

3. [acknowledge] This sign continued, addressed to people, whether familiar or not (parents, visitors, people on bus), and to the two cats of the house (who were definitely not responsive). There were also two non-interactional instances—playing with a new toy and playing with leaves in a tree while held up by M.

It is because this option was less definitely interactional than the others (and also much less frequent) that I have presented the options as in equal opposition to one another, rather than grouping (2) and (3) as a [non object-mediated] class in joint opposition to (1). In fact since (1) and (2) were unmistakably interactional and occurred in clearly defined situations, one could argue that (3) was really the odd one out.

Non-verbal responses. In addition to taking notice of being addressed, Hal could respond to M's: *Give it to Mummy* request, accompanied by an open palm gesture, by (silently) giving what he was holding to her—usually to have it returned to him in a little game of exchanges. He would also get the face flannel from its hook at bath-time and hand it over, on a verbal request such as: *Get Mummy the flannel.* Moreover, although there was no use of language by Hal in a regulatory function, there was a non-linguistic acknowledgement of language used to control him. The general adult prohibitive *No!* would, if accepted, lead to his desisting from what he was doing. If not, it would be responded to with tears. All these cases show his increased ability to take on a behavioural role in response to contextualized speech.

PERSONAL
1. There were by now three different expressions of affect.

1aa. [pleasure: general] At this stage this was another interactional-personal borderline. There were only eight recorded instances of these; two were definitely addressed to someone (after finding something delightful to play with), three were evoked by noticing the cat and this may or may not have been addressed to the animal, two were produced while playing with things given to or made for him, but not while looking at the adult, and one was delight at M's noisy nose-blowing.

Although the sign persisted for quite a long time, and overall appeared to be personal rather than interactional in nature, it was always minimally frequent which made it difficult to interpret with confidence. It was usually spoken softly and with a high rise–fall tone.

1ab. [pleasure: taste] This was a common sign, used in situations of enjoyment of food, or even occasionally in anticipation—when he was carried into the kitchen first thing in the morning.

1b. [relaxation] This continued on finishing a bottle of milk or after lying back sucking his thumb for a little. It declined in frequency throughout the period.

2a. [activity: with objects] A greater range of sounds here, which could all be interpreted as phonetic variants of the favourite [ga]. While tones were usually falling, there was a certain amount of variety including instances of rising tone; however, no contextual association with different tones was observed.

The language from 10½ to 12 months

During this period, the most noticeable new development was the emergence of the pointing gesture by Hal. In the very first instances the pointing was done silently, but almost immediately he developed a range of related sounds to accompany the gesture. Both objects and pictures were pointed to and the sign has been glossed as 'that's interesting', and interpreted as belonging within the personal function. This is despite the fact that many psychologists take it as axiomatic that the pointing gesture is an interactional one, functioning to achieve joint attention to an object. Hal's early pointing has not been given this interpretation because he was frequently observed sitting on the floor by himself with a book, pointing to the pictures and vocalizing without looking up or requiring any manifestation of shared attention. Bates (1976) recognizes this phenomenon, and describes it as 'pointing for self'. She sees it as developmentally prior to interactional or instrumental pointing, and she cites Werner and Kaplan's (1963) interpretation of the gesture as one 'to clarify the separation between the knower and the known' (Bates 1976: 102). My interpretation of this development as belonging within the personal function, where the self is defined in contradistinction to the environment, would clearly be supported by this view.

However, unlike Bates, I cannot determine any chronological moment when it clearly changed to a more interactional function. It was simply the case that once Hal started indicating by gesture, it was easier for the interested adult to keep track of his attention, and the natural tendency was then to keep offering him names. Thus, by the final day of this period, Hal's utterances in the following text might be seen as interactional.

12 months   (H has been grizzling, so M attempts to distract with a picture book.)

M: Now you read a book with Mummy (settling them with book). Look, there's the Mummy hippo, and the baby hippo standing in the water. (M or H turns page.) Look at the lovely pussy cats. (M or H turns page.) And the monkey, and the baby monkey . . . The little monkey holding on. (Last page is turned.) And the big rhino.

H: (turning page back) gà:

M: Yes, monkey

H: gà: (bangs page)

M: Monkey

H: gà:

M: Yes, is that your favourite?

This reading session is clearly a joint activity, the participants jointly attending to pictures, and M responding to Hal's vocal–gestural indication of interest. However, it is not clear whether Hal is in fact speaking in order to gain or maintain the attention of the other, requiring some indication of this to be satisfied. He does not look at the other—which is the main criterion of interactional speech— nor speak extra loudly as with the object-mediated interactional sign which has always been present. At this stage it might be viable to see Hal as learning that basically personal sounds will be received interactionally in the appropriate context.

We may note that in Halliday's account of Nigel, attention to pictures was exclusively interactional and the 'interest' sign within the personal function related at first not to things in themselves (nor pictures of things), but to things exhibiting a commotion of movement or sound.

Apart from these vocalizations accompanied by pointing, the

other main development of interest at this time was the possible emergence of an imaginative function. This grew out of his earlier sound play activity. By twelve months he was playing not simply with random vocalizations, but with all his self-created sign expressions. And if the imaginative function is interpreted broadly as language as creation, play or art, it may be possible to see its primitive beginnings here. This phenomenon is also an indication that Hal's expressions had become the object of conscious awareness. ([ga] clearly became so earlier as it was used in exchange rituals in the previous period.)

Notes on the language at 12 months (refer to Figure 4.3)

INSTRUMENTAL
The single sign here was still predominantly for demanding food, but also for other objects at times. It was also used now for an occasional service, such as having the tap turned on, or the door opened. There was one isolated example of indicating the desired item by pointing whilst uttering the sign. The form of the expression had changed to a monosyllabic one, at times with a level rather than falling tone.

INTERACTIONAL
1. [object-mediated] Unchanged.
2. [exchange] This was no longer the exchange of a sign operative in other contexts, but only of non-meaningful favourite noises of H.
3. [acknowledge] This had all but faded out by 12 months. On a few occasions a kind of low chuckle (represented [hə]) substituted for the velar affricate or fricative.
   Non-verbal responses. Hal by this time had a response to *Where's the pussy?* or *Where's the teddy?*, which consisted of looking round until he located the named object, perhaps going and fetching the teddy. These are the first names he appeared to recognize.

PERSONAL
1. [feeling] The [relaxation] sign had quite disappeared. The [pleasure] sounds continued as before, with [æ] being still very infrequent and marginally interactional.
2. [interest] The most striking development during this period was that H began using the pointing gesture (see pp. 62–3). The various expressions occurring here are listed in order of frequency from left to right.
   I have sub-categorized here only because the (2b) context favoured one particular vowel variant of the sign and did not have the [ɛ] variants found in (2a). Such an approach would

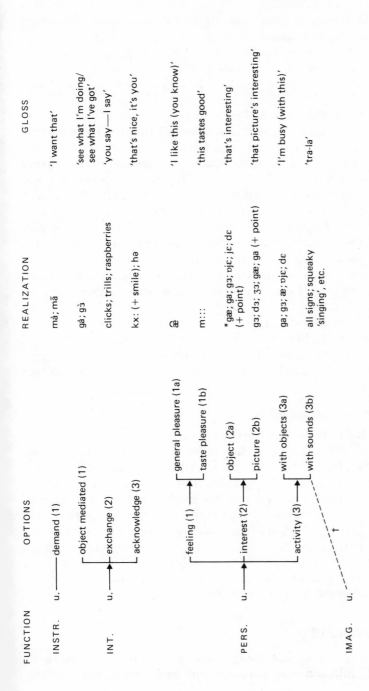

FUNCTION	OPTIONS	REALIZATION	GLOSS
INSTR. u.—demand (1)		mà; mā	'I want that'
INT. u. object mediated (1) — exchange (2) — acknowledge (3)		gà; g̀	'see what I'm doing/ see what I've got'
		clicks; trills; raspberries	'you say—I say'
		kx: (+ smile); hə	'that's nice, it's you'
PERS. u. feeling (1)	general pleasure (1a)	æ	'I like this (you know)'
	taste pleasure (1b)	m:::	'this tastes good'
interest (2)	object (2a)	*gæ; gɑ; gɜ; ɒjɛ; jɛ; dɛ (+ point)	'that's interesting'
	picture (2b)	gɜ; dɜ; ɜɜ; gæ; ga (+ point)	'that picture's interesting'
activity (3)	with objects (3a)	ga; gɜ; æ; ɒjɛ; dɛ	'I'm busy (with this)'
	with sounds (3b)		
IMAG. u. †		all signs; squeaky 'singing', etc.	'tra-la'

*Here and elsewhere, if the tone is not indicated, some variation is present and is discussed in accompanying notes.
†Dotted line on network indicates possible alternative interpretation of context resulting from emergence of new function.

Fig. 4.3 10½–12 months—protolanguage

suggest that the different expressions were not random phonetic variants. However, if there was a genuine contextual distinction here, it was not maintained for long.

In all cases the tone could vary between a fall, a wide fall and a rise-fall. There was no discernible difference in context, though to the adult they sounded like differing degrees of emotional intensity.

3. [activity: with objects] As far as the expression goes, there are no grounds for distinguishing this from (2) [interest] except that there is little restriction on the tone used—even rising tones occurred here. I have done so because the distinction does seem better validated in later months in terms of expressions, and because in terms of my admittedly adult perceptions the context seemed clearly different at this stage. H was not here pointing at things but, as I described before, apparently vocalizing his preoccupation with what he could do in relation to the environment, including such things as crawling up and down the back steps. Thus, it was the self in the environment rather than the environment as an object of contemplation which characterized the content of the sign.

4. [activity: with sounds] I see the first signs of the *imaginative* function emerging here from the earlier 'How loud can I sound?' kind of activity, because H began to recite to himself all his sign sounds one after another during private babbling sessions (see pp. 63-4).

Notes on personal network

Although Halliday treats [interest] as entirely comparable with other expressions of affect (pleasure, disgust, etc.), I have chosen not to do so in Hal's case for two main reasons. One is the distinctive factor of the accompanying pointing gesture. The other is that to interpret the options as primarily between [feeling] and [activity], as displayed in Figure 4.4, would be to interpret [interest] as more closely linked with [pleasure] signs than with [activity] ones, despite the fact that the latter share the same expressions. Although I have argued for [interest] and [activity: with objects] being different contexts, I think the overlap in expression warrants treating [interest] as different from other expressions of feeling.

The language from 12 to 13½ months

By 13½ months, Hal was using language in the four functions: instrumental, interactional, personal and imaginative, with at least

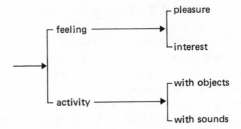

Fig. 4.4 Alternative network for fragment of personal system, 10½–12 months

two options within each. The regulatory function was at best a marginal one at this stage, although Hal did now improvise signals for
a continuation of a game. An example of such a signal would be his
saying *wheee!* to M to invite a repetition of M swinging him round
saying *wheee!* as she did so. But he did not then use this sound as
a means of initiating the game on a fresh occasion. Similarly, if he
had been being bounced, he would jig up and down for more
immediately afterwards. But again this did not transfer to another
occasion. Consequently, there was no signal used with the minimal
frequency required for a sign to be recognized, and these instances
were probably not symbolic at all—rather a case of Hal literally
and physically attempting to re-start the romp.

The personal–interactional continuum

In giving an account of the protolanguage for the previous period
(10½–12 months), vocalizations of interest in pictures or objects
in the environment were classed as personal in nature rather than
interactional. Before looking at the details of the language during
the 12–13½ month period, it may be worth considering the distinction between the personal and interactional functions in this
area a little more fully. To do this, I will discuss three texts, all of
which illustrate Hal's vocalization in largely personal contexts. They
show how language which is personal from the child's point of
view may none the less occur in what is a joint enterprise. The
interactional/personal distinction lies not so much in whether the
child is in contact with another, as whether a sign is spoken primarily to further the 'togetherness' or not. A consideration of such
texts may lead to the view that the two functions lie on an interactional continuum.

The first text is one recorded during bath-time.

13(6) (H in bath)
     M: Wash that face! Wash the cheek, wash the other cheek.
        Under the chin, round the nose. That's it. There we are.

(H puts the back of his hand to his mouth.)

M: Don't bite yourself.

(H continues to nuzzle at his hand.)

M: Tasty boy, eh! Tasty boy! (laughs)
   Yes, who's a tasty boy? Who's a tasty boy?

H: lalja (picks up nailbrush).

M: You going to scrub the screen again? Oh that's very
   helpful of you! Hal, get the flannel for Mummy. You
   going to get the flannel for Mummy?

(H ignores this routine, squeals, splashes.)

M: Oh, not going to be obliging today, hey?

H: a:ɒɔ

M: Too busy scrubbing, hm?

H: ɔ: jɛ ʔa (chatters as bangs with nailbrush).

M: Oh, gently!

H: (babble)

M: You don't think your Mum keeps it clean enough, hm?

. . .

M's initial running commentary is to distract H from the physical
fact of having his face washed, and thereafter she works hard to
create a conversation, constant rising tones and tags indicate the
unconscious working to get an appropriate response, which she ends
up providing herself (you're going to do this; you're not going to
do this—because of this and this). Here H is busying himself as it
suits him, while M keeps track, uttering comments, the content of
which is mostly beyond him, but the interactional nature of which is
heavily signalled by intonation: interactional from M's point of view,
that is.

This text illustrates the way random babbling and chatter occurs
at times even more often than recognizable signs; a problem discussed earlier, and the more H is talking for himself, the more likely
this is. Here, although M's presence is vital for H's peace of mind,
his speech is not directed to her at all and he never looks her in
the face.

In the following text M again tries to involve herself in his activity,
attempting at first to direct it, and is rather more successful in creating a joint enterprise.

(13)5 (M has gone into study to file some receipts. H has followed
   and begins unpacking the waste-paper basket.)

   H: ʋ'jè

   M: What're you gonna do with those little scrumpy bits, then?

(very high) Gonna put them back, hm? Put them back? Put them back in the basket?

(He does not, so M picks up waster-paper basket and puts over her head.)

M: (low) Where's Mummy gone? (high) Peep-bo! Where's she gone? Peep-bo! (repeating actions).

H: (giggles)

M: Where's she gone?

(H loses interest, turns back to rubbish.)

H: 'dàda 'gàga (picking up paper).

M: There's a bit of paper.

H: 'dàda (puts it in basket).

M: (high) There's a good boy. Put them all back.

(H puts another piece in.)

M: (very high) Good boy! Like to put this one back? (offering a piece of paper from floor)

(H does so).

M: There's a good boy. You goin' to put that one back? (offers piece of paper).

H: (does so) à

(. . . In similar way M hands over and H silently puts three more bits in.)

They end up doing something together, but once again Hal is not addressing M when he speaks. Here most of his utterances are ones which recur frequently in the context of his doing things with objects, recognizable as personal signs, and had he been playing quite on his own they would have been equally likely to occur.

Finally, let us consider some speech segments from a little later on that same day.

(M and H are looking at a picture book.)

M: (softly) There's a little calf and a dog (page is turned) and a hen and little chicks. Chick, chick, chick, chick . . .

H: (pointing) gæ̀ə (grunts) jɛ̀ə, ə'gà.

(H wanders off and starts to climb in toybox.)

. . .

(H later brings out another book.)

M: Shall we read the cat book?

(H opens it in middle.)

M: There's a bird and a pussy cat in a tree, and the pussy cat goes 'miaouw'.

(H looks up at M in wonder—both laugh. H turns the pages.)

M: A kitty cat and another kitty cat. He's winking at you.

(H turns back and points to previous page with bird picture.)
M: He's got a beak, sharp . . . (whispering) . . . pussy cat, yes.
H: (pointing) dèə.
M: (softly) Yes, there's the butterfly and a pussy cat. Where's
   the butterfly? It's on the flower isn't it? On the flower.
(H points.)
M: Yes.
H: (points) dɔ̀.
M: Yes there's a butterfly . . . on the flower.

Hal remains silent while M does quite a bit of talking (usually very quietly). He looks up at her when she makes an unexpected noise, but otherwise both are looking at the book, and when Hal makes a comment it is the same as he would make were he reading alone (though he does this much less now). When he points, either M may say something or he may do so himself. While utterances of this sort have been classified as personal, it has to be understood that they may occur very much in the context of an interaction—a shared activity.

All of these texts show M and Hal in interaction in the sense of doing things together, but perhaps only in the last case does it seem as if *Hal's* language, as well as M's, might be specifically contributing to sustaining the interaction rather than just the activity. It is in the last text therefore that the boundary between interactional and personal functions is least clear.

Notes on the language at 13½ months (refer to Figure 4.5)

INSTRUMENTAL
1. [require aid] This appeared to be a general distress signal when things wouldn't go, he got stuck, something was hurting him, a construction he was creating kept collapsing, etc.
2. [demand] This was still mainly a demand for goods (edible and other) and for a very small range of services, now including being lifted up within reach of the radiogram to fiddle with the knobs. The vocalic instrumental sign for assistance ([ə]) occasionally overlapped in use with the nasal sign ([ma]) for demanding objects. The nasal [demand] class now occurred with different tones. Originally taking a falling tone, it now usually had a narrower fall than other falling tone signs, or else it was level. An initial bilabial nasal was often lengthened or syllabic.
   There were occasions when Hal could be heard using an instrumental sign when not in anyone's sight. This seems puzzling, but Bates observed that her subject addressed the person less

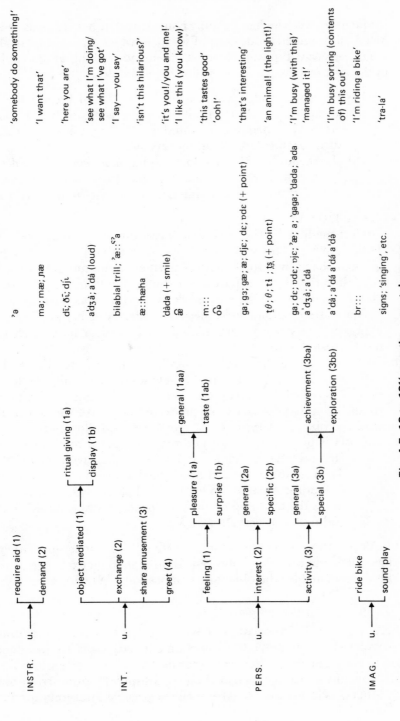

Fig. 4.5 12 to 13½ months—protolanguage

frequently once she had become confident that her sign was recognized and understood generally, than when first using it. Hal would anyway typically utter his demand looking at the object in the first instance as in the following examples:

12(15) H goes to fridge and reaches up to loaf of bread which is always kept on top. Looks at and reaches to bread saying *mā*; *mā*. Then looks round at M, beginning to grizzle; turns back to bread and repeats *mà*.

12(18) H reaches to M's handbag saying *mæ̀*; *mæ̀*. He looks at M, and then back at the bag, repeating *mà*. M gives him the bag, and while holding and looking at it H says *gà*.

INTERACTIONAL

1. [object-mediated] There were now two different forms:

1a. [ritual giving] This was always part of a ritual game of handing an item back and forth with a partner. Sometimes M verbally requested the object as part of the game, sometimes not. Although H now had a vocal sign to mark his performance in this ritual, he very often handed the object over silently as before. This sign expression was always articulated softly with a high pitch and level or rising tone.

1b. [display] Here as before, H would hold things up to M or F. The expression had changed, but the new sound was again one found in the personal [activity] context. It was a kind of invitation to the addressee to share his preoccupation with the self in the world of objects. A typical case would be the following:

13(1) H is playing with his hairbrush, putting it to his head, etc. He says quietly *a'dà* as he touches his hair with the bristles. Then he looks up and holds the hairbrush aloft addressing F loudly: *a'dà!* F smiles back. H then looks across at M, holds the brush up again and repeats loudly: *a'dà!* M smiles and responds verbally.

Very often, as in this case, a personal sign (or series of them) preceded, and probably followed, an interactional exchange of this kind, mediated by the object he had been playing with privately.

Note on interactional network

There are two different ways to view this part of the interactional repertoire. In Figure 4.5 the [object-mediated] signs are in opposition to the exchange of nonsense sounds. However, a defensible alternative would be to distinguish the (1b) [display] option from both the others, as in Figure 4.6. Although my original interpretation may

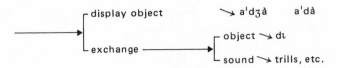

Fig. 4.6   Alternative network for fragment of interpersonal system, 12–13½ months

seem more natural given that the feature [object-mediated] was present from the start, the issue cannot be decided from a consideration of this period alone. Turn-taking exchanges are given considerable prominence in the literature on prelinguistic interaction, and thus from the point of view of an investigation which has already identified this as a useful format, the above presentation would be preferable. I have not favoured it because of the developments in the succeeding period when [display] is replaced by giving, taking or showing objects. This does not occur in ritual turn-taking and so the [dɪ̄] sign disappears. But very interestingly, the preferred expression for this giving/taking/showing activity tonally resembles [dɪ̄] in being [a'da] with a rising final syllable, or upjump to high level tone on final syllable. The impression is then that these two features of [display] and [exchange object] get replaced by a single one incorporating aspects of both (in both content and expression), and that the two should therefore be most closely linked at this earlier stage.

2. [share amusement] This was a kind of stage laugh. It was not a simple giggle of amusement, but was rather self-consciously addressed to the other in response to some behaviour on his own or their part which took his fancy. He clearly looked for some acknowledgement or response from the addressee. Example situations were: F blowing his nose loudly; playmate showing off by putting head into toybox; H exasperating M's attempts to dress him after bath.

3. [greet] His earlier form of acknowledging persons disappeared, and the new form was more obviously addressed to the other. F had attempted to teach Hal to say *Dadda* by pointing to himself and repeating the name. After this, H used it not only in general play (see personal function below),but while looking at M or F and poking either the addressee or himself. Occasionally he addressed himself in the mirror this way. The most typical use, however, was when M came home from work and gathered him up. He would then poke her nose or her glasses and say [dada]. (This was probably a result of a similar attempt by M to teach him to say *nose*, by pointing and repeating. He did not

learn *nose*, but apparently understood that nose-poking was a conventional way of interacting.)

Non-verbal responses. These expanded to include placing objects in a location (on table; in drawer, etc.) in response to a verbal request, usually one accompanied by a gesture. Hal could also be seen to understand at least two more object names: *ball* and *book*, and would hold out his hand to participate in *round and round the garden* on M's purely verbal suggestion.

PERSONAL

1aa. [pleasure: general] As before, there were minimal occurrences; these were: on being given something special; on finding some biscuit on the floor (two occasions); after M had built a toy tower; and on picking up a novel toy in a strange house. Only in the last case did he clearly look up at anyone.

1ab. [pleasure: taste] Used in enjoyment or anticipation of food as described earlier. Also, on two occasions, as if empathizing, as he watched pet food being ladled out or put down to the cat.

1b. [surprise] Perhaps in imitation of M, he developed an infrequent sign with high rise-fall tone that apparently indicated surprised interest. Example situations: leaf dropped off house plant while he was looking at it; tower of blocks collapsed unexpectedly; bubble popped suddenly.

2a. [interest: general] Largely as before, both objects and pictures were pointed to.

2b. [interest: special] This was overwhelmingly occasioned by the appearance of an animal. Originally, it was his own pet cats, often as he approached or fondled them, and I at first interpreted it as a greeting, 'hello cat'. Perhaps indeed it was at first, but it soon came to include other animals he saw, and to be used with the pointing gesture. It was extended to one toy—the dog's head on the end of his whistle, and rather mysteriously he also used it when pointing up to the light. Lights fascinated him, and he liked to be reached up in M's arms to try and touch the hanging shade. Often he would then point up and give the 'animal' sign.

3a. [activity: general] As before all the general [interest] expressions occurred here, so this may not be a viable separate category. There were a few expressions here not found also with the pointing gesture though, and the reduplicated syllables [gaga, dada] especially were favoured when his own capacity—to toddle unsteadily, manœuvre steps, etc.—was involved, rather than objects as such.

Whether or not this category needs to be distinguished, there were certain ways of behaving with objects that were very prominent and had their own favourite signs. These were:

3ba. [achievement] The principal context for this was H painstakingly or emphatically having set an object on a table a little too high for him, or getting hold of an object almost out of reach, or of special value (e.g. M's pen). It was distinct from an instrumental reach for an object in that he did not ever attempt to involve the other's assistance, and might in fact resent a well-intentioned attempt to do the deed for him. None the less he did use it at times on being given an object—for example, a banana that he had been watching F peel. And on one occasion it was on receiving an object he had requested himself.

3bb. [exploration] When H was getting hold of, or placing, an object with deliberation (the [achievement] context), the [adʒa, ada] expression was spoken clearly with falling tone and stress on the second syllable. He also used something similar when fiddling about, for example, rummaging in a cupboard, shifting objects about, unpacking containers, investigating the contents of M's handbag, etc. On these occasions [ada] was spoken quickly and more softly, sometimes with the stress on the first syllable, and with a variety of tones: fall, rise and up or down jump from level. One favourite variation was a quickly repeated series of two or three rises followed by a fall, as if finally satisfied with his investigation.

IMAGINATIVE

1. [ride bike] H adopted his older playmate's convention of accompanying a ride on his tricycle with motor bike noises. As this was imitative it is not possible to say whether it was genuinely pretend play or not.

2. [sound play] As before, playing with pitch levels, etc. and often now alternating series of front and back consonants, etc.

The language from 13½ to 15 months

The first word

This period is notable for Hal's first serious attempts to imitate the language being addressed to him, and for the appearance of his first genuine lexical item.

Imitations occurred in two contexts. One was interactional, and involved mooing, quacking, etc. when looking at animal picture books with an adult partner. The other context was that of personal [interest], when he pointed to objects and attempted to repeat names said to him when using a protolinguistic [interest] sign. (See the discussion of the personal system pp. 81–2 for more details.)

These imitations took place in specific contexts and may still be regarded as protolinguistic signs, but one item had the status of being a mother-tongue word. It is thus represented on the Figure 4.7 network as a lexical item rather than in phonetic terms. Its evolution over the six-week period was as follows: Hal suddenly abandoned his personal [interest:specific] sign [tθ] (see Figure 4.5), which had been used when pointing to animals (and sometimes lights). He began instead to use *puss* ([bɒʊ] and then [bɒəş, bɒş, bɒzæ], etc.), when he spotted his own cat about the house. This was not a 'proper name' though, as within a few days he was using it for other cats in houses he visited. (It was not used for pictures of cats for another five weeks.) He used the pointing gesture, and in the first week or so the word took a high rise–fall tone, after which it occurred with a variety of tones, although falling tone was most prominent.

Almost as soon as it appeared, this name was used with greater flexibility than simply ongoing 'interest'. It was very quickly used in anticipation and recall situations within the personal function as in the following cases:

ANTICIPATION
(i) Several times as H went into garden expecting to see his cat.
(ii) Several times as F carried H into the living room where cat was usually sleeping.

RECALL
14(2) H was standing on sofa pointing at window. He had found and played with cat on the sill a little earlier. He began to repeat *pùss, pùss, pùss* while pointing at the window. M looked out of the window, but saw no cat and said something to this effect. Ten minutes later, H repeated the scene, pointing and saying *pùss*. He then turned to M and repeated to her *pùss*.

This last example is particularly interesting as it shows Hal (I take it) not only considering a little event from earlier in the day, but sharing that experience with M after she has evinced interest in it. Thus, this is an example of an interactional use of language in fact, and moreover, an interactional mode (sharing past experience) not before seen.

In addition to these expanded personal and interactional occasions, there were instrumental uses of *puss*. The following example is of a text which occurred just three days after Hal's first recorded use of the word.

13(27) (H enters the kitchen whimpering.)
    M: (washing up) Hm? What're you doing?
    H: (turning to door) Pùss. (walks out and points into next room) Pùss.
    M: (following him) Are you looking for her?
    (H while looking at M points to window where the cat is inaccessible on window-sill behind a desk.)

At the time, I felt that H had 'told' me something for the first time, but on reflection I would interpret the above as an instrumental use, meaning 'I can't get to puss', rather than an informative 'I found a cat in there'. (He was lifted up to stroke her as the outcome.)

There were other instances of instrumental use, the following being about the only occasion when the general instrumental demand preceded a lexical item to make explicit the latter's functional interpretation:

14(18) H exits from M's bedroom in the morning, saying *Pùss.* Goes to living room, finds door shut, so can't enter. Returns to M saying *mà; mā; pùss; pùss.*

This example shows also the verbalization of intention in the first utterance, another expansion of the personal function.

Finally, it was used too in imaginative 'let's pretend' contexts. From 14(6) H would frequently pull up the edge of the bath mat he was sitting on and peep under, saying *puss.* This was an imaginative transfer of real situations of peeping behind curtains, under bedcovers, etc. to find her. As there was no question of her being in a bath full of water under a flat rubber mat, he was clearly pretend-playing in these cases.

Although subsequent lexical items did not generally follow this trend with anything like this speed, it is clear that the presence of a distinct representational content to a sign provides the first possibility of its being used freely in all functions. It also expands the potential of existing functions—interest in the environment can take on new dimensions not bounded by the here-and-now, and the joint recollection of past experience is a new interactional possibility.

Notes on the language at 15 months (refer to Figure 4.7)

INSTRUMENTAL
1. [require aid] As before, except that it now typically took a rising tone.
2a. [demand: general] Level or rising tones were common here too.
2b. [demand: edible] This sign was only ever used at this stage for

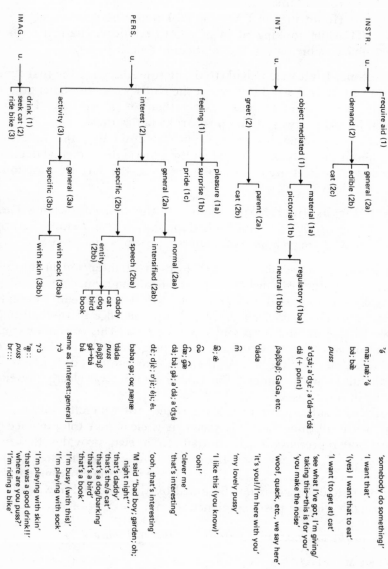

Fig. 4.7 13½–15 months—protolanguage

FUNCTION	OPTIONS	REALIZATION	GLOSS
INSTR. u.	require aid (1)	ʔɔ̃	'somebody do something!'
	demand (2) — general (2a)	mãː; ɲæ̃; ˀə̃	'I want that'
	demand (2) — edible (2b)	bə̃; bæ̃	'(yes) I want that to eat'
	demand (2) — cat (2c)	puss	'I want (to get at) cat'
INT. u.	object mediated (1) — material (1a)	a'dʒà; a'dʒɛ; a'dà→a'dá	'see what I've got, I'm giving/taking this→this is for you'
	object mediated (1) — pictorial (1b) — regulatory (1ba)	dá (+ point)	'you make the noise'
	object mediated (1) — pictorial (1b) — neutral (1bb)	βaβàβɛ̀β; GaGa, etc.	'woof, quack, etc., we say here'
	greet (2) — parent (2a)	'dáda	'it's you/I'm here with you'
	greet (2) — cat (2b)	m̂	'my lovely pussy'
PERS. u.	feeling (1) — pleasure (1a)	æ̃; æ̃	'I like this (you know)'
	feeling (1) — surprise (1b)	ɔ̃̀	'ooh!'
	feeling (1) — pride (1c)	đæ; gæ̃	'clever me'
	interest (2) — general (2a) — normal (2aa)	đɛ̀; bà; gà; a'dà; a'dʒà	'that's interesting'
	interest (2) — general (2a) — intensified (2ab)	dɛ̀; djɛ̀; n'jɛ̀; ɛ̀jɛ; ɛ̀ɩ	'ooh, that's interesting'
	interest (2) — specific (2b) — speech (2ba)	baba; gà; ɔɡ̀,ɲæ̃ɲæ̃	'M said "bad boy; garden; oh; night night"...'
	interest (2) — specific (2b) — entity (2bb) — daddy	bàda	'that's daddy'
	interest (2) — specific (2b) — entity (2bb) — cat	puss	'that's the/a cat'
	interest (2) — specific (2b) — entity (2bb) — dog	βàβàβ	'that's a dog/barking'
	interest (2) — specific (2b) — entity (2bb) — bird	gà→bà	'that's a bird'
	interest (2) — specific (2b) — entity (2bb) — book	bá	'that's a book'
	activity (3) — general (3a)	same as [interest:general]	'I'm busy (with this)'
	activity (3) — specific (3b) — with sock (3ba)	γɔ̀	'I'm playing with sock'
	activity (3) — specific (3b) — with skin (3bb)	γɔ̀	'I'm playing with skin'
IMAG. u.	drink (1)	ˀæ̃; æ̃	'that was a good drink!!'
	seek cat (2)	puss	'where are you puss?'
	ride bike (3)	br:::	'I'm riding a bike'

edible things. Initially in fact it was used only in connection with bread (including toast) and biscuits. It is possible he was trying to imitate these words and that the early instances such as the following were not demands but classifications.

14(24) H: bà (catching sight of biscuit barrel).
(M shakes head.)
H: (grins and reaches) bà; mā; mā.
M: No (removing it).
(H cries.)

14(16) M: Get some toast.
H: bà (running into kitchen).

14(18) (After lunch M offers to read a book but H goes back to table.)
H: mà; bà; bà.
M: What do you want?, etc.
H: (looks at her, points at biscuits) bà; bà.

The tone for [ba] was always falling, unlike the more established instrumental signs, and especially given the pointing gesture in the last text, which was very rare in instrumental contexts, H may in fact have been attempting to specify the content of the demand as bread or biscuit.

The sign [bà] was also one of the variants of the personal [interest] sign ([dà] being most common) which was used with the pointing gesture. It was not related to food in that context. In its instrumental use, it soon became generalized to all edible things, and eventually (next period) took over as the principal undifferentiated general instrumental sign.

2c. [demand: cat] Discussed p. 76 in consideration of first word.

INTERACTIONAL

1a. [object mediated: material] The giving to and fro game had disappeared (see Figure 4.5 (1a)), and so had the holding up of objects for attention (Figure 4.5 (1b)). This last was first replaced by H giving things to or taking them from M or F using the same [aˈdʒà] sign, suggesting that it might have been simply a new, more mobile form of the longstanding 'display' interaction. No turn-taking ritual was involved in these cases. But eventually he came to favour the handing over of objects exclusively, and the accompanying sign [aˈda] had a rising tone or upjump to high level, so that tonally as well as contextually it resembled the earlier [dī] sign.

1b. [object-mediated: pictorial: regulatory] H here developed a clearly interactional sign in the book-reading context. He had received some new books with pictures of farm animals, and was so delighted when animal noises were introduced into reading sessions, that for a time this was what they chiefly consisted of. He would stab the page with his index finger and say [dà] looking up at M for her to make the appropriate animal noise (or in other cases to say the nursery rhyme pictured). Sometimes he would point silently and look expectantly up at M. At other times he would scarcely look at the book at all, just at M as he turned the pages of high speed, pointed vaguely, shouting [dà] each time. As the feature name indicates, there was a regulatory flavour to this, perhaps especially as it was a request for a performance rather than a name. However, I have three reasons for placing the sign here:
     (i) Simply the intuition that control of the addressee was not really what was at stake so much as togetherness.
     (ii) The fact that the sign was one borrowed from personal (the indicating [interest] sign) as have been other object-mediated interactional signs.
     (iii) There are simply not enough distinct signs in this area in this corpus to develop any feel for what criteria could be applied to distinguish interactional and regulatory signs. Thus it would seem more revealing to interpret the sign within the well-established function of interactional.

1bb. [object-mediated: pictorial: neutral] This is where H himself assayed woofs, quacks and moos; sometimes spontaneously when looking at books with a partner, sometimes repeating after M, and sometimes in response to M's prompts of *How does the doggy go?*, etc. (also nearly always mediated by a picture book). He did this only with an adult partner, but not always looking at her/him.

2a. [greet: parent] As before, these signs were occasioned by the arrival home from work of F, or F and M together, or involved face-touching when he was picked up for a cuddle. There were two occasions when M arrived home alone and was greeted by H, who then continued repeating [dàda], clearly looking for F. This could be interpreted as a special [seeking interaction] instance, or it could be a personal statement of intention, anticipation, etc., since [dàda] was also his name for F, used as a comment as F left the house or when H heard him emerge from another room, etc.

2b. [greet cat] This was infrequent and short-lived, but while it lasted was quite consistent in use. When the cat came in he might choose to greet her with this sign, always attempting to fondle or cuddle her. Perhaps the cat's lack of enthusiasm for this demonstration explains H's abandonment of this sign after a couple of weeks, or perhaps the creation of the lexical item *puss* helped to push out this restricted use protolinguistic cat sign.

PERSONAL

1. [feeling] As before, this group were not very common and, as before, he would on occasion utter these signs while looking at someone, as if to add a 'don't you agree?' component.

1c. [pride] This new member of the group shared the high rise-fall tone of the others, and was an expression of satisfaction in such circumstances as putting the bath plug in place successfully, getting an awkward drawer shut, etc.

2. [interest: general] The expressions here continued to change and vary a little, and now for the first time the [e, ε] vowel group did seem contextually distinct in that it seemed always to be favoured when there was an element of unexpectedness in the sighting of the object, or of special delight in it.

These [interest] signs now occurred in many more conversation-like interactions, and Hal's response to a *Where's the ——?* question was to point and use the [interest] sign, as in the following text:

14 months M: Where's the light? Where's the light?
              (H looks at her intently, then up at light.)
           M: It's there, isn't it? Where's the light?
           H: dja̖ (pointing and looking up).
           M: Yes.
           H: dà (pointing again).
           M: Yes, clever boy.
           H: dà; dà; dà; dja̖; dà (pointing at another).
           M: Mhm, that one's not on.
           H: (walking about) gà (21 times).

In this text, although H does not directly address M, he is, in the first place at least, responding to her speech and thus maintaining the conversational interaction, so the borderline between personal and interactional functions is becoming more blurred.

Hal was also beginning to monitor M's confirmatory responses to his [interest] signs, as in the following case:

14(3) H: dæ̀ (pointing at bird in garden).

M: Yes, bird.
H: dà (pointing).
M: Bird.
H: dà (pointing).
M: That's a bird.
H: bà; bɔ̀ (pointing).

(N.B. A few days later [bà] became the regular form for *bird*). Again, he is not looking at M when he speaks, which is an important criterion for interactional utterances. Such an attempt by him to imitate a name given him is probably best seen as an indication that a learning function was developing out of the personal. That is to say, the repetition, as in H's final utterance above, was not so much to acknowledge M's utterance as for his own purposes of learning.

2b.   [interest: specific] As illustrated by the above text, H was beginning to attend to adult speech with a view to producing the mother-tongue forms himself.

2ba. [interest specific: speech] This feature refers to a few particular words or phrases spoken by M, which struck H in particular, either because of the context in which they occurred or because of their particular phonological qualities. H would always repeat these after they had been spoken to him, but not in order to prolong the interaction or initiate an exchange of sounds. They did not appear to be addressed to M, but were rather a private practising or thinking about what he had heard. At this stage they were not used other than in direct imitation except for *Oh!*, already adopted as a 'surprise' indicator.

2bb. [interest: specific: entities] Here are included those few names for familiar things in the environment which H was just beginning to develop. These were not yet of the same status as *puss*, since all except [dada] were restricted to accompanying a here-and-now observation. The name [dada], like *puss*, is not really fairly characterized just as [interest], since it was also used in seeking and recalling contexts. It was also of course well established as an interactional greeting sign, but in the latter case was not restricted to F and so cannot be said to be the same name used in different contexts.

3.   [activity: general] H still vocalized while busying himself with his own affairs, and by fifteen months there was no difference at all between the expressions occurring here and for [interest: general]. The reason I have not here grouped them under some

feature covering both, is that although the special [achieve-
ment] and [exploration] signs (see Figure 4.5) had disappeared,
there was still one expression peculiar to 'doing' as opposed to
'observing' contexts. This expression might be an approach to
sock as a name, though this is far from clear. It was used in two
situations which were distinct to the adult, but may not have
been to H. In one, he was playing with, walking around holding
or pulling off a sock (one of his favourite things), and in the
other he was pinching, pulling, stroking or feeling his skin or
that of someone else. The sound [ɣɔ] was the same in either
case, used quite frequently for a few weeks as an accompaniment to these specific ongoing activities.

IMAGINATIVE
During this period H began to invent clear 'let's pretend' occasions.
These developed from non-verbalized enactments, such as up-ending
his empty cup over the plants in the garden, having many times
watched M using a watering-can.

1.   [drink] the pretending-to-drink example is also a fairly direct
     pretend copy of something witnessed, including an exaggerated
     self-satisfied sigh.
2.   [seek cat] This has already been discussed (see p. 77). This
     mime had moved further into the imaginative realm and would
     not have been recognized without the accompanying utterance.

The language from 15 to 16½ months

During this time, the developments of the previous period were consolidated and extended. More mother-tongue words were learnt, and
Hal could now request certain goods and services by name, as well as
using names in both the interactional and personal functions, and
perhaps also in a regulatory function.

The interactional use of names developed from attending to
picture books with another person. At first he repeated names given
by the adult, but towards the end of the period he might name
things himself, as in the following case;

16(4) (H opens book.)
      H: Woof-woof (pointing at dog).
      (M points at cat.)
      H: Puss.
      (M points at bird.)
      H: Bird.
      (H points up in air.)

Of course, at other times Hal might simply attend to the pictures, leaving M to do all the talking while he sucked his thumb and listened. And occasionally repetitions or exchanges of quacks and moos took place much as before and were a recognizably interactional verbal romp. But the above text shows that the advent of names had changed the situation somewhat, and the *heuristic* function, which had begun to develop from the personal one in the previous period, was also developing here. Or rather, the *mathetic* macrofunction was beginning to evolve (see pp. 114–20).

In the personal function, Hal continued to use words while observing or manipulating objects, as he had begun to do in the previous period, and also used them to express an immediate intention connected with an object (see p. 90 for examples). These are intermediate steps in the development of true names which are functionally unrestricted and do not depend on the support of the here-and-now context for their meaning.

Notes on the language at 16½ months (refer to Figure 4.8)

INSTRUMENTAL

1a. [general demand: normal] The 'somebody do something' plea had almost faded out and was certainly no longer a distinct option. The ['ɔ̃] expression now simply alternated freely with other 'I want that' demand expressions. The most common of these was [bæ] or [ba] which had previously seemed a possible approximation of *bread* or *biscuit*. By now it typically, though not invariably, took a high level tone, as did the earlier [mæ]. The other two expression variants were generally rising in tone.

1b. [general demand: intensified] This impatient version of a general request was usually for food items that were taking too long to prepare.

2. [specific demand] H could now request a number of goods and services by name.

2aa. [specific demand: goods: initiate] Other than wanting to get at the cat as described in the last period, there were two specific objects for which he initiated demands by name. These were for his potty, kept on top of a cupboard in his room, and for M's glasses, always an object of fascination.

2ab. [specific demand: goods: respond] Although H had clearly been able to recognize a number of food names for some weeks, he never initiated a request for food by using the name himself —he simply used one of the general demand signs. It was as though names as a whole had a classificatory function, not to the forefront in instrumental requests, and this may relate to Greenfield and Smith's observation that: 'children ask for specific people and objects only after the naming function (Indicative Object) is firmly established' (Greenfield and Smith 1976: 104). Although my data do not support their claim in this form, I did observe that it took longer for receptively known names to be used instrumentally. However, if he was offered a favourite food—toast, banana or drink—by name, Hal did accept by repeating the name. In this responding situation perhaps the nature of the utterance as a demand was not so pressingly to the fore.

2b. [specific demand: service] Tones here tended to be rather variable at this stage; rising, falling and high level were observed. The initiating requests were items found in the personal [observation] context, and may fairly be regarded as mother-tongue words.

REGULATORY

This function can perhaps be put forward now, though with only two meanings, both very close to the interactional, and in one case with the word *puss* as the expression, which can no longer be seen as protolinguistic in character.

1. [get up] *Puss* was used, addressed to the adult, often with a rising tone, as H lay in M and F's bed in the morning. It was interpreted as a 'get up' request, since going into the living-room where the cat spent the night was the first activity of the day. He didn't really seem interested in the cat though, as in instrumental uses, but in getting the addressee to get up. The word was used in this context only a few times.

2. [sing] The regulatory, as against interactional use of [baba] was not entirely clear. It was used on some occasions as a favourable response to M's offers of *Shall we sing baa baa black sheep?* At other times, when M treated it as a request, he may have been trying to sing it himself, and sometimes he would repeat [baba] throughout M's rendition of the song as if to join in as best he could.

INTERACTIONAL

1a. [object mediated: material] The [aˈdá] expression used when handing objects to M continued, but the context had changed a little. It had now developed into an accompaniment to a joint task where H handed some object up to M to be put in its place

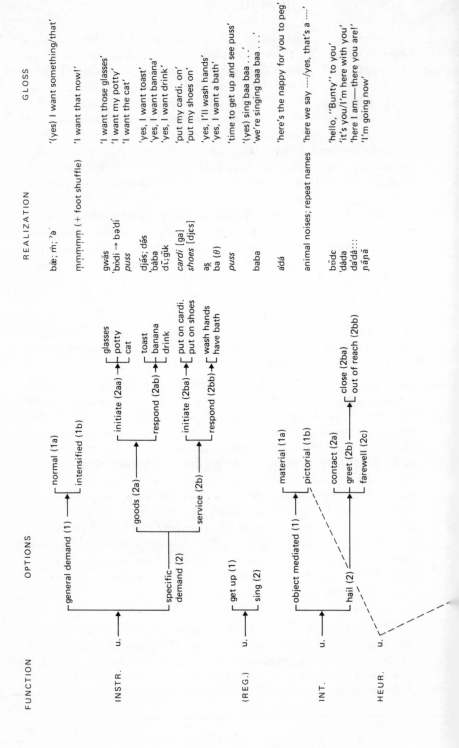

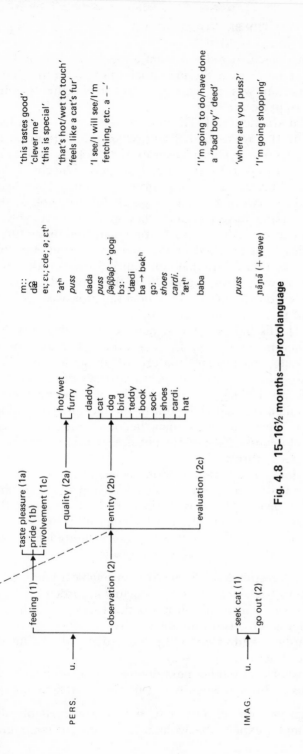

Fig. 4.8 15–16½ months——protolanguage

high out of his reach. It did not seem a regulatory demand for assistance, but more of a sharing ritual, and by far the most common situation was H handing items from the laundry basket for M to peg on the line.

1b. [object mediated: pictorial] The 'you make a noise' sign had faded out, but H now used the context of joint attention to picture books to repeat names given by the adult, as well as to play with animal noises. By the end of the period he could also name pictures himself. These instances of naming have been included in the network here although H did not look at the adult while speaking, largely because they appear to have evolved from the context of exchanging attention mediated by pictures, which was clearly established in the previous period, and this was the best way to indicate that continuity. However, the only names used here were those found also in the personal function, and as indicated on the networks, a new function was evolving out of both of these original functions.

2a. [hail: contact] His babysitter one rainy day decided to teach Hal to say her name *Bunty*. He was evidently more struck by the intimate, face-to-face nature of these lessons than anything else, and for a few weeks afterwards constantly addressed all his intimate circle with his version of *Bunty*. He always looked the addressee full in the face, often smiling, and seemed to mean no more than 'hello, it's me'. It was for moments of closeness, and not for physical reunions for which he used his [greet] forms.

2ba. [hail: greet: close] The normal greeting sign continued.

2bb. [hail: greet: out of reach] An additional version of the normal greeting had evolved. This was distinguished by stress on the second instead of first syllable and by elongation of the final vowel. It was always spoken loudly, sometimes shouted. Example contexts were:

> H is in car addressing M or F on street through car window.
> H is on top of back steps, GM down below in garden.
> M and H at one end of playgroup park. H sees and addresses babysitter and her son who are at other end.
> H is in garden. Addresses toddler next door who is up on sundeck of next-door house.
> H is in house. Hears toddler next door out on his sundeck.
> H is in house. Through window sees neighbour at her window.

Thus this sign was not exactly a summons—he certainly did not, for example, expect the woman next door to come into his house. It was still a greeting, but one which took account of a physical or spatial barrier to the addressee.

2c.   [hail: farewell] H now began to use his version of *night night* as a general farewell. At this stage it was used to mark his own leaving of the scene rather than anyone else's.

PERSONAL

1a.   [feeling: taste] This sign reappeared suddenly after a long absence. This was on the occasion of a stranger approaching H on the beach and offering him a chip. H took it in silent wonderment, and then uttered [m::] on tasting the novel food, after the donor had moved away. Thereafter it was used occasionally in contexts as before.

1b.   [feeling: pride] The [surprise] and [pleasure] sounds faded out, but [pride] continued as before.

1c.   [feeling: involvement] This feature is part of a reorganization which seems observable within the personal function as it moved to heuristic or mathetic characteristics. The [interest: general] and [activity: general] signs which were indistinguishable in expression in the previous period had largely disappeared in their earlier form. The sounds which now occurred in comparable noticing and doing contexts had a quality of pleasure or at least of emotional involvement, rather like the [intensified] sub-category of [interest] (see Figure 4.7). Wide falling tone was favoured, though regular falls and rise–falls were also used. The distinction was clearly no longer between 'noticing' and 'doing'. It was between this excited expression of affect or curiosity on the one hand, and the use of specific names in contexts either of observation, anticipation and occasional recall or of ongoing activity on the other. For this reason, the latter two contexts have been subsumed as [observation] and opposed to the truly protolinguistic sign which has been grouped with other expressions of feeling.

2.   [observation] I am using this feature name to indicate the comparability of Hal's use of language here and Nigel's use of personal language. However, this must not obscure the fact that Hal uttered these names not only as a passive onlooker, but also whilst doing things with objects or expressing an immediate intention, etc. The tone used was not entirely consistent but was falling in the great majority of utterances. Examples of the use of language realizing the feature [observation] were of the following kind:

Ongoing
['dædi] (teddy)—throwing his teddy bear down.
[djɛs] (shoes)—picking up M's sandals and walking about with them.
[bɒs] (puss)—stroking the babysitter's hair.
[bɒkʰ] (book)—fetching a book.
[bɜ:] (bird)—pointing at picture or at real bird.
[gʊgi] (dog)—pointing at picture or at real dog.

Intention/prediction
[gɔ:] (sock)—looking at F's sock drawer, before going across and taking out sock to play with.
[dada] (Daddy)—going down hall to bathroom where F is, then banging on door.
[babʊ] (bad boy)—looking at television; then going and pressing forbidden switch.
[ʔatʰ] (hot)—reaching towards light bulb in the (mistaken) expectation it will be hot.

IMAGINATIVE
1. [seek cat] The game of pretending to look for the cat continued.
2. [go out] Another 'let's pretend' game. H would put a bag or his beach bucket over his arm and walk out of the room into the hall waving goodbye to his audience, clearly 'going shopping'.

Overview of Hal's protolanguage and comparison with Nigel

By 16½ months Hal was on the threshold of Phase II of language development—the transition. The nature and significance of this change will be explored in the next chapter. The rest of this chapter will be devoted to reviewing key aspects of Hal's protolanguage up to 16½ months, and comparisons will be drawn between his language development and that of Halliday's Nigel, and also other children reported in the literature.

Onset of symbol use

The first vocal signs for Hal, as for Nigel, were in the personal and interactional functions and evolved between 7 to 9 months. However, whereas Nigel by 9 months had also developed two instrumental gestural symbols, Hal did not develop an instrumental sign until 9 to 10½ months, and never created any iconic gestural symbols. Pointing and reaching gestures were quite prominent, but only as an accompaniment to a vocal sign.

Number of functions

Although I have not made use of the heuristic function proposed by Halliday, because I have interpreted its emergence as a general shift towards a macrofunctional basis for the language, I have indicated those interactional and personal features which were developing into learning contexts, and this change took place at about the same time for both children. Thus, I would maintain that the absence of a heuristic function is simply a matter of emphasis in the interpretation rather than a pronounced difference between the two systems, though the lack of a 'What's that?' meaning in Hal's language probably made the positing of a heuristic function seem less warranted than for Nigel.

The lack of a regulatory function for Hal was, however, a genuine difference, and needs some consideration. For both children the greatest elaboration of linguistically realized options occurred in the more 'reflective' functions of interactional and personal, and the reason is surely that these meanings are more dependent on a symbolic means of expression. Regulatory behaviour was apparent in Hal's case. He did indicate that he wanted someone to continue a game or sometimes to stop doing something, but would do this in some improvised way that was either non-symbolic (e.g., deliberately removing M's hands from his trolley when she attempted to help guide it for him), or only marginally so (e.g., jigging up and down for a continuation of a bouncing-on-lap game, or saying *boom!* or *whee!* for a repetition of some poking or whirling game to which these were accompanying utterances by M). Perhaps these last would have developed into more obvious symbols had any particular romp persisted over a long enough period. Since this was an identifiable situational context, but one in which the most general meanings are so readily conveyed non-linguistically, it is perhaps not surprising that a child whose protolinguistic potential as a whole remained fairly un-elaborated (in comparison with Nigel) managed without a sign system here. It is interesting that Carter's account of one child's protolinguistic signs from 12 to 16 months, if interpreted in terms of functions, also has no regulatory signs (since I take it that 'Dislike' symbols glossed as: 'Get receiver's help in changing situation' are instrumental in nature) (Carter 1979: 79).

Size of protolanguage

At present we have no way of judging what is a 'normal' symbolic potential for a child in the pre-mother tongue period. At 13½ months,

Nigel had 32 signs (with 2 or 3 expression overlaps) and Hal had 17 (again with 2 or 3 expressions the same), while Carter reports only 8 distinct signs for her subject for the whole period of 12 to 18 months.

Scope

There are a number of ways then in which Hal's protolinguistic system is more limited than Nigel's and these are noted below:

1. Lack of regulatory language.
2. Lack of specificity in instrumental language until the general move into the mother tongue.
3. A general lack of the initiating/responding distinction which recurred throughout Nigel's system.
4. Fewer expressions of feeling within the personal function.
5. No distinctly interactional signs for expressions of feeling in which the adult is invited to share (cf. Nigel's 'shared regret', 'acknow- ledge reproof', etc.)
6. No distinct signs for responses to *Where's the* —*? Look at the* — utterances, where the adult draws the child's attention to objects in the environment.
7. No request for a name, i.e. no baby *What's that?* form.

It is perhaps worth noting here that Hal's [dà] was never interpreted by any of his circle as a demand for a name, and the only period when it was used clearly to demand a response was one where per- formance of moos and quacks or rhymes, and not names as such, was being sought.

A further difference between the two systems concerns the use by Hal of signs in a context not utilized by Nigel. This is what I have termed 'activity' within the personal function. Because Nigel did not create any signs in such a context, Halliday treated all interest signs as a sub-category of expressions of feeling until the onset of naming, when observations with a lexical content are separated off as a distinct class.

Similarities

Despite all the above there are striking similarities between the proto- languages of Hal and Nigel and aspects of protolinguistic behaviour reported in other studies.

1. As has already been mentioned, both children began developing a protolanguage at about the same age. Greenfield and Smith's two subjects were also reported to have produced their first consis- tent speech sounds at 8(19) and 7(22).

2. Instrumental demands, when vocally differentiated, did not on the whole concern playthings or food items (though the latter figured prominently for Hal as the focus of 'general' demands). Specific instrumental demands were usually for familiar things of special importance to the child, perhaps because of being involved in ritual situations, as with Nigel's *powder, clock, potty*; Hal's *glasses* and *potty*.

3. Both children used language as a means of establishing contact with a significant adult, though in Hal's case it took quite a while for such an acknowledgement of the other to be restricted to adult contexts of greeting. Interestingly, both developed phonological variants within the greetings context, though in Hal's case it was simply a change of stress pattern and vowel length, according to whether the interaction was intimate or more public. In Nigel's case a tone difference was used to convey a distinction in the response required from the addressee, and previewed a more general functional distinction later to apply across the whole language.

4. Both children from very early on enjoyed creating the most basic form of dialogue by exchanging sounds with another person. In Hal's case a single sound went back and forth; in Nigel's case the adult call–child response pair could be prolonged into an indefinite series.

5. Although Nigel did not use giving and taking of objects as a context for interactional utterances as Hal did, several other studies have reported this as a favourite style (e.g., Bruner 1975a; Bates *et al.* 1979a). In Hal's case the vocalization evolved from accompanying his role in a game of exchange to marking the performance of his part in a genuine joint task. In the latter case he used a sign-expression previously used in 'self in the environment' contexts, not interactional ones.

6. This leads to mention of one of the striking similarities between Nigel and Hal. And this is the use of personal sign-expressions conveying interest in the external environment, also in interactional contexts where the environment in some way mediated the interaction. In Nigel's case, pictures were reserved at first for interactional contexts, while interest within personal function related to sounds and movements. The two contexts are thus more obviously distinct than in Hal's case. For Hal it was physical objects which were at first used in both personal and interactional contexts, and later pictures were additionally used in both functions. (None the less, a distinction between a material and a pictorial object did seem to arise at certain points for Hal, as indicated

in the networks.) Often in Hal's case it was a sign-expression used
in a context of activity in the environment rather than contemplation of it (where these could be distinguished), which was concurrently used in, or later transferred to, an interactional context,
as if to emphasize the involvement of the self as well as the
mediation of the object in the interaction.

First names

Although Nigel's first possible imitation of an adult word occurred
as early as 9 to 10½ months, it was not a true name. It was an instrumental sign with the complex meaning 'I want my bird', just as his
first approximations to adult words within the personal function
meant all of 'I see a dog' or 'a dog—that's interesting', etc. Hal, on
the other hand, did not appear to try and imitate words until he had
really begun to grasp the notion of a name, though again not all of
his first imitations were genuinely different from protolinguistic
signs.

   As with Nigel, naming first arose in Hal's language as a development from expressing interest in objects (personal function), and
using objects, especially pictures, to mediate interactions with
adults. McShane's subjects also provide evidence for this interactional route to the understanding of names. He says:

> I would suggest that the child does not possess the concept of naming when
> he or she first learns to pair words with objects in rituals such as storybook
> reading. My further suggestion is that the words the child initially learns in
> these situations are learnt as a means of participating in a ritual activity that
> concerns talking about objects. The child first learns the words and later learns
> that these words are names. [McShane 1980: 49.]

Why McShane sees this conclusion as an insight to be put forward
in opposition to Halliday's account is unclear, but he differs perhaps
in laying such exclusive stress on the picture book context as the one
from which naming develops.

   In Hal's case the first word was not used with a picture for several
weeks, and Hal and Nigel both developed names also from protolinguistic signs used in the personal function. Here the child expresses
his interest in objects in the environment, and the adult, if attending,
typically names the object. The child's vocalization is not a request
for a name, but over time he comes to recognize that the adult's
word is not simply an acknowledgement of his interest but serves
to classify the particular object in question. At this point he begins
to repeat the name himself and to develop a similar capacity to categorize phenomena. He is then on the way to developing fully-fledged

names, although this will not be achieved until words are used in non-here-and-now contexts and for various functions, as happened with Hal's word *puss*.

In this way words were developed by Hal from personal [interest] and [observation] meanings, and in his case protolinguistic signs were produced in a context of activity with objects, also within the personal function. This context also developed new aspects with the advent of lexis, which helped to develop true names. From meaning simply 'I'm doing something with something', he came to be able to specify 'I'm doing something with a sock'. Once he took this step, imitating the adult word *sock*, he could very quickly also recognizably mean 'I intend to do something with a sock', an important step towards the development of a true name which would also be viable with a functionally different meaning, such as 'Let me do something with a sock'.

Many examples in the literature of 'first words' can be seen to be microfunctionally specific signs which happen to derive their expression from an adult word like Nigel's *bird*.

The following instances from different children are given by Bates *et al.* (1979), who recognize their nature and call them 'pre-referential words'.

da   = give Used by Italian subject only when giving and taking objects (interactional function).

bam!   Used only as an accompaniment to knocking over toys (personal function).

kitty   Used only to have a toy kitten returned after child has thrown it out of cot (instrumental function).

Menn (1978) also describes a number of word imitations used by her subject Jacob.

Jacob = Where's Jacob   Used only in peep-bo games (interactional function).

there   Used only when setting objects down (personal function).

bounce   Used only when bouncing (personal function).

Menn also describes the way one restricted sign [ioio], which was originally an accompaniment to rotating a wheel-like object, gradually extended its provenance. First, within the original personal function (to maintain Halliday's terms), it was extended to recalling and anticipatory uses (e.g., when pointing to tape spools which were stationary at the time), after which it was used as an instrumental demand (Menn 1978: 32). She observes too that not all words which developed in this way within the personal function went on to evolve instrumental or regulatory uses. This also parallels my data where even after the dawning of the naming concept and the use of several words without functional restriction, many 'words' were not extended across the functional range for a considerable time; e.g., *potty* meant at first only 'I want my potty', *hat* meant only 'I see/saw/will see; am playing with, do you remember?, etc., my hat'. This point will be elaborated in detail in the sections of this book dealing with the transition phase.

Sign-expressions

So far I have been generalizing about the functions and content of signs in different studies. It is also interesting to consider whether there are any general comparisons to be made concerning the expressions favoured.

Some sign-expressions clearly derive from natural physiological noises, and are self-imitations turned into symbols. For example, Hal's early greeting (x:] was the taking up of a sound sometimes occurring when smiling with a mouth full of dribble. The use of something like Hal's general instrumental sound ['ə] as a demand or command probably develops from a grizzle and has been quite frequently reported. Nigel had something similar in both instrumental and regulatory functions, and it is also reported by Ferrier as what amounts to an instrumental sign for her subject (Ferrier 1978: 474), by Carter as what she calls a 'General Want Expresser' (Carter 1978: 75), and by Dore (1973: 103) as a 'Request command'.

Other sign-expressions were doubtless picked up from mother-tongue expressions. In Hal's case [dada] began to be used after F had tried to teach him *Daddy*. In any case this will be a word frequently used to the child, and Greenfield and Smith report that one subject, Nicky, used [dada] as an accompaniment to ongoing action (as did Hal)—in fact as a first symbol (Greenfield and Smith 1976: 81). It is possible that Hal's [da] and [ada] sounds and the [da] and [la] of Carter's David, used with the pointing gesture, were like Nigel's [a::da] and Nicky's [ada], imitations of *What's that?* or at least *that* or *there*. Certainly, all these children in English-speaking environments used the sounds in comparable ways.

Nasal initial syllables seem to be favoured for 'wanting' signs. Greenfield and Smith (1976: 92) report [mama] as an early signal of volition, not necessarily associated with naming the mother. Hal used [ma, ɲæ] and [m̩mm̩m̩]; Bates's subject, Carlotta, used [nana] as a general request; and Nigel used [nã, m̂n̂ŋ] and [m]. Carter's David used [mm, ma, maɩ, mə] with a reaching gesture, as well as [na, næ, nə, noʊ] as disapproval indicators, which latter look like possible imitations of *no*.

Tone

One respect in which Hal differed from Nigel was in having a variety of tones as well as articulations for the same sign in certain cases. Where personal signs of interest and activity, but especially the former, varied between normal falls, wide falls and rise–falls, this may have corresponded to different degrees of emotional involvement. Where the instrumental signs varied between falling and non-falling tones, this seemed to relate to the gradual adoption of non-falling as the norm for this function. However, there did not seem to be any observable meaning correlation associated with different tones for personal activity signs, which, like random babble in this and other contexts, and like different instances of Hal's first word *puss*, occurred on a variety of tones. Interesting in this regard is Dore's (1973) observation that the tones which eventually carried functional meaning might be used at first 'without phonemic intent'. It was particularly noticeable with Hal's *puss* that different tones were used apparently indiscriminately for a while, although gradually level and rising tones were adopted much more frequently in situations when he sought an interaction with the cat.

There are one or two instances of signs with level tones in Halliday's data, but nothing which foreshadows the later systematic use of a rising tone until 15 to 16½ months. Hal had already by 12 months begun to show a preference for high level tone for the instrumental function which does tie in with this later use of tone. However, as with Nigel, it was not till 15 to 16½ months, at the earliest, that different tones could be regarded as freely combinable with the same word to convey functional differences. Menn (1978: 141) also reports an early use of functionally specific rising tone. Jacob apparently used rising intonation babble as early as 13 (22) to convey requests, and also rather interestingly used rising intonation in a non-interactional context of puzzling over an object. This last is perhaps comparable with Hal's personal [activity: exploration] sign where rising tones were favoured ([adá adá adà], etc.). In neither of these cases does it seem very likely that the tone was borrowed from adult usage.

Consistency of articulation of sign-expressions

One important issue concerning sign-expressions relates to their consistency. I have already touched on this in relation to tone; here I will consider the articulatory aspect. Halliday, like myself, often found a number of variants for an expression which were generally phonetically related, and in both sets of data, variation occurred in initial consonants and in vowels. Carter's data differ in that while vowels varied, initial consonants remained stable over the six-month period of her study.

These variations seem quite acceptable given the infant's lack of articulatory finesse. A question of greater moment is whether we should necessarily assume that the child will feel constrained to invent a new sound for every new meaning he has to express. This is indeed what we would naturally expect, given the nature of the sign as a content-expression pair; in principle, the only way to indicate a new meaning is by using a new sound. But it may be that some children are less inventive than others and rely more on features of the context to indicate the meaning.

Thus Bates *et al.* (1979a) report that one subject, Carlotta, accompanied both her first 'requests' and her first 'declaratives' with the same sound [ha], although a different requesting sound developed later. Another subject, Marta, succeeded an imperative [mm] with the sound [aji], which was used also 'deictically to point out novel events or objects' (Bates *et al.* 1979a: 125). From the description given, th ⌐rlier [mm] seems definitely instrumental, so if the 'declarative' use ⌐sonal in function then a single expression form is serving for two   ⌐ different meanings. As 'requests' and 'declaratives' are rather br⌐ categories to be working with, it is possible, however, that [aji] was used in regulatory and interactional contexts respectively, in which case the uses might in fact have been quite closely connected.

In my own data there is a point at which [bà], which was a variant of the personal interest sign [dà], also turned up as an instrumental sign. I have suggested that this may be explicable if [ba] was an imitation of the word *bread* or *biscuit* in the latter case only, but it may simply be that the different situational contexts were well enough established and easily enough distinguished non-linguistically that Hal did not worry about the temporary overlap in expression. Similarly, with the interactional greeting [dada] and the personal-activity [dada]. There could hardly have been any confusion as to intent in the circumstances in which the utterances were made. But here there were almost certainly some minor phonetic differences in the manner of utterance as well as in the context.

At present, the overlapping of expressions is probably best seen as generally relatable to overlap in meaning. This is because, for my data as well as Halliday's, the overlap chiefly concerns the spread within two functions of signs relating to combinations of the three focuses of self, environment and other. For Hal, the overlaps of meaning related to: (i) the environment as an object of contemplation alone or in conjunction with the other, and (ii) the environment as a source of exploration of personal skills or as a medium of interaction with the other. For Nigel, it was the environment as an object of contemplation alone or as a medium of interaction with another, and this joint attention to the environment of objects eventually led to a new role for the other as a source of information on the environment.

Orientational interpretation

However, an attempt to explain such overlapping expressions in these terms seems to lead to a view that something like an 'orientational' network is needed to complement the functional one. Halliday has himself described Nigel's language in some such terms in various writings (e.g., Halliday 1975a, Chapter 5; Halliday 1979).

At nine months, Hal's language could then be viewed in terms of his postulated world view, as in Figure 4.9a.

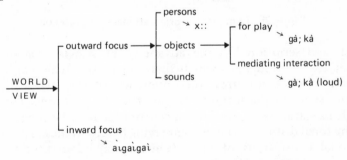

Fig. 4.9a 9 months—orientational interpretation

Of course, attending in particular to like expressions still does not mean that we should recognize no difference between displaying an object to another and manipulating it privately, even if the only difference in the symbolic expression is one of loudness and clarity. To take account of expressions to the exclusion of apparent differences in content can only lead to an impoverished description, given our present state of knowledge concerning what

does constitute a distinct context for an exchange of meaning
for an infant.

By 12 months, Hal's world view might look like that given in
Figure 4.9b. At this stage sounds, when orientated to, are for play,
while by 16½ months they could be seen as objects of contemplation, like material things.

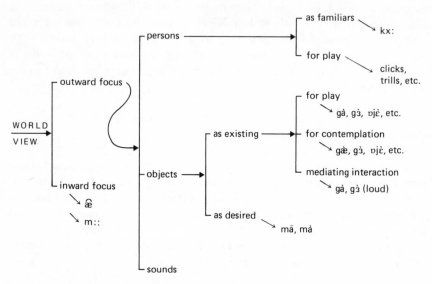

Fig. 4.9b 12 months—orientational interpretation

Such a description has the advantage of bringing together into
a closer relationship signs which share, or partly share, expressions.
However, it does not stress the uniqueness of [objects: as desired]
vs. other signs, in the former's frequent use of level tone. This is fair
enough in static terms, but evidence from the later language suggests
that the tonal distinction already emerging here, and the corresponding
functional contrast, is of more fundamental importance than this
description suggests. Thus, an account in these terms would be
a complementary one rather than a preferred one.

One possible advantage of a description in terms of the features
of the infant's world, rather than specifically the uses to which he
puts his language, might be that an analysis in such terms is more
directly relateable to studies of the infant's interactions before he
begins to develop language—when he can none the less be seen to
orient differentially towards persons and objects, for example. Thus,
for general purposes the 'world view' of the infant need not be defined,

even during the protolinguistic stage, purely by linguistic evidence. For Hal, for example, language was not used much at first as a means of control of other persons, or as the chief medium of play with the other. Yet there is no doubt that at nine months persons were orientated to as partners in boisterous, physical play, and control was achieved through crying and physical manipulation of an attentive adult partner.

Since I am concerned specifically with linguistic, rather than general cognitive development, etc., I shall not pursue a parallel description in such terms here. Descriptions such as the limited and provisional ones offered above in Figures 4.9(a) and (b) can simply be derived from the microfunctional presentation already offered. However, it is interesting that Hal's language seemed to reflect in its expression system both orientational *and* functional groupings, and a consideration of the former may be an approach which a non-linguist would find accessible for relating the proto-linguistic period to studies of things before the protolanguage and to things outside linguistics. However, since we do not have usable descriptions of adult language in such terms, it will be less explanatory for a purely linguistic developmental study than the micro-functional analysis I have prefe   d.

5 Into Phase II: from protolanguage to transition

The development of the first word pinpoints Hal's first move out of the protolanguage. The different status of a lexical item from a protolinguistic expression is very easily seen from an examination of the varied contexts in which the word *puss* occurred. From the start, it was a name referring to a particular class of entity, and not an inextricable fusion of interpersonal and experiential kinds of meaning as are protolinguistic expressions, which carry inseparable meanings such as 'I want' + 'that visible thing' or 'see this' + 'I've got something' or 'how interesting' + 'there it is'.

But although this turning point occurred between 13½ and 15 months, Hal's language as a whole certainly did not change abruptly at this point. What we find is that during this period he had one fully-fledged vocabulary item (*puss*), was developing the proper name *Dadda* and was just beginning to develop four or five other words, by imitating mother-tongue names with a protolinguistic meaning within the personal function, such as 'I see an X' or 'there's an X; how interesting'.

Then between 15 and 16½ months there were further changes:

1. Two more functionally unrestricted words appeared: (*shoes, cardi.*).
2. The meaning of a personal function proto-word was no longer restricted to 'I see an X' or 'I'm playing with X', but might be any of 'I'm going to see X', 'I saw X' or 'I intend to do something with X'; and there were also interactional meanings, such as 'we're looking at a dog here'. These developments indicate that even where the word had not occurred in an instrumental or regulatory function, the concept of a name was emerging just the same.
3. While the pattern of tone use was not yet clear, some of the functionally restricted mother-tongue imitations were becoming consistent in occurring with a particular tone. Personal ones took a falling tone, and *toast, glasses* and *potty* of the instrumental group took a level or rising tone, like the general protolinguistic demand signs.

Thus by 16½ months, a number of significant steps had already been taken by the child, and these were consolidated over the period 16½–18 months.

The language from 16½ to 18 months

In general terms, the 16½–18 month language can be character-ized as one using mother-tongue rather than invented expres-sions.

Goods, services and behaviours were requested by name, and offers responded to by repeating a name or using *no* for rejections and refusals. (See notes on instrumental and regulatory functions on pp. 106–7 for details.)

There were three principal areas where names were used in the interactional function. One concerned the establishment of con-tact with an addressee by labelling parts of the other person's face (see [object mediated:via face] p. 107 for examples). Another was sharing attention to picture books as before, and a new develop-ment was bringing a physical object to the addressee's attention as a form of greeting (see [object mediated:other] p. 107 for examples). Finally, there was the use of language to share an experience of being hurt or being chastised, such an experience occasionally being recalled from a short time before. (See [share state of feeling] p. 108 for illustrations and further comment.)

Within the personal function, entities were named chiefly when handled or observed, often in response to adult comments, such as *Go and find X, What's that?, Where's X?*, etc. Names of objects were also used in recall situations occasionally. (See [observation:entity] pp. 110–12 for details, discussion and examples of all these.) In addition to object names, certain properties of objects were referred to. And as well as naming a very few ongoing actions, he might also negatively characterize his own behaviour with *badboy*, or an event with *oh dear*.

By 18 months, invented sign expressions had largely disappeared, and an interpretation of Hal's linguistic potential in terms of separate microfunctional networks has become less viable for several reasons. However, in order to explicate this point, the language will first be analysed in terms of microfunctions as before. A number of text examples are included in the notes to the network (Figure 5.1), to help present the more extensive data set, and this microfunctional

FUNCTION   OPTIONS

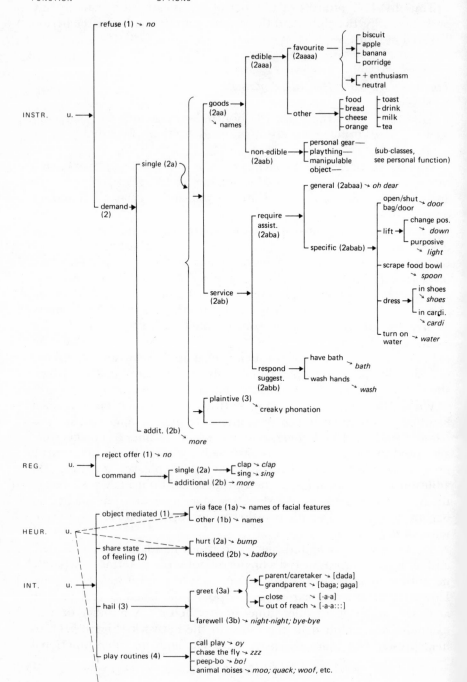

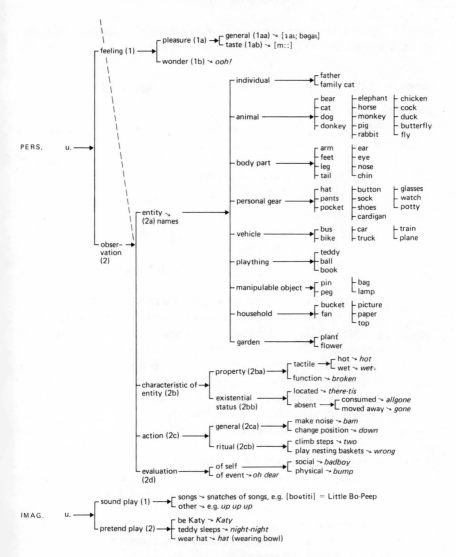

Fig. 5.1 16½–18 months—protolanguage

description will illustrate the emerging need for a 'macrofunctionally' based description.

Notes on the language at 18 months (refer to Figure 5.1)

INSTRUMENTAL

1.   [refuse] H now used *no*, which meant 'I don't want', in various circumstances. It might be a rejection of goods or services offered verbally or non-verbally, or the refusal of a suggestion, as in the following instances:

17(14) M: Want to pull the plug out?
          H: No.
17(22) M: Is Hal going to kiss teddy?
          H: No (throwing it into toy box instead).

In these cases, the meaning is 'I don't want to' rather than 'I don't want that' or 'I don't want you to do that'.

2.   [demand] H could now indicate required goods or services by name (2a), or request a repeat of either by the use of *more* (2b).

2aaa.   [goods: edible] There are two grounds at this point for regarding edible goods as a special class in opposition to other kinds of desired objects. One is the total absence of food names in non-instrumental contexts, and the other is the special phonology associated with a small sub-group of these instrumental names (2aaaa).

2aaaa. [goods: edible: favourite] H would now request food items by name, and three of these words occurred in a special phonological form, with a crescendo to diminuendo of intensity and an elongation of the final vowel. This indicated not impatience or anxiety, as in the case of his earlier proto-linguistic 'intensified' demand, but gleeful anticipation of his favourite food.

2aab.   [goods: other] Other requested objects were in the classes indicated on the network.

2abaa. [service: require assistance: general] This sign began as a personal one commenting on a sneeze and was copied from Grandma's *oh dear* in this situation. H generalized it to become a remark on any mishap, and then sometimes used it instrumentally. When used in the latter sense it did not have the personal tone pattern [ō ɒ dǐ] but usually had level tone on both syllables—sometimes with a small upjump or downjump on the second syllable. Sometimes the tone remained falling but from an upjump [ōɒdi].

2abab. [service: require assistance: specific] Specific services requested were to enable H to achieve something at present beyond his capabilities, such as scraping the remains from the food bowl, opening doors, turning on taps, etc.

2abb.   [service: respond suggestion] As before, there were one or two suggestions which H did not initiate but might respond to affirmatively by repeating the salient word.

3.   [demand: plaintive] Virtually anything except *no* and *more* could receive a plaintive voice quality, sometimes amounting to a pleading creaky voice.

REGULATORY
1.   [reject offer] As well as the meaning for *no* already discussed for instrumental above, Hal could use the negative to control the behaviour of the addressee as in the following examples.

17(28) M: Shall we sing?
       H: No.
17(25) M: (threateningly as H misbehaves at table)
          Do you want to get down?
       H: (calms down) No.

2a.   [command: single] Specific requests were still for musical performance only. The typical situation was for M to be clapping or singing with H and for him to request F to join in too. He persistently repeated his request on these occasions till F complied.

2b.   [command: additional] As well as requesting additional goods or a repetition of some service (e.g., 'lift me again to press the button'), *more* was used with a regulatory meaning of 'you do that again', as in the following:

17(20) Going up to lawnmower, asking M to push it again, as he enjoyed this.
17(25) Requesting a repeat of having his top spun.
17(27) Requesting a repeat of being held upside down.

INTERACTIONAL
1a.   [object mediated: via face] A very common occurrence at this time was the establishment of intimacy by means of touching and naming features of the addressee's face (and occasionally, body). This was usually with one of the family circle, and if other members were present, he might then go round touching and naming a feature for each person in turn. Another typical case would be when M was holding H in her arms while talking to someone else. H might then begin

touching the face of M's addressee, labelling as he did so.
The interactional nature of this labelling is illustrated in the
following two examples:

17(14) H spends some minutes intently observing another
toddler on the beach as if wanting to play with her.
Eventually he approaches and begins touching and
naming her facial features.

17(10) M has made it clear that she is fed up with H. He
wants to make it up and climbs on to her lap with
a book. He begins labelling a face in this, but quickly
turns and labels M's face, gazing sweetly into her
eyes in a clear attempt to win her over.

1b.   [object mediated: other] Naming and repeating names
occurred over books as before, but generally without any
eye-contact between H and 'addressee'. However, he would
now occasionally draw attention to an object in a more
obviously interactional way, almost as a greeting in fact.
For example:

17 months M enters the room, home from work. H delighted,
goes over to his tricycle, looks at M and says *bike*.

17(7)   M enters F's office at work with H in tow—this
is a novel situation. F greets him with *hello boy*.
H is silent for a moment, then says *book*, holding
up the book he has in his hand.

17(24) F enters H's bedroom in the morning. H points
up to the ceiling light and says *light*, only
momentarily switching his gaze from F's face.

2a.   [share state of feeling: hurt] When he hurt himself H expected
someone to say *oh bump!*, or to sympathize with his saying
it. Often, a little exchange of saying *bump* would cheer him
up. On at least one occasion he let M know that he had
hurt himself by approaching her for sympathy when she had
not witnessed the mishap, as follows:

17(22) M is in hallway and hears H grizzle in back room.
He comes out into hall and goes up to her com-
plaining *bump!*

It will later be suggested that this kind of occasion provided
one context for the development of informative language
(see p. 133).

2b.   [share state of feeling: misdeed] H's spontaneous uses of
badboy in the previous period were two occasions when

announcing an intention to do something prohibited, and two occasions as a running commentary to dubious behaviour. Six of the seven examples of use between 16½ and 18 months, however, appear to be interactional in nature. There were two instances such as the following:

> (i) M has smacked H for pinching her. H goes over to F upset and says *badboy* as if to enlist sympathy.

These occasions are very similar to that of *bump* above. Then there were the following incidents:

> (i) H leans over the arm of the chair while on M's lap to climb into the prohibited cat's 'sanctuary' in the corner of the room. He is restrained and told off. A little later he climbs on to M's lap again, then looks over into the corner and back at M and says *badboy*, recalling the earlier incident.
>
> (ii) H deliberately tips a drink he has asked for over F's coffee table. A scene ensues. That evening, several hours later, when being praised as a good boy, he looks over to the coffee table and repeats *badboy* several times, smiling impishly at M and F.
>
> (iii) H is chastised for biting M. When he has calmed down he returns to M, points to her 'wounded' arm, rubs the spot and says *badboy*, looking cheekily at M.

All these three involve recalling a shared experience from a little earlier, not at all as a reproach, but reinforcing re-established good relations.

The only other recorded instance of *badboy* is given below. It is a little different again, and is of interest in hinting most clearly at later informative language (see p. 133).

> 17(10) H comes in from the garden and hands M a seedpod and leaves torn from a young tree. As he does so he confesses softly, *badboy*.

3. [hail] This system remained as before except that the [bŏdɛ] sign disappeared, and his grandparents, who arrived for a three-month visit from overseas at the beginning of this period, were distinguished from parents or caretakers.

4. [play routines] There were four little games played with the help of language. Hal would pretend to call back and forth with his grandfather, yelling *oy*; play at chasing a pretend fly (another game created by GF); he finally signalled verbally an emergence during 'peep-bo' and still enjoyed quacking

and mooing games with a partner. All of these clearly have an imaginative element, but have been classified here because the factor of romping loudly with a partner seemed more prominent than Hal's awareness of the pretend aspects, which were largely introduced by the other person.

PERSONAL

1.   [feeling] This was the only area where a totally invented expression occurred. It was for pleasure or satisfaction, and was very frequent for a time, unlike the earlier pleasure and pride signs which had disappeared by this time.

2.   [observation] This feature has to be understood broadly as something like 'learning' or 'interpretation'.

2a.   [observation: entity] Two individuals were known by name —his father and the family cat. *Daddy* was quite a frequent comment to note F's exit from a room or else sounds of F from elsewhere in the house. The cat was for a week or two known as [ɛʃiʔɪz] as he heard *There she is!* so often addressed to him, but then he settled on her name *Katy*, used on noticing her, observing someone stroking her, while chasing her, etc. Other things were named as he handled them, prepared to fetch them, picked them up, put them down, or simply pointed at them. Very often of course it was pictures that were named with the pointing gesture. And during this period he would often point to a real object and then find a picture of the same thing and name each in turn, as if working out what constituted the provenance of the name. For example, on coming in from seeing the moon he would typically go straight to the book with a picture of the moon in and name that picture. Or on finding and naming a tail in a book, he would take the book over to the cat and sit pointing from the real tail to the pictorial one, naming each time.

It was not so easy to be sure exactly what lexical classes he was building up. Some names were used only here, and not instrumentally, which provides one broad grouping. Of these [animal] is suggested as a group because he had a clear expectation that anything here would have a characteristic noise, as well as holding naming sessions which included nothing else. Most of these names were in fact learned from picture books, and possibly the way things are grouped in books influences the child's taxonomic notions.

Face and body parts were named also in one specific

interactional context, so would seem to be a distinct, viable group. Then I have distinguished three classes of names also used instrumentally. One is [personal gear] —mostly names of clothes, but also *glasses, potty* and *watch*. These were used instrumentally before any other names, and in personal contexts were at times identified in turn as a group. The other two classes [favourite plaything] and [manipulable object] comprised names used in 'handling' rather than purely 'observing' situations. Toys were physically discriminated from other household objects in being kept together in a box on the floor. Teddies, balls and books were likely to wander round the house and get positioned out of reach, which may account for those names being used instrumentally while those of other playthings were not.

Finally, there are other objects in the house including some further toys whose names were not used instrumentally and so have been separately classed. One further group of toys—that of toy cars, trucks, trains, etc.—has been included in a distinct lexical class of [vehicle]. This is because real vehicles were also names, and their noises imitated when he played with toy ones.

The category of [garden items] is probably the most doubtful feature in this network, but may have validity as 'things not to be picked'.

I have said that H named objects chiefly when handling or pointing to them. Some such examples may not seem unambiguously personal in function. In all the following cases there may be some difficulty of classification into functional type:

16(17) M puts hat on toy donkey. H, watching, says *hàt.*
16(25) M: Where's the light?
        H: Light (pointing up).
17(1)   M: Go and get your donkey, Hal; go and get Eeyore.
        H: (fetching it) Eeyore [ʔɒʔi] ; (pokes its hat) hàt.
17(11) M: Ooh! What' you got? (as H enters, holding GM's bathing cap).
        H: Hàt.

All these are examples of H responding (with a name) to the adult's indication of interest in some object, whether expressed non-verbally, as a Wh-interrogative or an imperative. These could therefore be classed as interactional or personal, depending on whether or not their status as responses is regarded as crucial.

I have regarded them as personal, not only because H did not necessarily seek eye-contact with the addressee, but because his concern seemed to be with the objects rather than the interaction. If he was not interested in the object he might ignore what was said to him, as in the following example from a little later:

18(10) (H is on M's bed in morning, taking things from the bedside table and handing them to M.)

> H: Wàtch (handing it over), pèn (handing it over), glàsses (peering at table), còffee, allgòne, còffee, allgòne, còffee.
> M: What does this watch say? (holding it up to him).
> H: Glàsses (handing over glasses).
> M: Mummy's glasses (taking them).

(M of course makes the most of the interaction anyway in the final utterance.)

Nonetheless, the *effect* of the responses cited above was certainly to maintain interactional contact and this may have been a part of their motivation.

So far I have been discussing the naming of things in the here-and-now. Entities were also very, very occasionally referred to when not present, but in a way which is clearly interpretable as being recalled from a previous occasion, as in the following cases:

> saying *teddy*, pointing to the bookcase where he had been very surprised to find the toy 20 minutes before;
> saying *Katy*, and pointing to the spot where she had been lying earlier in the day when he had fondled her;
> saying *doggy* several times in the evening after an afternoon walk of special interest for the number of dogs met *en route*;
> saying *Dadda*, touching the fence where F had been nailing up loose planks with much noise a day or two before.

2ba. [observation: characteristic of entity: property: tactile] *Wet* was used on feeling and handling wet clothing or after turning the hose on himself. *Hot* was usually used as he touched something warm, but also in an anticipatory kind of way, reaching towards a lamp bulb, approaching the kitchen stove, etc.

[observation: characteristic of entity: function] *Broken* was generally used in running commentary when the car wouldn't start, a lamp switched off at the wall socket wouldn't switch on at the switch, etc.

2bb. [observation: characteristic of entity: existential status of object] The most common context for *allgone* was the consumption of food and drink, and it was quite often used when observing other people doing the consuming, e.g., F draining a glass, adults emptying a plate of sandwiches. It was also used at times for commenting on the disappearance of the bath water.

Gone was not used for food consumption but when hiding something under a cushion or after poking leaves through a cane-bottomed chair, etc. There was an element of 'I made it gone' in most cases, though sometimes he was remarking on the cat's departure.

There-tis was used at first when his hand was 'found' in a getting-dressed game; then most commonly on picking up an object or finding something he had been looking for; and finally, pointing to things located out of reach, especially aeroplanes.

2ca. [observation: action: general] *Down* was used initially at the end of 'Ring a ring of roses' and then to accompany his own jumping or sitting down, or climbing up actions, and occasionally to comment on a soft toy falling down.

Oh dear, as already described (see instrumental function), was used for about two weeks to comment on a sneeze or cough by himself or another, but by 18 months it had developed a more general 'something's wrong' meaning, and was then most often used instrumentally.

Bam! was generally uttered after hearing a bang. Sometimes he was responsible for the noise himself. On one occasion he whispered *bam!* to himself as he approached the open door, and then repeated it loudly and forcefully as he slammed it.

2cb. [observation: action: ritual vocal accompaniment] All the [general] instances above were used on occasions to comment on the behaviour of others. Here, however, are classed two other expressions used only as an ongoing accompaniment to his own action. When he climbed up and down the back steps he repeated *two*, having heard *one, two, three* so often in this context. Then, when he played with a set of nesting and building baskets he would repeat *wrong* because his grandfather would comment *right* or *wrong* on his efforts. Hal hadn't yet worked out the adult sense of this.

2da.   [evaluation: self] Although there was only one clearly non-interactional use of *badboy* during this period, this feature has been included here since both earlier and later periods witnessed non-interactional examples.

2db.   [evaluation: of event] This is the *oh dear* expression already discussed under 'instrumental'. At first, it was mainly said after he sneezed or coughed (see [action] above). But then it was used in the following kinds of situation: touching a page he had earlier torn; watching his ball roll under a chair; failing to fit one 'nesting' basket inside another; picking up a toy tractor and touching place where steering wheel should have been but was not. In all these instances he did not address anyone, but clearly some of these situations could easily develop into instrumental contexts, and more and more he would follow up a private [ōɑdi̇] with an instrumental [ōɑdī], [ōɑdi], etc.

IMAGINATIVE

There is an imaginative element in all the games included in the interactional function, but in those cases developing the interaction seemed to be to the forefront, and a less ritualized or verbalized interaction might develop from one of these.

However, he also invented his own little pretences: lying on the rug, saying *Katy*, as if acting her part; walking about with a washing-up bowl on his head, saying *hat*; and tucking a small teddy into a drawer, saying *night-night*. There were also 'occasional' pretences, such as when he carefully made a pile of pegs and then swooshed them on to the floor with a grin and an emphatic *oh dear!* (being not at all upset and promptly repeating the game).

In addition, he was beginning to learn snatches of songs and to play with the sound patterns of words, repeating *up up up up up* at various pitches and speeds, etc.

From microfunction to macrofunction

At 18 months a large proportion of Hal's utterances can, as before, be classified with a fair degree of confidence into one or other of the protolinguistic functions, provided that a regulatory function is now also recognized. However, I will now argue that a consideration of the language data suggests that some rather fundamental changes have taken place, which require us to recognize a different functional basis to the language at this point, where instead of five distinct microfunctions, the potential is organized in terms of two more general functions, termed by Halliday the 'mathetic' and the 'pragmatic'. The mathetic function is defined by him as 'the use of the symbolic system as a means of learning about reality', and the pragmatic function as 'the use of the symbolic system as a means of acting on reality' (Halliday 1975a: 106).

Obviously, the most striking innovation in Hal's language was the general abandonment of invented expressions in favour of mother-tongue forms. This move was startlingly swift. At 16½ months, Hal had fewer than twenty possible words. By 17 months this had doubled to over forty and by 18 months doubled again to about ninety. Only one invented sign expression was developed during this period (the pleasure sign [ʃaɪ, bɔgaɪ,] etc.), and there was no great persistence of the baby forms once vocabulary development was under way.

The first use of mother-tongue expressions has naturally always been taken as a milestone. However, the introduction of words does not in itself necessarily substantially change the system. I have already made the point that many 'first words' in the language development literature are microfunctionally specific feature realizations. And it is certainly true that most of Hal's words were not functionally unrestricted. None the less, I am arguing that the language has changed fundamentally, and a consideration of the data shows that there are three aspects to this:

(i) Considerable overlap among the lexical realizations as between certain functional areas, suggesting a washing out of some microfunctional boundaries.

(ii) The maintenance of a functional basis to the linguistic organization, but with the child's interpretation of the functional context made manifest in the realizations themselves.

(iii) An indication of changes in the nature of what language could now do for Hal, which are not best described as more detailed sub-categorizations of existing microfunctional features.

(i) Blurring of microfunctional boundaries

The first evidence I shall consider concerns the lack of functional specificity of the linguistic realizations as between the instrumental and regulatory functions on the one hand, and the interactional and personal on the other.

(a) The most prominent regulatory term was *more*, and this, like *no*, was used to realize parallel features within the instrumental function.

(b)   The phonological characteristic of non-falling tone was also shared by instrumental and regulatory functions only.

(c)   Virtually the whole of the interactional lexical repertoire was also used in personal contexts. For example, he would label facial features in an intimacy ritual, but also quite by himself when examining faces in books or of his soft toys. Similarly, other object-mediated interactions were expressed with the same repertoire of names as used in personal naming contexts; and, as we have seen, *badboy* and *bump* might also be used in either function. Although it is true that there was always an overlap between some personal expressions and object-mediated interactional ones, this wholesale sharing of lexis is very striking, and I shall suggest that it can be explained in terms of the development of a mathetic 'macrofunction'.

(d)   All these expressions in interactional and personal uses share either falling, or sometimes rising–falling, tones.

(ii) Linguistic coding of function

When considering the duplication of lexical realizations between different functions we see that a small proportion of the words found within personal occur also instrumentally. This often happened in the first place when a stated personal intention became frustrated, as in the following examples:

17(14)   H announces *sòck* as he goes to F's sock drawer. Unable to open the drawer, he repeats *sōck, sōck, sōck*, frantically pulling at the drawer and glancing over at M.

16(2)   H, sitting in high chair, drops something. He looks down and points to it, saying *there-tis* in a pleased way. Then finding himself strapped in and unable to reach it, he repeats *there-tis* in his plaintive creaky voice, as he reaches down, until F collects it for him. (This was the only such instrumental occasion with this expression.)

17(15)   H is pushing his stroller about the garden. It stops at some obstacle and he says quietly *ōh dèar*. He tries to push it over the bump but cannot, and repeats ever more frantically *ōh dēar, ōh dēar* until the problem is resolved.

What is obvious here is that, with the second utterance in each case, there was a switch in function, and this does not have to be inferred from purely contextual clues, as it is marked in the phonology of the expression. Thus, while there was no formal distinction between *more* used in regulatory and instrumental contexts, or between *badboy* used interactionally and personally, there was by 18 months a pretty well systematic phonological distinction between 'active' and 'reflective' uses of any word. The former received high level or rising tone (and/or a pleading voice quality at this stage, which faded out gradually after 18 months), while the latter received falling or rising-falling tone.

At the same time, it was only a smallish proportion (less than a quarter) of words which did freely cross this functional boundary and occur in both kinds of contexts, and even after he had developed this formal means of indicating the function of an utterance, he still maintained partially distinct pragmatic and mathetic lexical repertoires. During this period up to 18 months, for example, Hal would not name food items in his books, even though several favourite new Christmas books contained such pictures. He always simply turned the page straight over, and if the adult named a picture of food, he took it as an offer and went expectantly into the kitchen. Here we have then, incidentally, some evidence of the child filtering the language he hears to make sense of it in terms of his own system.

(iii) Changes in functional potential

It is not until representational content and function are separately encoded in any utterance—as lexical item and tone respectively— that we have purely language-internal evidence for functional distinctions operating in the language. It may then be argued that this dichotomous distinction emerging at around 18 months is not really a change or reorganization taking place, but that such an interpretation is simply the result of having imposed an overly specific functional framework on the earlier data. In this view, it would be better simply to look at the entire protolanguage in terms of some broad active/reflective dichotomy. This would certainly be a reasonable course, and the microfunctional networks have been displayed as a continuum from most to least active in order effectively to do this.

However, the more narrowly defined the initial functions are, the more closely we have to attend to the details of the specific situations in which utterances are produced. By doing this we have a better chance of discovering the relevant contexts for early speech, and thus for tracing the origins of later linguistic developments, as well as for building up a picture of the child's social world. As a heuristic then, I think the microfunctional approach is worthwhile, and it is also the case that the mathetic function as a learning one can evolve only with the child's move to share in the common tongue. Therefore, however much we wish to stress continuity in development there will be a real change in functional potential to be recognized at this point.

Thus, looking from the standpoint of the earlier linguistic system, we might characterize the 16½–18 month language as in Figure 5.2.

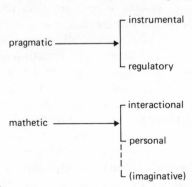

Fig. 5.2 One possible view of the early transition system

But the reason the potential has grouped itself in this fashion lies in the meanings of the macrofunctions themselves, which even by 18 months allow for the expression of meanings not easily, or most revealingly, expressed in terms of a microfunctional sub-category of a macrofunction.

If we consider the following texts, for example, it hardly seems adequate to classify Hal's utterances as interactional, even though he is clearly attending to speech addressed to him, including responses given to his own utterances. Nor can they readily be seen as personal, in the original sense of defining the self in contradistinction to the environment by reacting to or observing the latter.

16(27) H: (pointing to books in bookcase.) bʊ̀kʰ; bʊ̀kʰ
        M: (correcting) bɒ̀:kʰ.
        H: bɒ̀:kʰ.
17(28) H: Pòrridge (watching M stir it.)
        M: Yes I'm doing your porridge. It's just cooking.
        H: Coòking <new word>.
        M: Yes, porridge is cooking.
        (both go to M's bedroom. M gets dressed.)
        H: (to himself) Còoking; còoking; pòrridge.
17(26) (H is wrenching about the feet of a new wind-up duck.)
        M: No, no. Don't do that Hal, no, no, no, no, no. It'll get broken.

H: Nò, nò. Bròken. Nò. (eventually gives toy to M.)
(That evening and for the rest of the week when bathing
with same duck, H repeats the wrenching action and says
again *Nò, nò, bròken*, looking at the toy.)

In these texts we see H adapting his speech to M's correction,
struggling to interpret what she says to him (even though he doesn't
succeed in the second example, adopting *cooking* as a thing-name
for a boiled egg shortly after), and in the final example he was again
clearly mulling over the prohibition he received and the explanation
of cause and effect which accompanied it. Such cases are a far cry
from protolinguistic expressions of interest in the environment. Here
Hal was not simply observing aspects of the physical environment, but
concerning himself with the way they are expressed and interpreted in
the shared language, and with using the language to better understand the things, processes and relations of his experience.

There were still occasions of course when a simple expression of
togetherness, or alternatively, of interest in the environment was
clearly foregrounded, but his potential now went far beyond
this, and the reason that interactional and personal occasions shared
the same vocabulary is because both these uses of language were now
serving a more general function in the child's life. This was in the role
of language for learning, language used to sort out experience, to
classify the things, processes, feelings and values which make it up.
Thus, whether H said *hat* in response to M's *What have you got?* or
spontaneously and to himself, he was classifying the object; whether
he said *badboy* to M, bringing her attention to an earlier misdeed,
or to himself preparing to perform one, he was verbalizing his understanding of the social rules.

Similarly, whether he said *oh dear* on seeing his teddy fall off the
bed, or in fun swishing things to the ground, he was considering
and representing linguistically what counted as a mishap in his
experience. I regard the imaginative function as less obviously subsumed by the mathetic, because while imaginative contexts *were*
often learning ones for him, a 'lets pretend' situation always remained
unambiguously recognizable as such. It contributed to the mathetic
whilst remaining an identifiable use throughout.

On the pragmatic side, the greatest extension of potential at first
is the addition of clear regulatory meanings, but Halliday's study
shows that this may not typically be associated with the macrofunctional generalization, since Nigel had regulatory meanings from
10½ months. But being able to use regulatory language to respond
to a threat, as in:

> M: Do you want to get down <i.e., stop misbehaving or I'll put
>   you down.>
> H: No <i.e., Don't do that.>

is probably not the kind of regulatory language that could be used
before the approach of the transition.

Other than this, the seeking of the presence of an individual or
a restoration of intimacy was soon to be a possibility. This is probably
best seen as evolving from the interactional rather than instrumental
or regulatory functions. And soon too he could initiate requests
for a bath or an outing, because after 18 months he was no longer
restricted to the instrumental-regulatory meanings of 'give me',
'help me' and 'you perform', but evolved a more general category
of 'I want to do' as an aspect of the pragmatic function of acting on
the world with the aid of language.

A macrofunctional analysis, 16½–18 months

Now that there is a purely linguistic criterion for determining the
functional context of any utterance by the child, and now that there
are lexical realizations of options deriving from the mathetic or
pragmatic functions. I propose to focus my attention for the rest
of the case study on the development of the lexico-grammatical
system itself. In other words, I shall concentrate on the systemic
relationships demonstrably realized in structure and lexis, with the
expectation that sooner or later there will be points where stratification of this 'semantic–grammatical' network into two distinct levels
of semantics and grammar will be desirable to capture different
kinds of relationships.

First, however, I shall discuss what appear to be the broad areas
of learning which were carried out through mathetic language, and
the range of modes of action achieved through pragmatic language.
The resulting categories are thus contextual ones but restricted,
like protolanguage categories, to those which appeared relevant
from a consideration of language in use.

Taking the *mathetic function* first, I observed the following
three main areas of learning:

1. The material world—things
                        processes
                        qualities
                        locations
                        causal and additive relations, etc.

2. Social world   —prohibitions
                         evaluations
                         parameters for greetings and valedictions
3. Language   —phonology
                         semantics

Hal's learning about the material world was clearly expressed in his language, and the desire to classify the phenomena of the physical environment was undoubtedly the strongest motivation underlying the lexical 'explosion'. His learning about the social world was noticeable at this early stage in his linguistically expressed preoccupation with what was and was not permitted behaviour, and with whom, how and when to express greetings and farewells. Of course, these particular social norms were ones explicitly verbalized to him by adults in his daily life.

There are also many texts throughout Phase II where Hal's attention was focused on the language itself. At first this was a fairly passive consideration, amounting to repetitions of corrected versions of his labelling or pronunciation. Naturally, since learning about the material world means in the first place learning how to classify things by means of language, it is not always possible to distinguish a concern for the material as against the linguistic. But there were occasions, as we shall see, when it was the phonology, some structural form, or the grammar of interaction that he was concerned with, and in these cases the material world was not at all at stake. In the last case of course, we may see the learning of language intersecting with the learning of *social* norms, rather than material ones.

Whether or not it is possible to distinguish these as distinct systemic contextual choices, it seems clear that they do not each have a distinct linguistic grammatical potential realizing them, if only because learning about language necessarily involves using the same repertoire as learning about anything else.

Other relevant factors in the consideration of mathetic language concern the linguistic mode of learning, which might be:

(i)   By representing a presently observed event, object, state, etc.
(ii) By prediction or recall of events, entities, etc., through language.
(iii) By the expression of either (i) or (ii) above, or of the evaluation of self or the observation of linguistic forms to himself.
(iv) By the expression of any of the above to another person.

Furthermore, any instance of learning through language might be a response to purely physical or mental phenomena, or might be a response to a linguistic event.

In addition, some child language researchers have also distinguished between the child's linguistically expressed observations of
his own actions as against those of others. Greenfield and Smith,
for example, claim that infants verbalize their own actions first,
then those of objects on which they are acting and then those of
other people. They explain this in terms of decentration: 'To express
the action of another requires a leap in the ability to perceive the
world from the perspective of another person.' (Greenfield and
Smith 1976: 159.)

The data from Hal do not in fact support their claim as to the
developmental pattern of 'action' utterances, and in any case commenting on what somebody else does, does not necessarily involve
looking at the world from their point of view. None the less, it is
certainly true that the great majority of Hal's comments concerned
his own actions or objects he was handling, or locations he was
heading for or placing objects in, just as the great majority concerned
the here-and-now rather than recall and prediction.

The first question to be considered, then, is how much of all the
above should be represented as systemic choices in the grammatical
network. None of the distinctions mentioned above, which were all
contextually observable, received any distinct lexical encoding. No
particular area of the vocabulary was reserved for recall situations
or for comments on other people's behaviour or for comments
addressed to another person, and nor were there any phonological
distinctions employed to realize such choices.

Obviously, an ideally complete account of language development
would represent all such choices, tracing the change in frequency
patterns between the marked and unmarked options in each case,
but I feel that a formal representation, staying as close to the grammar as possible, is entitled to ignore all of these factors, which is not
to claim that they are unimportant or that they are not genuine
options at the contextual level.

I shall throughout the case study be attending to the changing
nature of the context, which is a requirement if we are to understand either the transition from the protolanguage or the gradual
move into the adult system. However, the only choices not realized
in the lexico-grammar which will be built into the formal description
will be those which *are* grammatically realized at a near future
point, and those which can be ascertained from a consideration of
utterances in linguistic context, such as the initiating vs. responding
status of utterances.

On the *pragmatic* side, I observed the following range of interpersonal intents expressed through language at 18 months:

  (i) The gaining or rejection of goods.
 (ii) The gaining or rejection of assistance to carry out an action or repositioning of self.
(iii) Getting another person to repeat an action or service.
(iv) Refusing suggestions for action.
 (v) Accepting suggestions for caretaking routines.
(vi) Getting another person to perform musically for him or with him.

Most of these intents were distinctly expressed by different areas of lexis, though all rejections and refusals were alike expressed: *no*.

Where the linguistic mode of *learning* was predominantly by representing something to himself, the linguistic mode of *achieving* was naturally predominantly by addressing another person. However, in cases (i) and (ii) above, especially if the pragmatic utterance followed from the temporary frustration of a stated expression of intention, an addressee was not necessarily overtly appealed to. Hal sometimes simply persisted in pursuing his intention whilst expressing a pragmatic demand, and achieved his original goal unaided. This may of course simply mean that he assumed a relevant addressee would be attending, since this is what his experience had led him to expect. Bates *et al.* note in this regard that: '[The] pattern of alternating eye contact often becomes less frequent . . . as the child becomes more confident that his signals work.' (Bates *et al.* 1979: 35.) Alternatively, we may interpret the pragmatic tone as signalling that some general response from the environment was required such that his goal be fulfilled, rather than meaning specifically 'addressee respond'. Whichever interpretation is favoured, it seems clear that it is not the same choice of addressing the other versus addressing the self as can be observed in mathetic contexts.

Finally, like mathetic utterances, pragmatic ones can also be distinguished in discourse as occurring in response to language or not. And the recognition of this as an option is also justified at this stage by the presence of some response-only items, and before long it is also encoded in tone (see pp. 750-7).

Figures 5.3 and 5.4 represent the 16½-18 month language in terms of these two intrinsically defined functions, termed 'macro-functions'. There are peripheral aspects of the linguistic potential such as the greetings system and ritual accompaniments to some games, which are not obviously interpretable in terms of either of the two functions and have been omitted from the reorganized description. The reason that the mathetic network chiefly embodies the personal

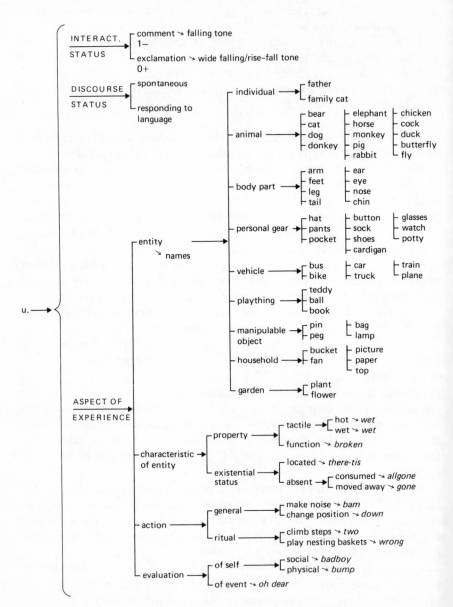

Fig. 5.3 16½–18 months—mathetic potential

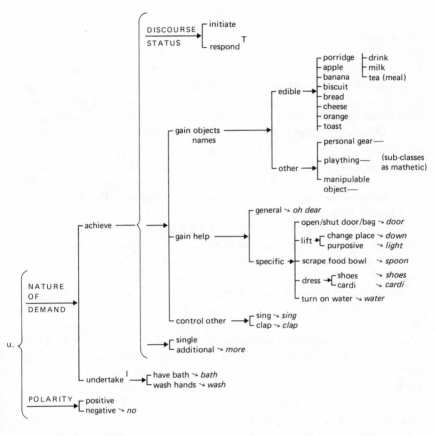

conditioned realizations:
[achieve] / [positive] / [single] ⤳ Realizations as specified on network
[achieve] / [positive] / [additional] ⤳ *more*
[achieve] / [negative] ⤳ *no*
[undertake] / [positive] ⤳ Realizations as specified on network
[undertake] / [negative] ⤳ *no*

Fig. 5.4   16½–18 months—pragmatic potential

(or personal-heuristic) microfunctional one, is that the feature [obser-vation] in the latter was already necessarily encompassing a meaning virtually corresponding to the macrofunctional one of learning.

The transition to adult begun

Halliday has used the term 'transition' to describe the stage of language development between the protolinguistic one and language that is adult-like in nature. Phase II is transitional not just because it stands temporally between protolanguage and adult language, but because it is in some ways essentially protolinguistic in character and in others essentially like adult language.

The protolanguage may be characterized in the following way: every new meaning is ideally expressed in a new sound, and no representational aspect of meaning is distinguishable from the functional meaning of the sign as a whole. The meanings derive from uses the language serves in the child's life, but the contexts in which language occurs exist independently of language, and the most general meanings which derive from them, such as 'I want that' or 'I like that', may be expressed without symbols.

Adult language may be minimally defined as a linguistic system which allows any utterance to have some representational function, and which simultaneously but distinctly encodes the status of the utterance as a verbal transaction with another speaker: as a question, statement, command, etc. Moreover, the most important of these latter interpersonal meanings are entirely dependent on language both for their expression and their acknowledgement. There is a lot more to say about mature human language than this of course, but in these crucial respects we can see that the baby protolanguage has to both develop an independently codable experiential content and also to express this simultaneously with linguistically defined acts of meaning—speech acts, in effect.

The introduction of lexis is the first step in the development of independent representational content, and the systemic (i.e., oppositional) use of tone is the first simultaneous encoding of experiential and interpersonal meanings. While a few score lexical items which carry a tonally expressed status of either 'reflective comment' or 'active demand' is a long way from the adult grammar of TRANSITIVITY and MOOD, still the crucial first steps have now been taken. By making formally salient just two ways of using language—to learn about (reflect on) reality and to act on it, the transition language has begun to develop a grammar which simultaneously encodes systems for talking about things and for talking to people.

The macrofunctional representation considered

If the capacity to combine a limited kind of speech function choice with a limited number of experiential options is a highly significant shift towards adult language as I have claimed, then the formal grammatical description may well be expected to reflect this aspect of the language in particular. Yet analysing the language as a potential with respect to each of the two macrofunctions, as I have done, does this only implicitly, in that it allows a comparison between lexical realizations of mathetic and pragmatic features to show to what extent the same lexis occurs in both functions.

A description in these terms has the advantage of allowing a ready comparison with the protolanguage, showing most clearly how the transition stage is a development from it, and stressing the way in which the newly evolved macrofunctions are similar in nature to the earlier microfunctions. However, this must not obscure the fact that they are not entirely similar. A mathetic function cannot arise until the child has something of the mother tongue. He cannot learn through language (thus also learning the language) until he begins developing a lexico-grammar—though he may be able to express a reflective state of mind protolinguistically. The mathetic function is not one which arises and may be achieved independently of language, like the original microfunctions. The pragmatic function for Hal at this early stage is still much more comparable to the microfunctions in this respect, though it will soon move in the direction of accepting and even seeking a linguistic rather than a purely extra-linguistic response.

There are several reasons why I have not chosen to emphasize the simultaneity of the speech function and experiential content systems—which would in effect be treating the macrofunctions more as adult metafunctions—in my formal description. First, it has to be stressed that having developed this exciting potential, the child does not by any means exploit it to the full straight away. The fact that certain linguistic items, or classes of items, are still restricted to a single 'speech function' is evidence for the relevance of the macrofunctional context, and its kinship to the earlier infant functions.

It would therefore be quite misleading at this stage to assume that if any member of an experiential class can be freely used as either a 'comment' or a 'demand', then so can all other members.

In other words, a representation of the kind given in Figure 5.5 has to be rejected. To be more accurate, a non-macrofunctionally specific network would need more complicated wiring to indicate functional restrictions. A fragment of the language described earlier in Figures 5.3 and 5.4 is recast in this form in Figure 5.6.

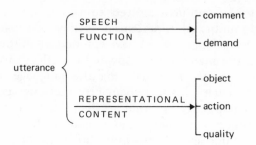

Fig. 5.5   A simplified 'metafunctional' representation of the early transition language

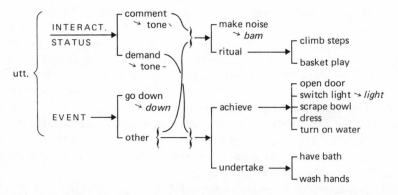

Fig. 5.6   A simplified 'metafunctional' representation of a fragment of the early transition language indicating functional restrictions

A description such as that given in Figure 5.6 has the advantage of placing *dōwn* and *dòwn* in an appropriate opposition, which the individual macrofunctional networks (Figures 5.3 and 5.4) cannot do, but it thereby treats *dōwn* and (switch) *līght* as distinct classes of demand, and *dòwn* and *bàm* as distinct classes of comment, although contextually this would not appear to be justified.

Since the language is in process of changing from one kind of system to another, it is not surprising that a necessarily static representation is faced with the choice of reflecting most clearly either the kind of system the language evolved from or the kind of system it is evolving into.

The macrofunctions can be looked at in one way as 'advanced' microfunctions, each with its own grammar; a view which will provide the insights that it is in pursuit of language as learning that lexis and Process·Medium structures are chiefly developed, while in the pursuit of the function of language as action come the first systems of POLARITY and PERSON, as well as a distinction between initiating and responding moves, etc.

From another viewpoint, the macrofunctions can be seen as 'primitive' metafunctions. If this is done, the significance of the moves away from the original functional contexts is stressed. Consequently, the way the system is moving towards one which has no restrictions on its functional capacity, because the entire grammar has simultaneous choices of experiential and interpersonal options (or sets of options), is foregrounded.

As the aim here is to explore the kinds of linguistic systems built up in the service of the two macrofunctions, the preference has been to stress continuity in the formal description, and to present the language in terms of two functionally distinct potentials, until such a point when the language data make this approach genuinely untenable.

Comparison with Nigel and subjects from other studies

There are three characteristics of early Phase II language which are strikingly shared by Hal and Nigel, and, as far as one can judge, by other infants who have been intensively studied. These are:

1. A functional distinction between language as reflection and language as action.
2. The encoding of this distinction by means of tone.
3. At least a partial differentiation of the lexical (and possibly structural) repertoire between the two functions.

There are a few differences between Hal and Nigel which can perhaps be mentioned first. For one thing, they differ in that Hal adopted the tonal distinction earlier and was already developing it in the protolanguage itself, whereas Nigel adopted his falling vs. rising distinction quite suddenly at 19 months (Halliday 1975a: 88). Another difference is that Hal did not have as simple and unequivocal a two-way tone choice as did Nigel. Within mathetic,

Hal used normal, wide and rise–falls—the latter two having an exclamative quality—and within pragmatic there were both high level and rising tones. I was not able to discern any clear difference in meaning here; it may have been that forms like *more* which tended to favour the rising form did so because they were so often addressed to the child in this form. All these tones found during the transition period were present in the earlier protolanguage.

There were also a few items which did not get re-processed through his own tone system. For example, *all gone* mimicked at first the singsong of the typical adult pronunciation to him; and when labelling a face, *eyes* usually occurred at first with a rising tone, which was presumably copied from adult listing intonation, since facial features were invariably named to him as *ēyes, nōse, mòuth*, etc. (This was one of the first adult intonation patterns he adopted with adult meaning.)

It may also be the case that some meanings did not get inter- preted as either mathetic or pragmatic in function, and it is the greetings system that is the most marginal case. These utterances took falling tone and may be interpretable as mathetic since they were clearly involved in learning the *language* (he clearly rehearsed *bye-bye Daddy* structures for use here). But if falling tone is an unmarked tone generally, these may simply lie outside the main functional system. Nigel treated greetings, as well as interactional 'I say—you say' routines, as pragmatic, coding them with rising tone, fitting his pattern of rising tone for 'response called for'.

When we come to consider other studies undertaken outside the systemic framework, there is quite a lot of apparent corroboration of some aspects of the transition language as described by Halliday and myself. David Ingram (1971: 889) quotes the following state- ment by Stevenson made in 1893:

When a very young child says 'water' he is . . . [using the word] . . . with the value of an assertion, something like 'I want water' or 'there is water', the distinction in meaning between the two expressions being shown by the child's tone of utterance.

Other writers, such as Lewis (1936) and Bates (1976), distinguish between 'manipulative' and 'declarative' or 'imperative' and 'declara- tive' respectively, but do not suggest that these are explicitly coded distinctions. Greenfield and Smith (1976) distinguish 'volitional' and 'indicative' modalities, suggesting that tone of voice may be used to carry the distinction linguistically. Of Dore's (1973) two principal subjects, one used level tone contours on requests and commands and the other used rising contours to request both things and behaviours and the presence of others, while McShane (1980: 73) found that requests made by his subjects typically had 'a characteristic rising intonation'. Another study of interest here is that of Lise Menn, since she too observed functionally distinct tone patterns before the mother-tongue period, for giving and requesting objects, attention getting and 'curiosity' noises accompanying private explorations (Menn 1978: 134). She also found she had to class level and rising contours together and says of Jacob:

He began to almost always use rising contours for utterances in which he wanted an adult to do more than share a focus of attention, while on the other hand those proto words and words that accompanied ongoing activity usually showed falling contours and were interpreted as narratives, declarative in mood, by adults. [Menn 1978: 147.]

There is no shortage in the literature of observations of functionally specific words or structures at this period. Carter (1979: 86) mentions *more, mine, have one* and *here*, which all appear to be exclusively pragmatic in function as used by David, while *look* and *there* he used only to point out objects. Bloom's (1970) account shows Alison using *stop* only as a reflective comment, while *no* was a clearly pragmatic refusal. Nelson's (1973) study of the first fifty words acquired by eighteen different children also reports that early words were quite consistently used to express a particular function. However, she was not working with a two-way functional cut and some of these first words may perhaps have been microfunctionally, rather than macrofunctionally, restricted.

Gruber's (1975) work also supports something like a mathetic/ pragmatic distinction, but his subject used structural rather than tonal means to achieve this. Gruber examines the first ten weeks of multi-word utterances for one child and claims that all fulfil one of two performative functions: indicating or demanding. Furthermore, the evidence for this is not derived solely from behavioural context, but from the linguistic structures themselves, of which one element must be either a reference to speaker or addressee or a word referring to demand (such as *want, have, get*) or indication (such as *see*).

In general, we can say that the maintenance by the child of different sets of words for particular uses at the early—usually 'holophrastic'—stage of mother-tongue speech is quite well attested. This provides evidence that the mother tongue does develop initially from a functionally based language system as Halliday has suggested. As yet, however, it is not clear how general a phenomenon it is for the child explicitly to encode something like a mathetic/pragmatic distinction, whether by means of a choice of tone or a functionally specific operator accompanying a lexical choice, or by any other means.

While many researchers have contributed to our growing knowledge of the infant's first mother-tongue speech forms, Halliday's further contribution has been to offer a coherent explanation for the phenomena observed, in terms of the metafunctional nature of adult language. Although the illocutionary use of tone has been observed by a number of writers, it is generally noted as a useful guide to empirical classification of utterances, without any theoretical significance being recognized. Systemic theory, by characterizing the linguistic system in terms of simultaneous sets of oppositional features, can recognize a turning point at the stage when different representational contents (expressed in lexis) and different illocutionary functions (expressed in pitch, tone, voice quality, etc.) occur in different combinations, by those children who take this route into the adult system.

In addition, in his use of the term 'mathetic', rather than one derived from adult grammar, such as 'declarative' or 'statement', Halliday provides an explanation for the sudden increase in lexis which may occur. This is that the child is using language to help make sense of his environment—an environment of objects, persons, activities, routines, prohibitions, qualities, sounds (including language sounds), temporal, spatial and causal relations, and doubtless much else besides. McShane (1980) sees the lexical explosion as a phenomenon in need of explanation, but rejects Halliday's account. At first he appears to interpret the mathetic function as the use of language to learn names, and he then continues:

It is unclear what naming teaches the child about the environment. The realisation that things have names is not a discovery about the environment, but a discovery about the relationship between language and the environment. [McShane 1980: 25.]

This remark indicates that his dissatisfaction with Halliday's work is based on a misinterpretation. The mathetic function is neither the use of language in order to learn names nor 'the insight that things have names'. Indeed, an insight can hardly be a use of language, although many insights about the language, as well as about social norms and the accepted view of the structures and relationships of the material world, will arise through language developed in the service of the mathetic function.

6 Eighteen to nineteen and a half months

The emergence of the informative function

Halliday describes the notion of giving information as the understanding that language may serve as an alternative to shared
experience as well as an expression of it. He has stressed that while
the adult typically sees information giving as the definitive use of
language, the child comes to this notion slowly. His subject, Nigel,
was at first only able to 'tell somebody something' if that person had
already witnessed or shared the experience with him. Even when he
did begin to use language to inform, he kept this as a distinct option,
realized by a different lexico-grammatical structure from talking
about things already known to the addressee (Halliday: 1975a).

This case study would certainly support Halliday's contention that
the child's move into the mother tongue is motivated by the desire
to classify and interpret the various phenomena of experience,
rather than in order to tell people things. None the less, the informative function began to emerge for Hal between 18 and 19½ months,
earlier than for Nigel. The two closest occasions before 18 months
were those classified in the microfunctional analysis as realizing the
interactional feature [share state of feeling]. On one occasion Hal
approached M saying *bump* immediately after he had had a fall
which she had not witnessed, and on another occasion he brought
in something picked from the garden and gave it to M saying *badboy*. These in turn developed from less informative sharings, particularly in recall (see pp. 108–9 for all these texts). Then, during the
18–19½ month period, he would sometimes express regret,
acknowledgement of misdeed, self pity and/or a need for sympathy
after being chastised, by naming the chastiser to someone else
present. For example:

18(15) M tells H off sharply. He goes to Granny, a witness to the
scene, and says *Mùmmy* softly to her.

Often his chosen confidant(e), while present in the room, was not
attending the preceding scene, so that Hal's utterance virtually
served to inform them about it.

And finally, at around 19 months, there were the following informative texts:

19(1) H and M are in bathroom. H pulls cat's tail, causing her to flee out of the window. A few minutes later he says to F in the bedroom *tàil; tàil; tàil; pùssy; tàil; pùssy; tàil; pùssy; badbòy.*

19(8) M is in bedroom. H enters and says *nàughty; pèe; nàughty; pèe.* He takes M's hand and leads her to kitchen, saying *nàughty; pèe; pùssy.*

(F explains that H had peed on floor while playing with tins of 'pussy' food and had been told off by F.)

19(9) (M is in bathroom. H enters.)

H: Nàughty, nàughty.

M: Naughty? What've you done that's naughty?

H: Pùssy.

M: Oh, you've been naughty to the pussy have you? Do you want to pee?

(M puts H on loo and fiddles with window; H's attention is drawn to it.)

H: Pùssy; outside <= that's where she goes out>.

(H then points back to door and reverts to his original news.)

H: Pùssy; tàil.

M: Oh, you pulled the pussy's tail, did you?

All of these were spoken to someone who was not present on the occasion of the related incident, and are striking in that they concern incidents of socialization—discovering what is and is not acceptable behaviour—and this remained a prominent factor in informative texts for some time. Hal was therefore imposing on his addressee a role not just of hearer, but possibly also of sympathizer, and in this respect these may be seen to be a development of 'shared feeling' occasions, and even to have something of a pragmatic flavour.

However, I do not mean to suggest by this last remark that the primary function of such narratives is to manipulate the addressee. I see them as lying in fact within the mainstream mathetic function. Hal seems to be reporting incidents to somebody else, partly as a means of representing them to himself in order to understand them better. Exploration of the social world was probably less easily achieved on his own. An acknowledgement by the addressee, while not the primary point, was perhaps helpful to him as a confirmation of the interpretation he had arrived at from the interaction with the other adult. At any rate, phonologically these informative utterances resembled other mathetic utterances and were selected from the same lexical repertoire.

Information giving was also to develop from another interactional context. This was the naming of an object to hand as a means of mediating an interaction, especially in an adult greetings context (see p. 108). During this period he continued occasionally to do this, generally now mentioning whatever he had been attending to before the entry of the other person, as in the following case:

19(11) M and F return from work while H is finishing his meal. Pieces of apple are on the plate in front of him. M comes in first, and H exclaims *Mùmmy! Àpple!* F then comes in and H turns to him with *Dàddy! Àpple!*

Then just at the very end of this period, such a situation provided an opportunity for him to discuss the whole event preceding the meeting:

19(14) M returns from work to find H in garden with Matthew. H rushes up to her, saying *pùll; Màtthew; sànd* <i.e., Matthew has been pulling Hal and/or sand in the trolley.>

Information giving for Hal did not then involve any decisive leap into a new understanding. It was a smooth and continuous development out of the personal and interactional protolanguage, as may be illustrated in the Figure 6.1 summary.

One characteristic of these information-giving utterances is that, more than most mathetic ones, they were concerned in a minor way with the social relationships of the interactants (in the speech situation) as well as with the domain of learning. There was in fact one other development at this time which also hinted at a greater involvement of the addressee in the mathetic function, and this was the creation of jokes by Hal. For example:

19(2) H often tested the temperature of an adult's coffee cup with his finger and said *hot* on finding it so. He has been round to each person's cup in turn doing this. Now he ostentatiously touches his beaker of juice, withdraws his finger mock-hastily and says *còffee; hòt*, looking round at his audience with a grin.

The incident is still a consideration of what things are hot, what are not, and what happens when you touch something hot, etc. —still mathetic in fact—but again a role is assigned to the addressee in such a case.

AGE IN MONTHS	PERSONAL	INTERACTIONAL
9	Exploration of (capacities of the self in relation to?) the environment Express feeling +	Drawing attention of other person to self and object
9–10½		+ Expression of feeling sometimes addressed to other
10½–12	Pointing out objects	
12–13½		Express shared amusement
13½–15	Naming of object under attention #	Getting other to perform by focusing joint attention on picture of animal
15–16½	Commentary on aspects of ongoing event. Comment on immediately past events*	# Naming of objects under joint attention * (rare) Recalling of past event to another, e.g. 'Pussy was here earlier'
16½–18	Reconsider social rule, e.g. 'It's naughty to do this' 'Mummy said No, no, broken when I did this' =	Share feelings e.g. * (i) 'I hurt myself' (ii) 'Aren't I being naughty?' =* Recall shared experience, involving emotions e.g. 'I was a bad boy, wasn't I?'
18–19½		Enlist sympathy e.g. 'Mummy told me off'
	Tell somebody something to aid private consideration of salient experience e.g. 'I pulled cat's tail'	Tell somebody something to underline interpersonal contact e.g. 'Nice to see you; I've been playing with Matthew'

+ # * = These symbols indicate cross connections between interpersonal and personal meanings

Fig. 6.1 Outline of development of information giving

Other mathetic utterances

Hal's naming of things took place either when an object was being handled, observed or alluded to in an anticipating or recalling context, or else with an apparently classificatory intention, accompanied by a pointing gesture. Interestingly, he developed one new nonsense word at this time, and it served specifically to label pictures of things in books for which he did not have or could not remember the name. Although all his other baby signs had disappeared, he appears to have felt the need to make this new one up (it changed form two or three times) in the light of his new understanding that everything has a name.

He continued to name in succession different instances of some class of object, but rather than going from a real object to a picture, he now compared one pictorial representation with another. For example, he might spread out around him all the pictures of giraffes in his various books, pointing to and labelling them in turn. This kind of behaviour certainly suggests that he was indeed practising naming as a tool for classification, and not simply as an aid to remembering names in order to be understood.

It is generally from observations of classificatory naming that (tentative) lexical classes of entity can be deduced. Some further evidence is provided on those occasions where Hal was uncertain about a name, as in the following cases:

19(26) H looks long and hard at a large woman on a bicycle, pointing at her silently. Eventually he says *bòy*, and then looks up at M as if to seek her reaction to this label.
(He has only used *woman* in immediate imitation as yet.)

19(7) H is walking along with M. He pulls his T-shirt and says *shìrt* two or three times. Then he looks up at M and pulls her dress silently. M responds *dress; Mummy's dress and Hal's shirt*. H beams and repeats *shìrt*, pointing to his shirt, and then *drèss*, pulling at M's dress.

18(8) M corrects Hal's *bus* to *car* as Hal points to a car. When the next car passes H remembers and corrects himself *bùs; càr*, and then at every succeeding vehicle that passes—including trucks—he says very emphatically *càr*.

The fact that Hal confused *bus* and *car*, and over-generalized *boy* as an uncertain attempt to categorize a woman, suggests the lexical classes which were evolving. Similarly, the switch of attention from his own attire to that of his companion, suggests that he had some concept of garment or clothes and immediately recognized *dress* as a cohyponym of *shirt*. This occasion was the only one to date where he appeared to request a name, and he did so only non-verbally.

Observations of Hal's naming behaviour also give a clue that the meronymy relation was being developed at this time. He had few superordinate terms, but where he did, he sometimes liked to label the whole and then one or more parts, pointing as he did so, e.g. *car; wheel* or *dog; tail*.

Before turning to consider pragmatic speech at this time, the networks displaying the mathetic potential are presented in Figures 6.2 and 6.3, and a few brief comments on the networks follow.

Notes on mathetic potential, 18–19½ months (refer to Figure 6.2)

INTERACTIONAL STATUS

Although the development of the ability to impart information is a crucial one, there was no grammatical difference between generalized comments, which might be self-addressed, and the very rare informative ones described at the beginning of this chapter. Although the two could be distinguished on contextual grounds at this stage, and the extreme rarity of the informative utterance was noted, Hal at no point in the future coded the distinction linguistically, and I have therefore not included it in the network as a distinct sub-system of [comment].

ASPECT OF EXPERIENCE

[entity] As can be seen, food names were now used in mathetic as well as pragmatic contexts.

[characteristic of entity: personal association] This was the naming of the individual associated with an object handled or pointed to by H. He had originally begun doing this occasionally a few months before, saying *puss* when indicating the cat's bowl, but this had faded out in the meantime.

[characteristic of entity: disappearance] *There-tis* had dropped out of the system and *gone* and *allgone* now appeared to be in free variation, used to comment on consumed edibles, cessation of noise, the moving out of sight of objects and beings, etc.

[sound] *bam!* was no longer used accompanying his own slamming activity, but generally as an observation on any kind of banging noise heard, including the toast popping up from the toaster; *noise* was used as a more general category for everything from electric drills to gurgling stomachs.

[location] At this stage, *table* and *drawer* were only ever used in contexts of Hal placing objects on to or into them, and never

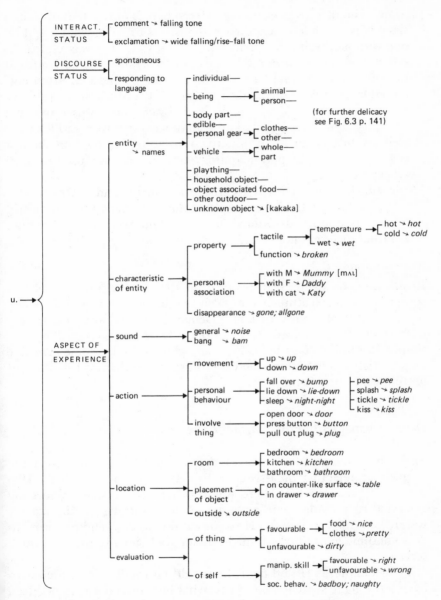

Fig. 6.2 18-19½ months—mathetic potential

in observing and classifying situations as were those nouns treated under [entity].

[action] The three-way grouping offered here is only a tentative one, since it is much less easy than with objects to judge what might be oppositional from the child's point of view. *Up* was clearly in direct opposition to *down* because for several weeks he confused the two, and when he had worked out the distinction, often corrected himself when he made an error. Of the other classes [involve thing] was expressed by a noun, and always one not used to name an entity. I have represented here all those action words which were well established in his productive repertoire, although in the last week or so of this period quite a few others were used once or twice only.

[evaluation] I have chosen to treat *nice, dirty,* and *pretty* at this stage as distinct from *hot, cold* and *broken,* since they so clearly carried a purely attitudinal meaning and were used therefore in rather different non-'exploratory' contexts.

Note on Figure 6.3

Realizations of all the features at ultimate delicacy are names corresponding to the feature name given on the network. A serious and detailed systemic study of lexical semantics would almost certainly not produce an analysis in this form. However, my goal here is simply to display Hal's lexical spread, while outlining some plausible major classes, and this seemed the most straightforward method of presentation for this purpose.

Developments within the pragmatic function

The main change here involves the category concerned with the 'gaining or rejecting of assistance to carry out an action'. By 19½ months it is clear that there was a difference between requesting a service to provide some amenity, such as turning on the tap for water, building a tower for H to knock down, etc., and requiring to do something *himself* which might incidentally involve some enabling service.

For example, if H said *light*, he would be totally dissatisfied with having the light switched on or off; what he required was to be lifted or in some way enabled to do this action himself. There was thus a clear behavioural distinction between 'I want you to do' and 'I want to do' (though neither a behavioural nor linguistic one between 'I want to do' and 'You enable me to do'). Success in this

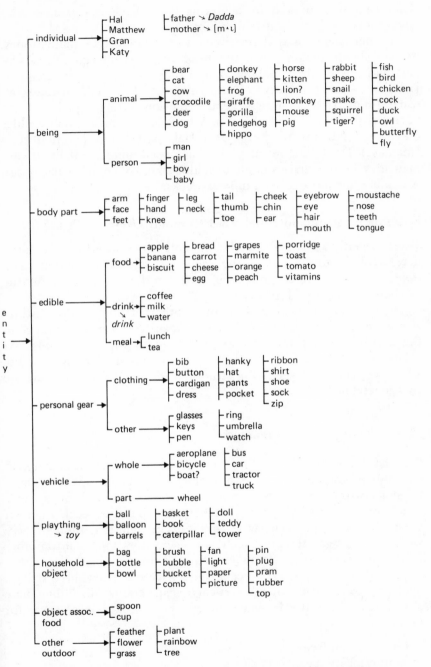

Fig. 6.3 18–19½ months—mathetic potential: entity network

latter case was marked by achieving the behavioural goal, not by having got the other to attend to him.

Another change is that two items were produced on falling tones, though clearly pragmatic in function. One was infrequent and was [mā:mà], used when seeking M, and the other was a very frequent [nà::] or [nòɷ] negative. The former was distinct from the more usual [māmā], used as a general attention-getting signal and not necessarily directed at M, and it may have been copied from his older playmate. (NB for mathetic uses Hal used [mʌ ɩ] rather than [mama].) The falling *no* may also have been mimicry of his friend, or it may be the first example of falling tone favoured for responses, which became more general in later weeks.

Notes on pragmatic potential, 18–19½ months (refer to Figure 6.4)

There are only a few additional comments which seem to be required here. One is to note that the range of objects demanded [gain object] had extended, but still included fewer classes than the mathetic category of [entity].

The [achieve action] and [control other] features have distinct sets of realizations. He could not yet mean 'you sleep' or 'you go in the garden', nor 'I want to sing', 'I want to wipe my hands'. At a later date, the same actions might be required of himself or the addressee, and he developed a structural means of distinguishing the two general meanings.

Successive single-word utterances

One development over this period, evident from texts already cited, was the production of little monologues which comprise 'strings' of single-word utterances, where each word is uttered on a single tone contour, usually with a slight pause between each one. Of these, 80 to 90 per cent were mathetic in function, though there were a few pragmatic ones, such as *flower; more* (= I want another flower) or *basket; tower* (= make a tower with these baskets).

Several researchers over recent years have discussed these strings. Scollon (1976) calls them 'vertical constructions', including here also cases where the language of another speaker intervenes, for example:

    Child: Fan (repet.)
    Mother: Fan! Yeah
    Child: Cool   [Scollon 1976: 160.]

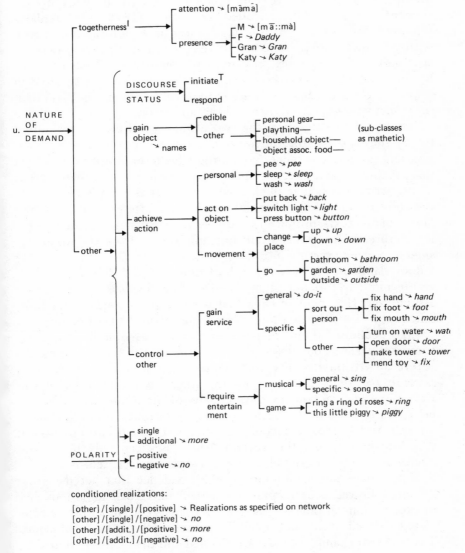

conditioned realizations:

[other] / [single] / [positive] ⤳ Realizations as specified on network
[other] / [single] / [negative] ⤳ *no*
[other] / [addit.] / [positive] ⤳ *more*
[other] / [addit.] / [negative] ⤳ *no*

Fig. 6.4 18–19½ months—pragmatic potential

Greenfield and Smith (1976) have also considered single-word strings. From their standpoint of seeing single-word utterances as the verbal encoding of one situational element, they have addressed the question of how we can predict which situational/syntactic element will be verbally encoded. Greenfield (1978: 443) explains this using the principle of informativeness in the information theory sense of uncertainty—uncertainty exists where there are possible alternatives. She analyses only running commentary kinds of texts. In one, the child remarks *car* on hearing one go by; *bye-bye* in response to his mother's *Where's it going? What's it doing?*, and then *car* whilst whining for his own toy car, and so on.

Greenfield explains that the two utterances of *car* are accounted for by the fact that the car in each case is not in the child's possession and is therefore 'uncertain', although she does not explain how this psychological uncertainty relates to the information theory sense of the term. Nor is it at all clear what range of alternatives is open to the child for encoding a demand for an object, for example. Furthermore, many texts produced at the single-word stage are impossible to interpret in her terms at all. Example strings from Hal would be: *allgone; coffee* (peering into cup) or *bang; door; Dadda* (on hearing a door slam). In the latter case, both the door and Daddy were non-visible and therefore uncertain in terms of her analysis, but one would assume that Hal encoded *bang* first because the sound was the most salient aspect of the situation to him rather than the least certain.

Like Scollon, I found that word order was variable in apparently comparable cases, but it was generally true that an object was named before an attribute of any kind. Thus it was more often *milk; nice, shirt; pretty, flower; broken* than the other way round, although this was only a general tendency. And in any of these cases he might well be handling the object, which according to Greenfield would make it unlikely to be verbally encoded. In sum, Greenfield's proposal is not very convincing, and the question she raises can only be seen as a relevant one if her general theoretical stance is accepted.

More interesting is Bloom's (1973) evidence that her daughter, Alison, followed a developmental path from verbalizing a sequence of observations in time—'chained' utterances—to describing a completed defined event 'holistically'. I observed both kinds of string. The first two examples below are chained and the next two holistic.

18(28) *Oh* (spotting fluff on leg), *gone* (as M picks it off), *there-tis* (spotting it again on floor).

18(4) *gone* (as tissue drops to floor), *down* (climbing off bed to fetch it), *up* (climbing back up).

18(28) *Badboy; Dadda; no* (= I was a badboy and F said '*no*').
18(11) *Bang; door; Dadda* (after hearing a door slam).

However, in Hal's case, the holistic, recounting kind of string appeared at about the same time as the running commentary kind.

Undoubtedly, stringing single words together is an extremely common strategy for creating texts at a point before any grammatical structures are used. But from the little evidence we have, there do not seem to be any obvious common developmental patterns of text organization in these strings. This may be because the data are not strictly comparable; only Bloom, of the writers mentioned above, restricts her discussion to single words in monologues, i.e. self-sustained texts.

Although it is not really possible to make comparisons on this point from the published data, it may be that Hal's preference for creating such strings within the mathetic function will be a common one. If this proves so, one reason would probably be that speech in the mathetic function, even in the early stages, is marginally less context dependent than pragmatic speech, and therefore longer strings are more likely.

That mathetic strings should be more prominent initially seems predictable given that the mathetic function involves discovering, or imposing, some patterning on the flux of reality, by means of language. It is relevant to note here that in Hal's case, grammatical structures were also developed earliest in mathetic language. And many of the single-word strings are precursors of grammatical structures such as Attribute^Thing or Process^Medium, basic linguistic patterns which encode the disparate and innumerable phenomena of the world. Putting words together in strings shows the child beginning to relate objects and their qualities, or happenings and the principal participants involved.

Some single-word strings are not obviously forerunners of simple clause or group structures (see, for example, some of the informative texts of the next period, Chapter 7, pp. 148–9). These strings encode more complex events that can be glossed in the adult language only by a clause complex or series of clauses. Halliday has suggested that the beginnings of the narrative genre can be seen developing here. This may be relevant to a consideration of Bloom's ideas on chained and holistic strings. She suggests that chained utterances are just the first step by the child towards the more advanced holistic conception of things or events as wholes, with different, equal or unequal, aspects to them. If most children do follow Alison in developing chained strings before holistic ones, this may be a good explanation.

But if Hal is typical in developing both side by side, then it may be that chained 'running commentary' strings are important in their own right as precursors of the narrative genre, where sequenced events are described in a recall situation rather than as an ongoing commentary.

7 Nineteen and a half to twenty-one months

During this period the first structures appeared, and like the first words, these were macrofunctionally restricted. None the less, developments in the functional possibilities within the mathetic and pragmatic functions over this period show that contexts for language were less exclusively one or the other than was at first the case.

Developments within mathetic function

1. Self-addressed speech

An important strand of mathetic speech continued to be self-addressed; these were often reiterations by the child of what had been said to him. The function of such utterances, as in the following text, was surely to help the child process what had been said to him, and it would be unwise to dismiss them as mere uninteresting 'repetitions' (cf. Greenfield and Smith 1976: 36).

20(18) H: Bòy (pointing at girl in street).
     M: It's not a boy, it's a girl.
     H: Gìrl; bòy.
     M: A girl.
     H: Bòy; gìrl (repeats this to himself in a low mutter several times).

At this stage I noticed too that Hal could attend to names even whilst primarily concerned with getting goods & services, as here:

20(15) H: Mīlk (reaching for a bottle of juice).
     M: Orange (giving him some).
     H: (drinks, then stops and points at bottle) Òrange.

And he could of course receive information other than simple names, as the following examples show:

20(11) (H is playing inside with flower from the garden.)
     H: Flòwer; flòwer; flòwer; flòwer (as he pulls the petals off on to chair).

M: Oh Hal, you do make a mess.

H: Mèss; mèss; mèss; mèss (rubs at petal stuck on his hands) tōwel; tōwel (runs off to bathroom to get one, but all are in wash, returns to M) tōwel.

M: In your bedroom, Hal. There's a white towel there. In the bedroom.

H: (to himself) Bèdroom; tòwel (runs off to M's bedroom. Returns with pair of towelling shorts. Rubs at petals) nàughty; nàughty; nàughty; mèss.

20(24) H: (wanting to go out back door) Outsīde; outsīde.

F: It's cold outside, Hal.

H: Outsìde; còld. Outsīde. Còld.

The mathetic language in the above examples, even where it occurs in response to an adult utterance, does not have the adult function of acknowledging to the addressee information received. I cannot therefore agree with Rodgon (1976: 94) that overt repetition is generally an early attempt at a dyadic communicative interaction, displaying the child's awareness of the speaker–listener relation, plausible though this might sound as a hypothesis.

2. Informative speech

However, there continued to be a lesser proportion of mathetic speech which *was* more concerned with the speaker–addressee roles. There were, for example, further cases of information giving, which may be contextually, though not linguistically, distinguished from other mathetic speech. A greetings context still supplied one motivation or opportunity, though it was still only rarely taken up:

20 months (H greets M at front door on her arrival from work.)

H: Càr; càr.

M: Yes, we've come in the car.

H: Càr; tòwer!

M: Oh, you've been playing with cars. Is that what you're telling me?

(H leads M into living-room to see Lego cars with towers built on them.)

20(2) (F goes into H in morning.)

H: Bùmp; nòise; bìrdie; nòise.

Sharing the experience of being chastised, perhaps to enlist sympathy, was prominent still, providing another kind of occasion for informative speech.

20(13) (H comes in to M, clutching pencil.)
      H: Nàughty; bàd; nàughty <i.e. F has told him off for scribbling in F's book>.

20(24) (H enters room where F is, crying.)
      H: Eyebròw; nàughty; pùss.
      M: (coming in) What's the matter?
      H: Nàughty <i.e. H was naughty to cat who scratched his 'eyebrow'>.

20(25) (H enters room where M is.)
      H: Don't tòuch; dont tòuch; dont tòuch; Dàdda; don't tòuch <i.e. H reports what F has just said to him.>

Moreover, Hal did now occasionally proffer more general information, as in the next text:

20 months H has had bath with M and commented on the noise of the water gurgling away. Later, when dried and dressed, he says to F *wàter; gòne; nòise.*

This last example, where an event is reported after a lapse of time, was still untypical. On the whole, the use of language was still very much concerned with the here-and-now.

As might be expected from the above statement, Hal did not really produce informative speech in responses as yet. He could of course reply appropriately to *What's that?, What's he doing?, Where's X?* kinds of questions, but he did not respond to questions that sought to focus his attention away from the here-and-now, unless he received a great deal of prompting and encouragement. (And this was generally only possible if the questioner was not genuinely seeking information but—having shared the experience—was seeking a shared recapitulation.)

3. Argumentation

One further development in mathetic language where the speaker-hearer relationship is relatively foregrounded, concerns little arguments over classifications. Sometimes this was simply in fun:

19(15) H: Pùssy (pointing at rabbit in book).
      M: No, it's a bunny rabbit!
      H: Pùssy.
      M: It's not a pussy . . ., etc.
      <both names were familiar to Hal>

But at other times, as in the next example, he was apparently in earnest.

20(6) H: Bòy (pointing to girl in picture).
       M: It's a girl.
       H: Bòy ; bòy (very fast).
       M: It's a girl.
       H: Bòy; bòy (fast).
       M: It's not. It's a girl.
       H: Bòy; bōy (anxiously).
       M: All right, it's a boy with long hair and a skirt.

Developments within pragmatic function

During this period there were three important areas of development in the pragmatic function.

1. Pragmatic responses contained a more prominent level of experiential content than before, and began to take falling tone.
2. Pragmatic language was used to obtain linguistic as well as behavioural responses from the addressee.
3. Pragmatic language was very occasionally used as a means of exploring the social and linguistic world.

1. Pragmatic responses

As soon as there is lexical coding, the majority of demands necessarily contain a specified classificatory element. However, the typical pragmatic dialogue initiated by M in the previous period would take the form of specific suggestions, which H could either accede to or reject. For example:

18(24) M: What do you want for tea?
       H: Tēa.
       M: What about boiled egg?
       H: Ēgg.
       M: Do you want some milk?
       H: Nò.

Now his responses carried more spontaneous specification of content, as in the next two examples:

20(7) M: What do you want for lunch?
       H: 'máto; cheēse.
20(20) M: What shall we sing?
       H: 'Oh dear màtter.'

This may be related to the fact that H now distinguished about 60 per cent of the time between initiating demands on level tone and responding ones on falling tone. At first, a falling tone response was often immediately succeeded by repetitions in a level tone. For example:

19(23) M: Do you want some bread?
        H: Brèad; breād; breād.

In the context of an immediately preceding adult offer, the 'I want' aspect carried by the level or rising tone could presumably be downplayed in favour of the experiential aspect, so that in effect there was no longer such a sharp distinction between 'I want lunch' and 'I'm talking about lunch'.

2. Nature of addressee response

Hal's increasing ability to accept a linguistic response to a demand, rather than an object or behaviour, has already been illustrated by the following text, cited earlier.

20(11) (H is playing inside with flower from the garden.)
        H: Flòwer, flòwer; flòwer; flòwer (as he pulls the petals off on to chair).
        M: Oh Hal, you do make a mess.
        H: Mèss; mèss; mèss; mèss (rubs at petal stuck on his hands) tōwel; tōwel (runs off to bathroom to get one, but all are in wash. Returns to M) tōwel.
        M: In your bedroom, Hal. There's a white towel there. In the bedroom.
        H: (to himself) Bèdroom; tòwel (runs off to M's bedroom. Returns with pair of towelling shorts. Rubs at petals) nàughty; nàughty; nàughty; mèss.

Here, on failing to find what he wanted, H returned to get M's help, and accepted verbal instructions rather than physical aid. And another previously cited text, repeated below, shows him accepting a linguistic response, even when it meant *not* getting what he had demanded. (Possibly he was distracted here by working out for himself the explanation implied.)

20(24) H: (wanting to go out back door) Outsīde; outsīde.
        F: It's cold outside, Hal.
        H: Outsìde; còld. Outsīde. Còld.

On this point, we can compare the following text at 18 months with a comparable one from the period under consideration.

18 months (At breakfast table.)
                H: tōast; tōast; tōast (looking round at F at toaster).
                F: Toast?
                H: Tōast; toást; ṁ.
                (F brings toast to table.)
                H: Tōast; tōast.
                F: (Buttering it) Yes, toast is coming.
                H: Tōast; dāddā.
20(2)   (M and H are out on a walk.)
                H: Drink; ōrange.
                M: OK. We'll go to those tables (indicating an outdoor cafe a little way off), and have a nice drink of orange.
                H: Drìnk; tàble; nìce.

In the first case above, even in the face of both physical presentation of the object and verbal offer, H maintained his demand until actually receiving the food. In the second, he accepted the deferment of gratification on the basis of the linguistic offer alone, and showed again signs of telling over to himself (mathetically) what had been said, the better to understand it.

There were also very rare but clear cases of Hal actually *seeking* a specifically verbal response, in the form of the granting of permission. Examples follow:

20(9) H: Tōuch (looking at M while putting hand out to stationary car).
20(9) H: (playing with radio lead.) Pùll (looks at M) púll.
        M: No.
        (H puts lead on cupboard instead.)
20(27) (H has pencil poised above piece of paper.)
        H: Páper (looking at M).
        M: Yes, you can write on the paper.
        H: Pàper (doing so).

3. Use of pragmatic language to learn

It may well be that in these very rare examples of permission seeking Hal was quite as much concerned with learning the rules of behaviour, as with being allowed to do something. And there was another class of demands for a linguistic response which seem even more readily interpretable as an attempt to explore social norms. Examples are given below:

19(28) (H climbs precariously on to seat of tricycle.)

M: Careful!

H: [kaxu] (M turns attention to something else.)
[kɒθə] ; do-it.

(M is baffled until, seeing H is at bike again, she realizes she is being asked to say *Careful!* again.)

19(19) H says *nāughty̆* very loudly as he climbs on to the table, looking at M. M agrees that that is naughty and hauls him off. H is not upset.

20(10) H says *nāughty̆*, as he pours salt on the table, looking round at M, who laughingly stops him and admonishes him.

20(20) H calls *dōing* as he stands on chair. He repeats *dōing* until M realizes she must say *What are you doing?*

These are interpreted as attempts by H to investigate the kinds of situations which call forth warnings and admonitions by means of playful enactments which require the addressee to play a role.

There was also a single example of Hal requesting M to perform verbally so that he could explore *linguistic* norms:

20(11) H: Doing; doing (pushing open picture book at M).

M: (puzzled for a moment) What's he doing? <i.e. character in book> Is that what I say?
(H beams.)

Finally, there were a few examples of pragmatic language being used as if to check on a name. Here we can reconsider the following text, cited earlier as an illustration of argumentation.

20(6) H: Bòy (pointing to girl in picture).

M: It's a girl.

H: Bòy; bòy (very fast).

M: It's a girl.

H: Bòy; bòy (fast).

M: It's not. It's a girl.

H: Bòy; bōy (anxiously).

M: All right, it's a boy with long hair and a skirt.

The pragmatic tone used on the last utterance seems to have a meaning something like 'Isn't it "boy"?'

There are also a few tape recorded examples of a pragmatic tone where a mathetic one would normally seem called for, as in the following two texts:

19(2) M: What's this?

H: Cārrot.

M: Carrot

H: Càrrot.

19(2)   M: What's that there?
      H: Gräss.
      M: Grass, yes.

In these cases, the names were very recent in Hal's vocabulary, which may explain the pragmatic tone as one indicating uncertainty or need for verification.

Then there were one or two clear, but rather unsystematic requests for names, which occurred at the end of this period. These are given below.

20(28)   H: (points to picture of beaver in picture dictionary) Béar.
         (M is not really attending and doesn't respond.)
         H: (pointing again) Māma; béar (looking at M).
         M: No, that's a beaver, darling. A beaver.
         H: Bèaver.
         M: Beaver.
21 months M: (pointing at same beaver) What is it?
         H: (wriggles, and looks coy) [bajajaja . . .]
            (babbles, looks up at M) bear <tone not noted>.
         M: No, what is it Hal? What's that? (points at beaver).
         H: (indecipherable, then) Māma (points at beaver) mōre;
            māma (takes M's finger and puts it on beaver).
         M: It's a beaver.
         H: (pleased) Bèaver.

His strategy, then, was on the first occasion to offer a name with a high rising tone, as if for verification. On the second he used more general pragmatic signals, the closest he could get to 'you tell me', since he had no lexical item for *say* or *tell*, nor any Wh forms.

There was one further example of this kind of thing.

20(14)   (M and H are looking at a night scene in a picture book.)
         H: Moòn!
         M: Moon, yes.
         H: moōn; moūn; móre; móre.
         M: More?
         H: Mòre; moūn.
         M: (suddenly realizing he is pointing at stars in picture)
            Oh, these are stars, these are little stars, stars in the sky.

Again Hal used *more* as if to say, 'go on talking', and as in the 20(28) example, was perhaps offering the name *moon* for verification, though this time with the usual level demand tone.

The mathetic/pragmatic distinction

Given the developments described in this chapter, it can no longer be accurately stated that for every utterance the context may be unequivocably interpreted as either one of reflective learning or active achieving. As we have seen, a mathetic utterance sometimes now involved achieving a linguistic interaction with an addressee, whether it was to gain acknowledgement of information given or to gain participation by the other in argument. On the other hand, pragmatic utterances might now involve manipulating the addressee in order to learn, rather than to satisfy material needs.

Two points need to be made here. One is that the majority of mathetic utterances were still self-addressed and very little concerned with the roles of the speech situation. Correspondingly, the majority of pragmatic utterances were concerned with material demands for goods-&-services and not with any kind of information seeking or investigation of reality. The second point is that even the more complex utterances were still being assigned to one or other function by the tone used.

Thus we have to see the context for most instances of productive language as either mathetic or pragmatic as before, and this is borne out by the fact that a good part of the systemic potential was still functionally restricted. However, at the same time that a proportion of lexis was available for use in either function, some situational contexts would appear to have had both reflective and active components, though the use of tone indicated which component was dominant.

Formal description of the language, 19½–21 months

First structures

Thus far, developments in the nature of the functions themselves have been discussed. Turning our attention now to the more formal aspects of the language during this period, the first point to be made is that there were now just a few syntagms appearing in the language. Almost all of these occurred within the mathetic function. As with single-word utterances, only those which occurred spontaneously, rather than in immediate imitation of an adult utterance, have been included in the network (see Fig. 7.1).

It took Hal a little practice to master the production of two words on a single tone contour. For example, at first (for a few days) he could not come out with *bye-bye Daddy* without rehearsing the items separately: *bye-bye; Daddy; bye-bye; Daddy; bye-byedi; bye-bye Daddy*. And then, having produced the syntagm, it tended to revert to being a single unit again, and no matter who was fare-welled it would come out *bye-bye Daddy* (again for a few days). Similarly, *nice* was used by M in the structure *nice book*, which was how the adults tended to refer to a special illustrated book of his. Having several times used *nice book* appropriately, he couldn't at first manage *nice* with an alternative name. One day he sat eating a boiled egg and said *egg; nice; egg; nice; nice book; nice book . . .* tailing off in confusion, when it seems clear that he had originally been aiming at *nice egg*. Such rehearsals and occasional failures only took a few days, after which he may fairly be said to have taken the first steps towards the development of constituent structure.

Some structures produced were clauselike: either Process and Medium ones (*make tower, open door*) or concerning the location of an entity (*dadda cot*). There was also one instance of an attributive one (*radio off*). A larger number were nominal group-like (*hot porridge, blue shirt*, etc.). For the first two or three weeks during which these structures arose, they were used infrequently, at least half the occurrences being immediately after hearing the structure from the adult rather than in spontaneous production.

This step of combining units into a syntactic structure was for-merly seen as the single most crucial step in language development, and can be regarded in various ways. If language is viewed primarily in syntagmatic terms, then perhaps the main opposition set up in the system would now be 'complex' vs. 'simple'. This would align *make tower, radio off, Dadda home* and *blue shirt* as being alike in struc-tural complexity, and all would be opposed to single-word forms such as *make, off, home, tower, shirt*, etc. However, when the lan-guage is viewed as here in terms of oppositions of features assigned from a consideration of functional context, then the closest links are seen as between *off* and *radio off*, *make* and *make tower*, *shirt* and *blue shirt*.

It will be seen that, in Figure 7.1, structural realizations of features are not presented as structural functions such as Modifier or Head. This is because we cannot assume that the moment there are occa-sional, even spontaneous, examples of a Modifier^Head structure, the child has formed a generalization, such that any realization of the feature [entity] can be modified, and any non-modified realization warrants being regarded as a Head only of a potentially endocentric structure.

The way the data are described in the network (see Figure 7.1) simply shows that here and there amongst the classes of [entity], the possibility of some specific modification arises. The only structural functions implicitly assigned are starting/ending ones (by the . . . convention). This is an 'uneconomical' way to describe the data since all the structural realizations are presented as individual choices. But it was deliberately chosen in order to suggest that the generalization implied by the structure has not quite been achieved. My proposal is that the same kind of option only gradually spreads across the system. As it does so, more and more classes of things, for example, become open to qualification, and simultaneously there is less and less restriction on the specific modifications for specific classes.

Although it is not possible to point to any particular moment when the generalization was achieved by Hal, in the first week or two of the *next* period (21-22½ months), there were dozens of these structures recorded rather than just occasional instances. And with that increase, an increase in the scope of collocational possibility was apparent, so that Hal could talk of a *big ladder* and a *big pee*; of *noisy Daddy, noisy bird* and *noisy bike*, even of *poor Daddy* and *poor drink* (when it was spilt). Of course a few newly learnt collocations tended to be restricted at first, e.g. *bright* only with *moon* or *star*, but this was probably because he had not quite worked out the meaning of an Epithet learned in a collocation, and it does not invalidate the general point.

In sum, then, the picture of development I am giving is as follows: the child begins by naming specific entities, qualities, actions, locations, etc., or classes of these. Then, by juxtaposing different items in a string (see pp. 142 ff), a relation between different specific items can be implied at the time the string is uttered. Under the influence of the language used to him, the child then makes specific relations explicit by consistently expressing them in the structural patterns of the adult language. However, at first the child behaves as though, for example, the activity of opening is in a specific consistent relationship only with doors, or as if the quality of colour is in a particular relationship only with clothes, and is not necessarily comparable with another quality, such as size or temperature.

A structure such as Modifier^Head or Process^Participant encodes a more general kind of information than do individual lexical items. I have suggested that, in the first instance, particular lexical items are related on the adult model, but that it is only when a sufficient number of like items are related to others in the same way that we can talk of the child generally interpreting actions as involving a participant of a specific kind, or as interpreting objects

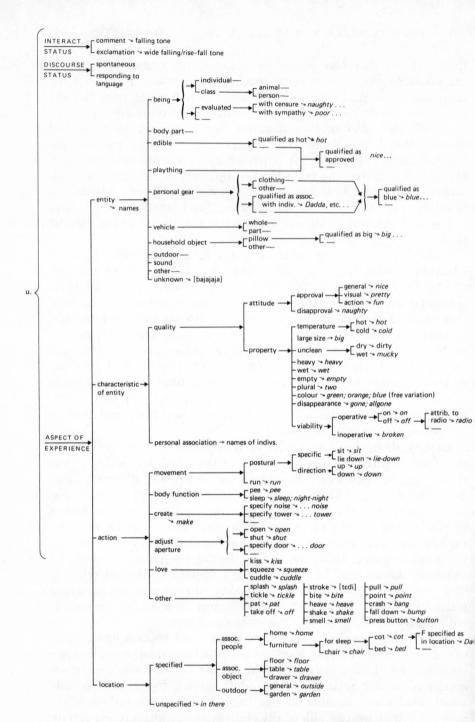

Fig. 7.1 19-21½ months—mathetic potential

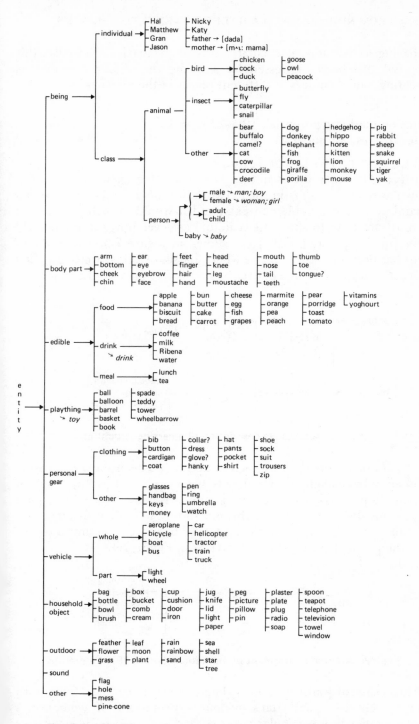

Fig. 7.2 19½–21 months—mathetic potential: entity network

as having as features, particular kinds of properties. Formally, this proposal has been expressed by showing the child's grammar as repeating 'same' choices at different places in the network.

Notes on mathetic potential, 19½–21 months (refer to Figs. 7.1 and 7.2)

ASPECT OF EXPERIENCE features
[entity] Although the structure *blue shirt*, for example, has been shown as related to *shirt* in the network, both *blue* and *shirt* occurred separately in comparable contexts, and it would probably therefore be most accurate to show the structure as developing simultaneously from [quality] and [entity], as shown in Figure 7.3. The development has been presented as one where classes of things were qualified in certain ways, more as a matter of simplicity, than of principle.

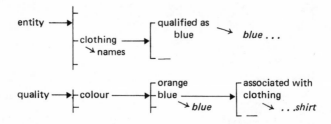

Fig. 7.3 Alternative description of emerging structures

The rationale for the way each structure has been shown as arising from an individual choice has already been explained (see pp. 156–7). The developmental nature of the grammar is being stressed in Figure 7.1. If one did not wish to do this but simply to look at the grammar for this period in its own terms, it would be more economical to display the [entity] part of the network as in Figure 7.4.

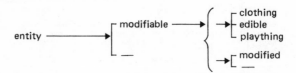

Fig. 7.4 Alternative fragment of mathetic network, 19½–21 months

The classes of [entity] proposed here are again deduced from both naming behaviour, and Hal's evident expectations of what things went together in a particular context, and now also by what classes are modified in what way. The feature [sound] has been added as a sub-class of [entity], rather than being treated as a separate class in opposition to the latter, because of its occurrence in the structure *make noise* as a participant, where the language the child is learning treats this phenomenon as a nominal, a 'thing'.

Hal continued occasionally to use a nonsense word, now [bajajaja], to classify pictures where the name was known, though this was fading out.

Figure 7.2 expands the [entity] network to give a picture of Hal's expanding lexical repertoire. Although I have presented it as a simple taxonomy, some items are now entering more than one class; e.g. *fish* is both [being] and [edible], *car* should be both [vehicle] and [plaything]. Entering an item in more than one place suggests that the two *fish*, for example, were different words for Hal, realizing different meanings. This may actually have been so in this case, but if not, it will be necessary to abandon the simple taxonomic approach and to employ some kind of componential analysis such that fish in the pond and fish on the plate share meaning features which are thus realized by the same lexical item. No attempt has been made to expand the scope of this account in order to do this, bearing in mind that it would also need to be applied to the non-nominal area, because for the period under study, a straightforward taxonomy seems to offer a satisfactory display of the lexical repertoire, and this research is by no means focusing specifically on the lexical level.

[characteristic of entity: quality: attitude] Terms previously classed as a distinct category of [evaluation] are included here, since like other [quality] terms they might now occur modifying an [entity] realization. They are maintained as a separate sub-class of [quality], not just on general semantic grounds, but because only this sub-class will later be available to modify proper nouns.

[characteristic of entity: quality; property] Whereas at 19½ months there were only words for variable properties of an object, there were now at 21 months also terms for immutable qualities such as size and colour. He also used the word *two* for dual or multiple instances of an object, especially when he could lay the items out side by side. (It would not be used for a second occurrence in time, e.g. of a car passing by, or a dog barking or of any action performed.)

The *there-tis* sign which previously formed a closed system with *gone* and *allgone* disappeared, perhaps because the latter terms were soon to be used (there were one or two imitative instances even now) in an attributive-like structure—*doggy gone*, etc.—not available for *there-tis*. Since other [quality] words would later also occur in relational structures of this kind, there seems no strong justification for continuing to see *gone* and *allgone* as a separate case. On the whole, the [disappearance] and [viability] realizations occurred with an element of change of state in the meaning which was not prominent in other kinds of quality words, but while this indicates a general extension of the potential here, I am not proposing a formal systemic opposition.

[characteristic of entity; personal association] Personal names were used to point out objects typically associated with specific individuals —items of clothing, F's razor, M's glasses, etc., and also occurred in Modifier^Head structures. They are distinguishable not only in meaning but in the way they function grammatically as the language develops, and are thus a genuinely distinct class. Since the proper nouns realizing this class also occurred with a different function as entity names, the simple lexical realization system provided on the network is not adequate here. It is not in fact possible entirely to avoid introducing a structural function into the realization path to describe the 19½–21 month language. A function such as Modifier or Possessor is required to take account of the lack of bi-uniqueness between form and function here.

[action] There was a considerable increase in the number of possibilities here, though I could not find very clear principles for assigning these to classes, and have done so only where apparent contextual similarity is supported on other grounds—such as a corresponding class being found in pragmatic uses, or having the option of adding a specific participant element, or later a circumstantial one. One additional class which has not been explicitly brought together, of course, comprises the three 'action' words which occurred in a proto-clause structure. Again, types and tokens were both so minimal that, as with the developing nominal group, the likeness to the earlier system is stressed here.

[location] The sub-categories here appeared justified from observations of Hal's use of these terms. The [associated people] group alone on two single occasions gave rise to an attributive-like structure: *Dadda cot* (on finding F there unexpectedly during a hide-and-seek game) and *Dadda home; cuddle* (on observing F come in). The [associated objects] group were used only when placing or locating an object in one of these locations, or when moving it from the place, while the [outdoor] group was one which also functioned pragmatically as a class.

in-there [njɛə] was a general deictic term which appeared for the first time.

Notes on pragmatic potential, 19½–21 months (refer to Figure 7.5)

DISCOURSE STATUS features

As has already been mentioned (see p. 150), Hal began to realize the initiate/respond distinction by means of tone choice, moving gradually to a situation where demands in response were systematically expressed with a falling tone. This may be interpreted either in terms of the more informative nature of a response, giving rise to mathetic tone, or as a reversion to the unmarked tone, owing to a recognition that the demand status is implicit, given a discourse position following an addressee offer. (Cf. Nigel's use of unmarked, falling tone where pragmatic status is expressed by gesture, reported by Halliday 1975a: 53).

NATURE OF DEMAND features

[call] Requests for interaction were now defined in terms of particular actions required, and the general 'concern yourself with me' signal [mama] disappeared. People were summoned by name and both [mʌι], which was previously exclusively mathetic, and [mama] were used for M, with generally level or rising tone, though sometimes mimicking adult sing-song calling intonation. There were also two names for F, depending on whether Hal was calling him on his own behalf or for M. In the latter case, he used [matῑ] (= Martin) rather than [dada] and always with adult calling tone. This would seem to be an interesting example of 'decentration' or early role play. Hal still did not respond verbally to his own name being called, or acknowledge a response to his own call.

[other: focus on object] If we consider the particular intents which could be contextually observed and which were expressed in pragmatic language, it is possible to distinguish the gaining of goods for possession from getting to see or do something with an object. For example, *paper* could mean 'I want to have that paper' on one occasion and 'may I write on the paper' on another. The contextualization provided by strings of successive words often corroborates the observation that a pragmatic object name was no longer necessarily encoding a desire for possession. For example:

> *flower; point; flower*
> *book; read*   = you read
> *fan; see*   = let me see

However, there was no longer any distinction in vocabulary used to express objects of desired possession and objects of desired action, with the exception of the [body part] class which occurred only in the sense of 'you fix up my hurt/dirty hand', etc. Consequently,

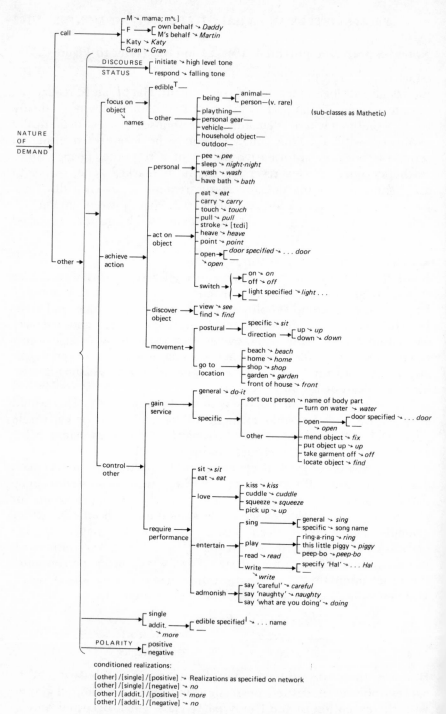

Fig. 7.5 19½–21 months—pragmatic potential

conditioned realizations:

[other] /[single] /[positive] ↘ Realizations as specified on network
[other] /[single] /[negative] ↘ *no*
[other] /[addit.] /[positive] ↘ *more*
[other] /[addit.] /[negative] ↘ *no*

with this exception, names of objects used pragmatically are brought together in the grammatical network under the broad class of a demand focusing on an object.

One particular class of object, that of [edible], could occur in a structure with *more*, giving *more drink, more bread*, etc., and has thus been distinguished from the others as before. Although *more* as a single utterance could still occur demanding a repetition of any kind, the structure *more X* always had the meaning 'I want to have more (to eat)'. However, the name of a food item alone was not necessarily a request for food to eat, as the following example shows: *porridge; porridge; see.* Here, Hal wanted to watch the porridge being stirred.

[other: achieve action] and [other: control other] There is also a certain amount of overlap in realizations as between the [achieve action] and [control other] options. However, the distinction between 'I do' and 'you do' was soon to become a structurally realized one, so there is no question of ignoring it as a relevant meaning choice at this earlier stage. However, it would be possible to represent the options along the lines of Figure 7.6. I have not done so, simply because as long as most of the choices were still person specific, the Figure 7.6 representation is less easy to read than the original less economical one. In any case, certain overlaps and loose ends are inevitable, and should be acceptable, when artificially freezing a developing system. A comparison with the 21-22½ month pragmatic network will, however, show that the system after 21 months moved in the direction indicated below, with representations of actions simultaneously selected with choice of 'doer'.

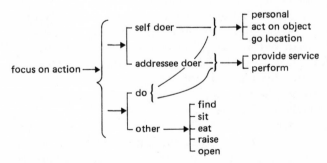

Fig. 7.6 Alternative representation of fragment of pragmatic network, 19½-21 months

Functional restriction of lexico-grammatical realizations

The language was moving all the time further from the protolinguistic form of a self-contained potential for each function. As can be seen from the mathetic and pragmatic networks, most of the lexical items used by Hal were found in either function, so that this representation as two distinct grammars is an idealization. None the less these were not yet two parallel systems—there were no quality words within pragmatic, there was no mathetic negative, and the rather minimal move into syntax was genuinely functionally restricted. Just as most single word strings were produced in mathetic contexts, so were the majority of structures. The only nominal group-like structure within the pragmatic function was *more X*, which cannot be taken as parallel to mathetic examples like *blue shirt* since each structure was exclusive to its own functional context. (Single *more* was also still exclusively pragmatic.) The other two structures occurring pragmatically were *write 'Hal'*, which was only found in pragmatic uses, and *open door*, which was functionally unrestricted.

General summary

The period from 19½ to 21 months was notable for the production by Hal of his first syntagmatic structures. This step no longer has to be seen as the only crucial milestone on the language development trail, but it is certainly an important one. It allows the encoding of more general meanings than does the iteration of individual lexical items, and in due course it provides a means for the simultaneous realization of different sets of features.

An examination of the words and structures uttered on different tones suggests that by 21½ months the language was less functionally restricted than before. Then an examination of contexts of use of utterances suggests that these were changing in character so that mathetic utterances could not only serve to explore and classify environmental phenomena, but begin to operate within a more defined speaker–hearer relationship. At the same time, pragmatic utterances were not only concerned with acting on the environment, but more and more with making reference to it and even on occasions with exploring and learning about it. Thus, the gradual freeing from functional restriction of the lexical realizations over this period can be recognized as the formal reflection from the 'output' of the changes in the nature of the functional context inferred from close observation of individual occasions of speech.

The breaking down of the mathetic/pragmatic distinction

It is during this period that many utterances cease to be obviously *either* mathetic *or* pragmatic in their function. Changes in the child's tone system render many utterances ambiguous, and contextually many examples of speech show the child's concern both with specifying aspects of experience and with interacting in a speech situation.

In discussing pragmatic responses in the previous period, I described how responses to adult offers began to adopt falling tone. It was also noted that Hal's pragmatic responses might supply a specific request as a response to a general offer. For example:

M: What do you want to eat?
H: Fish.

However, the most common kind of offer at this stage was probably still one where the adult specified a limited range of alternatives. For example:

M: Do you want to go home now, or do you want to go on the grass.
H: Go on gràss.

It was in responding to these that Hal gained practice in using longer utterances in the pragmatic function, but the real point is probably that the offer in the form of a choice question can focus attention on the experiential content, more or less taking the desire for granted. Thus, goods-&-services exchanges of this sort were getting a much greater component of information giving. Given this fact, and the current tone system, one might interpret the falling tone used by Hal in the following exchange as signifying that he was giving information (mathetic) or responding to M's implied offer of help (pragmatic).

22(4) (H is grizzling.)
M: (sympathetically) What's the matter with you? What's the matter with you?
H: Bùmp.

And the following example shows that H could respond to an offer or command by inference, by offering relevant information.

21(29) (Last bedtime ritual. H is not reluctant to go.)
       M: Shall we throw the teddies to Daddy?
       H: Teddy on tàble <= we will have to fetch the favourite teddy from other room first.>

As a final note on falling tone in pragmatic utterances, it should be mentioned that Hal took up the adult imperative *look!* during this period, complete with falling tone. Sometimes it was said after doing something noteworthy with his toys, and sometimes much more clearly as a demand for attention, holding something up to M, obliging her to respond (verbally). Given its tone, one could interpret this as a precursor of the use of adult tone 1 for imperative-like commands which he adopted in the next period, and therefore as essentially pragmatic, or simply as an exclamative kind of mathetic utterance which was addressed to another person.

Alternatively, of course, one can see such indeterminacy as a further clue that the language no longer had the functional basis that it did earlier, and there are certainly many indications that this was so. Such a doubtful case as *lòok!* could only arise when mathetic utterances were addressed to other people, with experience having taught the child to expect a verbal response on such occasions, and when pragmatic utterances looked for verbal, rather than behavioural, responses.

Further important evidence that the organization of the language was changing lies in the fact that most of the linguistic items which had hitherto been monofunctional (e.g. *no* and *more* as pragmatic only, and Epithet˜Thing structures as mathetic only) were now found in both functions. Although there were still some restrictions, to maintain a separate linguistic potential for each function so that every utterance is a realization of distinct features in either one or the other function is clearly becoming much more unrealistic.

In addition, it should be noted that Hal had now developed a little formula for offering food to a parent—namely *some Múmmy* or *some Dáddy* (with *some* as [səm]). While this is related to the pragmatic utterances in that it was necessarily interactive, and concerned goods rather than information, it was obviously not a demand, as pragmatic utterances had been hitherto.

From all this we can see that the original distinction between mathetic and pragmatic uses of language was becoming more complex in various ways. Hal, by this point, was moving towards a linguistic system where lower rank items were available for either mathetic or pragmatic structures, and where clauses were beginning to have a balance of experiential and interpersonal aspects. However, he had not yet developed a means of marking the interpersonal status of his utterances to replace the tonal distinction which was becoming inadequate. This he began to develop now.

First adult MOOD forms

Wh interrogative

It was during the period 21–22½ months that Hal used his first Wh interrogative forms—*Whats that* and *Whats in/on X*. These were not requests for a name, and there were only two examples during this period of the *ad hoc* name requests noted in the last period (see p. 154. On these occasions Hal placed M's finger on the picture he was interested in, looked up at her and said *Mama*. The Wh forms were not used in such situations. They were related rather to a kind of role playing that Hal carried out extensively a little later, where he seemed to be exploring the nature of linguistic exchanges. At this stage, the Wh forms served to introduce a mathetic comment, and were testimony to his understanding that using language to reflect on the world, 'talking about things' is an interactive process, a matter of exchanging information. Example texts follow:

21(17) H points at picture of flowers in book and says *whats that; whats that; whats that; flower.*

21(25) M and H are playing with toys and shopping bag. They put teddy, etc. in bag. H walks off and then returns to M and opens bag, saying *whats in-there; whats in-there; whats in-there; whats in-there; teddy.*

22(2) F asks *What's that?* pointing at picture in book. H can't remember and looks round room for something to name, pointing in an arc, repeating *whats that* till his finger comes to F, whereupon he says with a grin *whats that; Dadda.*
<i.e. Hal recognizes F's request for a name. As he can't respond to that question he re-questions himself to make his answer appropriate.>

22(11) H holds up his thumb with a plaster on and says *Whats on [ə] thumb* three or four times.

All these examples show Hal's awareness of the Wh form as a response-demanding one—indeed he had been responding to it for months—and although the information-giving form itself was not formally distinct from a pragmatic one, Hal made its status unambiguous by embedding it in a self-created adjacency pair.

Whether these Wh forms are to be regarded as pragmatic or mathetic is again problematic. They have been placed in the mathetic network on the following grounds:

(a) they had falling tone—but this was in imitation of adult speech and tone was no longer criterial;
(b) they did not seek a response from the addressee—but then Hal was playing the part of the addressee himself;
(c) they were in a sense practice forms, helping Hal learn how to use language interactionally, and from the start learning about the language was one of the threads in the mathetic function of learning about reality.

In favour of seeing them as pragmatic forms are the counter arguments given above, and perhaps the fact that the only explicitly coded initiating/responding system was found within the pragmatic function, as were the informal, other-addressed information-seeking instances already mentioned. While they have been treated as mathetic in the functionally specific analysis (see Figure 8.1), it is in fact probably best to see this phenomenon as Hal's way of bringing the two functions together. Talking about the world was being embedded in a dialogue construct, which had an initiating, essentially response-demanding form and a responding informative one, but was not yet being employed to sustain actual dialogue with an addressee.

Imperative

The Wh interrogative was not the only adult MOOD form to be developed at this stage. Hal also began to use the imperative, and once again the form is being regarded as essentially mathetic in character. It too was self-addressed, as in the following examples:

21(4)   H peers at M's glasses and says *Mummy glasses*, and then *dont touch!*
22 months While sitting near taps in bath, H says *Mind head!*
21(14)   H says *be careful! dangerous*, while looking at F's tools.
22 months H yells *dont open [ə] fridge!* as he slams it shut after opening it.

Before this, he had occasionally quoted such an admonition in an information-giving report, for example saying to M, *dont touch; Dadda; dont touch* after F had told him not to touch the TV (see

p. 149 20(25)). But now, the imperatives, while still quotations, were addressed as reminders to himself, clearly functioning as an aid to learning the rules of behaviour. They can be regarded as memorized formulae since he did not at this stage produce any 'original' forms; nor of course would there be any need for him to do so, as long as these utterances served a private reminding–learning function. He simply repeated the utterance in exactly the context he had originally 'received' it in.

Again it could be argued that these imperatives were pragmatic in that Hal was seeking a response (non-verbal) from himself, but he could also be regarded as taking what he recognized as an adult language-as-action form, and addressing it to himself in order to reflect on its meaning. It seems to link with two familiar aspects of Hal's mathetic language. One is his concern with social norms as an aspect of reality to be understood, a concern which initially spurred him to produce informative texts focusing on his misdeeds. And the current strategy of private quotations as reminders to himself also links with a longstanding 'language for learning' strategy, which was the verbalization of instructions or privately formed intentions, as an aid to carrying them out, as in the following examples:

18(8)   M: Show Daddy the flowers, Hal.
         H: (to himself as sets off) dàda.
20(11) M: In your bedroom, Hal. There's a white towel there. In the bedroom.
         H: Bèdroom; tòwel (setting off).
21(2)   H: Bring wàter (going over to hose to do so).

The direct quotation of language used to him in correction, whether of information or behaviour, was another aspect of this. The early text cited before (see p. 118 17(26)), where H repeats *no; no; broken* after M's warning, concerned the latter, while the following example from the current period is one of many concerning the former. This was the first occasion when H used the mathetic negative form *not X*.

21(20) M gets H up from midday sleep. He sees there is someone in the living room and enters eagerly, saying *Dadda*. M corrects him with *No, that's not Daddy; it's Debbie*. About half an hour later he looks searchingly at Debbie and repeats *not Dadda*. Four days later, he repeats two or three times, apparently out of the blue (perhaps Debbie's name had come up in adult conversation), *not Daddy, Debbie*.

A week later he could produce spontaneously *not orange; apple;*

and on sitting down to a dish of yoghourt, he said *not soup*. However, he continued to use the reminding quotation as a way of keeping things straight, as the following later examples (23 months) show:

23(1) H: Doggy (pointing at calf in book).
       M: No, it's not a dog. It's a cow, moooo cow.
       H: (later, returning to this page) not a dog.
23(13) H: (pointing at his nipple as undressed for bath) Pipple.
       M: Not pipple; nipple.
       H: . . . (after bath) Pipple; not pipple; not pipple.
. . . H: (a week later, getting undressed) Nipple; not pipple.

Summary of evidence for breakdown of the functional dichotomy

This chapter began with a claim that the mathetic/pragmatic functional distinction was becoming eroded. Evidence for this lies in the following developments:

1. The weakening of the original tonal distinction in that:
   (i) pragmatic responses (and occasional emphatic initiations) took a falling tone;
   (ii) calls had adopted adult calling tones;
   (iii) the newly acquired item *look*, if taken as an attention seeker, had not been re-processed through Hal's original tone system but adopted directly from adult speech;
   (iv) mathetic utterances might adopt non-falling tones for textual reasons following adult practice, e.g. listing.
2. There was now a large-scale sharing of lexico-grammatical forms between the two functions.
3. The informational or experiential element was becoming more prominent in pragmatic utterances.
4. The interactional role was becoming a more relevant factor in mathetic utterances with the development of Wh interrog^(pseudo) declarative pairs, and the increase in information-giving speech, both marking the increasing importance of the addressee generally.

All these developments mean that the situational context was no longer being defined by the child as almost exclusively mathetic or pragmatic. Instead, as was apparent at times before 21 months, situations were getting interpreted as having a component relating to field (what is going on and what is being talked about) and

component relating to tenor (speaker–hearer relationships), though
ne or other might be clearly dominant.

Factors in support of maintaining a functionally specific interpretation

t would be wrong, however, to suggest too sudden or too complete
. change at this point. Just as the move from protolanguage to transi-
ion did not occur from one moment to the next, so the language
vas now at certain times or in certain respects quite adult-like, and
.t other times or in other ways still much the same as before. There
tre therefore certain advantages in continuing to look at the language
n the same mathetic vs. pragmatic terms as before, if we wish to
iighlight continuities in its use. For example, on the mathetic side
>ne can relate previously described behaviour, when 'same' and
related things were grouped in naming sessions, with a current
trategy of observing how things are *like* other different things. This
:ould be in respect of some specific characteristic, as here:

21(25) H: (approaching dog) Pat dòggy.
   M: (as he does so) It's all soft isn't it?
   H: (patting) Pùssy (stands back and points at dog.) Dòggy
      <i.e. it feels like cat, it *is* a dog.>
21(15) H: Bâll (delightedly, on finding the orange he has thrown
      bounces and rolls.)

n other cases comparisons were implicit, as in the *not soup* example
given earlier (see p. 172). Sometimes likenesses were noted in a play-
:ul, imaginative way, as for example when mouthing the pillow and
:xcitedly naming the resultant wet patch as *camel!* or *sheep!*, etc.

On the pragmatic side, we can see that the 'I do' vs. 'you do' dis-
:inction, which was previously validated only contextually, now had
i formal means of differentiation, namely *Hal X* vs. *Mummy/Daddy X*,
:he latter type becoming in fact the preferred form of 'you do' com-
nand.

Moreover, it would simply be an overstatement at this stage to
suggest that the systemic potential was functionally *unrestricted*.
As we shall see, transitivity structures evolved a little differently
within the two functions; the mathetic nominal group was more
elaborate than the pragmatic, and even where systems and forms
occurred in both contexts, a highly frequent choice in one function
might still be a rarity in the other. And finally it should be said
that Hal's original tone system which realized the two-way functional choice had not been superseded yet, and nearly all pragmatic
initiations were still encoded with high level tone.

Formal description of the language 21–22½ months

There are two important developments to be discussed as a preliminary to the formal analysis of the language at this stage. One is the development of a rank scale of three levels: clause, group/phrase and word; and the other concerns the nature of the development of TRANSITIVITY structures.

Development of rank scale

In the previous period, we saw embryo group and clause structures emerging (e.g. *blue shirt; make tower*), and by 22½ months, a hierarchical relationship can be observed, with a Modifier^Head structure operating as a constituent in a mathetic prototype relational clause like ((*new shoes*) *dirty*) or a pragmatic utterance like ((*more Ribena*) *in-there*). At this stage, however, participants in [action] clause types were realized by single lexical items. These will be treated as nominal groups with Head only.

Prepositional phrases also occurred as clause constituents, as in *dirty suit in drawer* or *put on Daddy*, but these were not yet fully developed. He would often use a name directly as a locational circumstance, as in *sit potty, pee bath*, and the preposition occurring with any particular noun was fully determined. If the location was *drawer, box*, etc., then the preposition, if present, was *in*, if *table* or a proper noun or body part, then the preposition, if occurring, was *on*.

It should perhaps be made clear here that a speech functional definition of a clause has been adopted in the description to follow, so that anything realizing a comment, a self-exhortation or instance of information giving on the mathetic side; or a call, offer or demand on the pragmatic, counts as a clause. (Any such clause may comprise only one group, and any group may comprise a single word.) I have not at this stage distinguished between 'major' clauses (containing a Process/Predicator) and 'minor' clauses, as in systemic descriptions of adult language, because it seems premature to see this as a choice comparable with the adult one. During this period, the likelihood of a structure occurring depended more obviously on whether the utterance occurred earlier or later in the period than on anything else. Moreover, a (non-imperative) Process alone was still a relatively common production, and it would be difficult to exclude these from a classification as 'major' along adult lines, although this is an immature form and one not acceptable in the adult system.

Development of TRANSITIVITY structures

In mathetic contexts the following utterances are representative of process forms in the 21-22½ month period.

Put on table
Saw dog
Say 'bye-bye'
Daddy coming
Mummy sleep
Pee on grass
Hal pee
Cut apple
Take toast
Switch off radio
Buy bread
Bring water
Carry box
Bite apple
Take off shirt
Press button
Point flower
Teddy jump

An examination of the above data reveals that with the minimal exception of 'mental' processes (namely *see, say, write*), which were developed previously in exclusively pragmatic uses, all other processes occurred mathetically with an optional Medium. In other words, where two inherent participants were involved, the Actor appeared in intransitive structures and the Goal in transitive ones. Thus, if we wish to capture a generalization about which participant occurred in these early structures, an ergative interpretation of clause structure is best, since it allows us to describe the facts simply, by saying that a Process·Medium structure had developed.

Turning now to pragmatic structures, the following kinds of data have to be accounted for:

Hal bring
Bring stick
Hal get up
Mummy sit
Mummy cut
Mummy cut fingernail
Cut fingernail
Hal buy bread

Hal take
Press button
Hal press button (see Figure 8.8 for full details)

As can be seen, the distinction between 'I want to' (enable me
let me) and 'I want you to' (you do) was often now made explicit
by the use of proper names: e.g. *Hal pee* or *Hal buy bread* vs.
Mummy sit; Mummy cut (fingernail). This means that although the
only participant to be encoded in a mathetic process was the Medium
(intransitive Actor, transitive Goal), in pragmatic language both
transitive and intransitive Actors were produced.

We could say then that the first Agents appear in a pragmatic
context, in examples like *Hal press button, Daddy wipe hands*. But
this ergative interpretation seems a little forced. The mathetic data
strongly suggested an ergative approach to process structures, since
some generalization concerning transitive Goals and intransitive
Actors (i.e. Mediums from the ergative view) appeared to have been
made by the child—since only these are encoded. But an examination of pragmatic clauses during this same period shows that here a
specified participant is not necessarily a Medium. Moreover, in a
two-participant clause where only one participant is encoded, that
one is most likely to be the Actor (ergative Agent) (e.g. *Mummy cut,
Daddy get*).

One possibility is that we are looking at the development of some
kind of 'Subject' notion here. In an adult goods-&-services clause
where the mood is imperative, the one modally 'responsible'—the
Subject—is the addressee. And what Hal was specifying (with
a proper noun) in these pragmatic clauses was sometimes a Medium
and sometimes an Agent instead or as well, but most often the one
who was to fulfil the desired action. In other words, he may have
been specifying the interpersonal role of Subject.

However, it is true that, even in adult, the imperative MOOD
Subject and the TRANSITIVITY Actor roles are still very closely
allied, and it may be more revealing to continue to consider the
clause functions in experiential rather than interpersonal terms.
Halliday's interpretation of the experiential structure of the English
clause is perhaps unique in assigning dual transitive and ergative
experiential functions to all clauses, although some process types
are more readily accommodated by one or other interpretation.
Furthermore, he regards no language as being exclusively ergative or
exclusively transitive in its experiential organization. Dixon has
discussed this question in a paper entitled 'Ergativity', where
he uses the terms 'accusative' and 'accusativity' where I have

ised 'transitive' and 'transitivity' above. He discusses verbs rather
han clauses and claims: 'It is certainly the case that every language
mingles "ergativity" and "accusativity" in the structure of its
exicon.' (Dixon 1979: 109.)

He points out that 'accusative' languages tend to ally transitive
and intransitive Actors as Subject, giving this element unmarked
case and making it the pivot for operations of co-ordination and
subordination. 'Ergative' languages, on the other hand, ally intransi-
ive Actors and transitive Goals (i.e. Mediums), giving this element
inmarked case and making it the pivot for most syntactic operations.
He notes, however, that 'even the most ergative language' will align
ransitive and intransitive Actors (and *not* Mediums) in the impera-
ive, allowing this element to be omitted, for example, as in English.

If it is true that all languages combine in some degree the ergative
and the accusative models of reality, and also that the imperative
construction is one typically favouring an accusative interpretation,
hen this perhaps supports a view that the macrofunctionally based
difference in favourite clause structures in Hal's language data from
21 to 22½ months may relate to the development by him of alternate transitivity models.

Halliday has said:

The ideational component of meaning arises in general from the use of language
to learn [mathetic macrofunction] while the interpersonal arises from the use
of language to act [pragmatic macrofunction]. [Halliday 1975a: 53.]

However, I am here suggesting that the pragmatic macrofunction
may also play a part in reality construction and the development
of the ideational or experiential component.

The pragmatic mode clearly concerns the notion of 'do something'
and the transitive (accusative) model of reality favoured here may
be seen as appropriate when semantically glossed as 'somebody
does something (Actor + Process), and this action may be extended
to or directed at another participant (+ Goal)'. The mathetic mode
concerns understanding or making sense of reality, and the ergative
model which is favoured here—at least in this data set—can be
glossed as 'something is affected by or involved in an action (Medium
+ Process)'.

Obviously these ideas can only be tentative; but they do lead to
the notion that the transitive (accusative) model may be the 'natural'
goods-&-services way of looking at the world, while the ergative is
the more informational. And, especially if the two typically develop
in this way during the transition period, this in turn may explain
why all languages embody both models.

Representation of TRANSITIVITY structures

Having considered the nature of the TRANSITIVITY structure during this period, the form of representation used in the claus networks (Figures 8.2 and 8.8) may need clarification. Let us take the following small sample of mathetic speech as representative:

Med.	Pro.	Loc.		Pro.	Med.
(Katy)	walk	(on grass)		pat	(dog)
(Mummy)	sit			eat	(bread)
				bump	(head)
				carry	(book)

[( ) brackets denote optional element]

These data can be economically described, as in Figure 8.1.

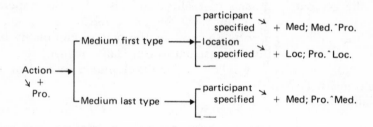

Note: Where — options are chosen, processes are distinguished according to how the pattern when a Medium *is* specified.

Fig. 8.1   An 'economical' description of TRANSITIVITY structures, 21–22½ months

However, it will be seen that in the comprehensive description of the mathetic potential given in Figure 8.2 the network specifies for each individual process or small group of processes whether or not a participant or locational element is possible. This is in order to indicate Process·Medium collocational restrictions, and to give approximate frequencies for the principal choices made (such as ± Loc). This is not just to provide a more exact representation of Hal's system, but to give a better idea of how the development of the generalization embodied in a structure such as Process·Medium actually occurs. It seems as if the first step is that particular specific concatenations are produced (e.g. *make tower; open door* in the 19½–21 month period), and that this is a marked option as against a single-word utterance *make* or *open*. Two developments then take place: one is that the marking pattern flips over to make something more like the adult pattern the norm, and the other is that rather than learning each structure as an individual pair, the child grasps the generalization that by and large any participant can be brought into a particular relation with any process. These changes occur very swiftly, but it seems possible to discern three steps:

1. Isolated pairings into structures (i.e. developing an option to choose a particular way of interpreting events—as things affected by actions, or actions in which entities are necessarily involved—but making it available for only one or two kinds of action).
2. These spread to involve more and more processes, but with different single vs. structure probabilities and different degrees of freedom in the pairings. This is the stage I am attempting to represent here by describing the system in terms of the child repeating the same choice at different places in the system. Presumably the frequency with which the participant is specified depends partly on the nature of the process and the likelihood of situational context discouraging explicitness, partly on the frequency of the process form in the child's discourse—favourite ones developed the structural form more rapidly than others—and partly on the extent to which a process was favoured for accompanying rather than recounting talk. *Kiss* and *cuddle*, for example, were used almost entirely as a running commentary, which may explain the infrequency of an accompanying participant element.
3. The probabilities even out to the adult norm (which will not of course always be 0 as against 1, as in the case of −Med (0) to + Med (1)). At the same time constraints on what goes with what in the structures relax into an adult pattern. At this point, a simpler network is possible, and the child can be said to have learned or developed a particular generalization.

Note that at the second stage there may also be a few cases of structures being produced whose elements did not occur separately. Hal, for example, produced *post letter* and *turn[ə]page* before 22½ months, though it was not clear whether these were genuinely part of his productive system, occurring as they did in close proximity to an adult model. If they were, they were learned as structures because of the mutually exclusive collocations (and because he had already achieved step 1 above).

I made the point during Chapter 3 that these probability weightings should be seen as a general guide only. Even if the researcher attempted to record every single instance of a selection of developing forms, it seems unlikely that there would be enough data on which to do any serious statistical analysis. For example, there may well be only a few dozen instances of the form *take* from the time it occurs only as a single-utterance to the time it occurs only in a Pro·Med structure. Less favoured forms (or less talkative children) may produce even less to go on. For this reason I suspect that as long as we are interested in the developing paradigmatic system as a whole such approximate probability weightings may be the best that can be attempted.

Notes on mathetic potential at clause rank, 21–22½ months (Refer to Figure 8.2)

INTERACTIONAL STATUS features

[(informative) comment] it seems as if the mathetic 'comment' was gradually turning into the speech function of information giving. That is to say, a greater proportion of utterances were now in fact giving previously unknown information to the hearer, it was getting a little easier to solicit information, and Hal's utterances were much more frequently unequivocally addressed to specific addressees. Moreover, Hal was becoming conscious of the informative nature of typical adult declaratives as his 'practice' adjacency pairs show (see p. 169). None the less, the running commentary was probably still the most frequent type of utterance, and the private commentary persisted and was especially noticeable where Hal was processing information or directives received, and with the emergence of the self-addressed imperative forms.

Feature specifications, Fig. 8.2	Text
[exhort self: prohibition]	(H is peering at M's glasses.) *Mummy glasses. Don't touch.*
warning]	*Be careful* (picking up knife).
[(in form.) comment: neutral/entity]	(i) (H has made a mess. Goes to cleaning cupboard) *Brush.* (ii) *Stone* (putting one on top of sandcastle).
exclam./entity]	*Two pen!* (excitedly laying a second pen alongside one he has just found).
neutral/action:mental]	H: Boy M: Boy? H: Saw boy
neutral/action: placement: location spec.]	*Put in rubbish* (collecting bits of paper he has torn up). *Put in rubbish* (returning to M from having done so).

(inform.) comment:

exclam./action: placement: location spec.]	*Put on top!!* (on managing to balance something on top of Lego structure).
neutral/action: other: Med. first: movement: postural]	*Lie down* (lying back to have his shoes put on).
(as above): sit/ location spec.]	*Sit on Mummy* (doing so).
neutral/action: other: Med. first: movement: locomotion: location spec.]	(i) *Go on [ə] grass* (pointing and running on arrival at picnic spot). (ii) *Bump. Fall off* (tearfully to M when she enters after hearing him fall).
exclam./action: other: Med. first: movement: location: participant spec.]	*Teddy jump!* (tossing teddy off bed).
neutral/action: (as above)]	*Daddy coming* (anticipating F's return).
neutral/action: other: Med. last: general: participant spec.]	(i) *Buy bread* (telling F on return from shop with M). (ii) *Bring water* (fetching hose). (iii) *Cut apple* (watching F do so).
neutral/action: other: Med. last: restricted: participant spec.]	(i) *Do bib up* (as M does so). (ii) *Hurt finger* (complaining).
neutral/action: other: Med. last: general: accompanying]	*Point; point; point* (as he touches a series of flowers with index finger).
neutral/characteristic of entity; part-whole] (as above): whole spec.]	*Got horn* (pointing to deer's antler in picture). *Dadda got chin* (touching it).
neutral/characteristic of entity: quality: attribution]	(i) *Dadda busy* (returning to M after failing to get F to play). (ii) *Katy hungry* (observing cat mewing for food).
neutral/characteristic of entity: quality: simple]	(M talks of H's behaviour the previous day) *Naughty.*
exclam./characteristic of entity: quality: simple]	*Big!* (as M puts a fat cushion under him at table).

[(inform.) comment:

neutral/characteristic of entity: naming: simple: pos.]	(i) *Bright moon* (pointing up into sky).
	(ii) *Mummy drink, Hal drink* (pointing in turn).
neutral/characteristic of entity: naming: simple: neg.]	(i) *Not telephone* (pointing at heater).
	(ii) *Not orange; apple* (holding up fruit).
neutral/characteristic of entity: naming: classification: declarative]	(i) *That's boy* (pointing at child).
	(ii) *That telephone* (reaching to it).
neutral/characteristic of entity: naming: classification: interrog. introducer]	*What's that; monkey* (pointing in picture book).
neutral/characteristic of entity: locational: participant not spec: pos.]	*In-there* (peering inside post box toy).
neutral/characteristic of entity: locational: participant not spec: neg.]	*Find slippers* (setting off down hall). *No* (looking into bedroom). *No* (peering under hall stand).

Examples of mathetic realizations at clause rank

As it is not possible to provide lexical realizations on the clause network for the period 21-22½ months, some sample forms are provided below, together with feature specifications from Figure 8.2:

[exhort self] I have treated these imperative forms as a distinct speech function, which means regarding them as formally unrelated to other comments using the same lexis. This is necessary, given the fact that they are memorized formulae produced in highly restricted contexts. On the whole, in fact, different lexical items occurred here; *be careful!*, *don't drop it!* and *mind tap!* had no 'declarative' commenting equivalents. *Touch*, which occurred ritually in *don't touch*, was otherwise found only in pragmatic contexts, so the only possible problem is with *don't open [ə] fridge*, since *open X* was also a familiar mathetic comment. It may be unsatisfactory to treat the two forms as unrelated, but it can be justified on the grounds that Hal had learned the imperative clause as a ritual phrase for a specific context. And though doubtless the fact that *open X* was already in his receptive and productive system helped him understand the adult directive, the parroting of *dont open [ə] fridge* does not really demonstrate that he had grasped a specific formal relationship between the two (commenting and imperative) forms.

ASPECT OF EXPERIENCE features

[entity] As before, there were occasions when Hal simply referred to things or people in contexts which were not obviously of the classifying type, such as when responding to M's mention of being home soon with *drink; Katy*, meaning 'we'll give Katy a drink then' or 'I'll have a drink and see Katy then'.

[action] In contrast to the situation at 21 months, virtually all realizations of this feature could now occur as structures. These were of two elements, either Process·Medium (or occasionally Actor Process or Process Location).

[action: placement] *Put* stood alone in having a virtually obligatory Location element, but in no case was there an alternative Process· Medium structure (NB: although he did produce three element structures, such as *Dadda got nose*, there were no recorded examples at this stage of a Process·Medium·Circumstance mathetic form).

[action: mental] With minimal exceptions, the participant in a structure here was always a Medium in terms of adult language, i.e. intransitive Actor or transitive Goal. The exceptions to this were a group of mental processes (or two classes of 'mental' and 'verbal' processes; see Halliday 1984b). What is perhaps more relevant here is that all these structures were developed first in a pragmatic function where the generalization that the participant was always a Medium did not hold. *See X* had for many weeks been a frequent demand, meaning 'let me see —', and now during this period there were three recorded tokens of *saw X* as a mathetic form. (Two were apparently recalling, and one possibly anticipating, something to be seen by himself.) In addition, two verbal processes *say* and *write* appeared for the first time in a very occasional mathetic use.

[action: other] There were about forty processes not in the [mental] group. The structural forms here all involved an optional Medium. I have grouped these initially as [Medium first] vs. [Medium last] types, since I wish to claim only that Hal had made the generalization that virtually any entity can be seen entering into one particular general relationship with virtually any action process.

[action:other:Medium first type] Hal did not yet refer to himself in mathetic utterances of this kind, but the Medium had to be an animate being. All such processes concerned movement or bodily function, and if there was no participant specified, there might be a Location element expressed in some cases.

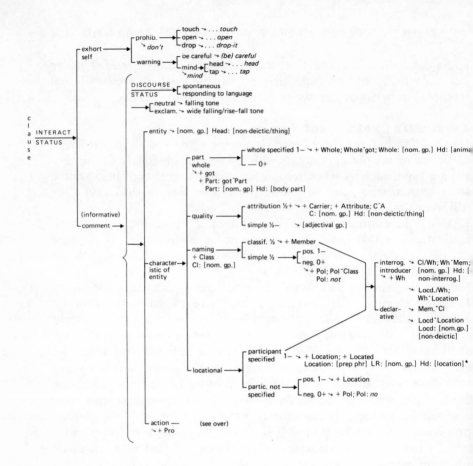

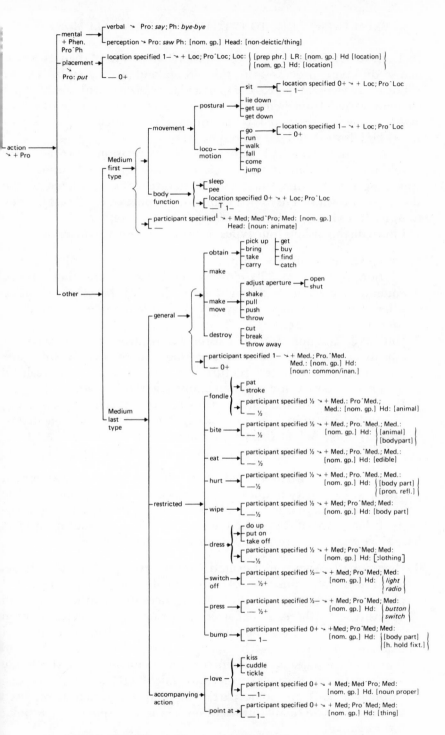

Fig. 8.2 21–22½ months——mathetic function; clause rank

[action:other:Medium last type] There were more than twice as many different processes in this group and no examples yet of a Location element here. The particular realization of the Medium element varied from being almost unrestricted in the case of *get* or *make*, to being restricted to a nominal class such as [edible] or [clothing] for *eat* and *put on* respectively.

[characteristic of entity] Various types of relational process were developing here, and at this stage when the structural forms were appearing for the first time, each structure is being related to the single-word form still used in a comparable context, e.g. *Thats [ə] dog* to *dog* and to *not [ə] dog*; *porridge hot* to *hot*, etc.

I have distinguished four types of proto-relational clause:

1. [part–whole] This was to develop into a more general possessive relation, but was, at 22½ months, restricted to itemizing parts of animate beings, as in *deer got horn*. Initially he would point to a being or a picture and say *got X*, but very soon preferred the three-part structure.

2. [quality] The non-structural form was realized as an adjective or adjectival group, e.g. *big* or *very big*. There was by this time also a Carrier^Attribute structure, with the Carrier always realized by a named entity and never an exophoric *this* or *that*.

3. [naming] The simple form, with only one specified participant, was either a nominal group or a negative structure, e.g. *big dog* or *not [ə] dog*. A [classification] clause took a form such as: *thats [ə] dog*, with the first element always expressed as a Deictic.

It is true that when H said *thats Mummy* or *thats [ə] moon*, pointing at the entity in question, he was in fact identifying a unique referent, since there is in fact only one Mummy and one moon. However, I have not distinguished identifying and attributing clauses here since the two were formally indistinguishable at this point.

4. [locational] Where no Located element was present, the clause, when positive, consisted of a nominal group or prepositional phrase. I am treating the first occurrences of a mathetic *no* as in opposition to these. It occurred as a running commentary when Hal failed to locate something he was looking for. He might, for example, announce that he was going to get a teddy, and would then peep into each room in turn, announcing *no* if the teddy was not there. A similar procedure might take place on looking through a book for some particular picture. *No* was never used at this stage to deny information or as a response to a polar interrogative.

PROTO-MOOD features
The [naming] and [locational] clauses were alike in having a Wh interrogative form. Unlike the [exhort self] imperative imitation, the Wh interrogative was a productive form, and is therefore represented as in direct opposition to the information-giving [declarative] form of these clauses. The interrogative has not been treated as a primary speech functional (INTERACT. STATUS) distinction of Hal's overall mathetic system because of its restriction to two specific clause types, and because, as explained earlier, it was not an information-seeking form proper (see pp. 169–70). I regard the Wh form as an introducer of an (informative) comment at this stage, sharing its speech functional status.

I have termed the system's features [interrog. introducer] and [declarative] because they were Hal's imitations of adult Wh interrogative and declarative forms, and because he was exploring the dialogue functions these forms congruently encode in adult language rather than adapting the forms to more idiosyncratic ends as did Nigel (see Halliday 1975a). However, it should be noted that the key adult MOOD realizational contrast of Su.^Fi. vs. Fi^Su was not a relevant one here. Moreover, although in adult language the Wh function must conflate with other MOOD functions, here it seems possible and more economical to conflate it with TRANSITIVITY functions to produce *What*.

Notes on mathetic group/phrase rank

Nominal group (refer to Figure 8.3)

The adult nominal group has both an experiential and a logical structure. The latter, with the functions Modifier and Head, concerns the potential for recursion in the syntagm (see Halliday, 1984b). At 22½ months, Hal's group did not have a potential for more than one Modifier, so there is no recursive wiring in the network. The terms Modifier and Head have been chosen simply as general function labels.

MODIFICATION
There were three experientially distinct kinds of Modifier which have been treated by means of features conditioning the realization of the Modifier element, rather than as realizing independent experiential functions, since there was only one Modifier place at this stage.

The first kind of modification in Hal's language was of the Epithet^Thing type; modification in the form of qualification,

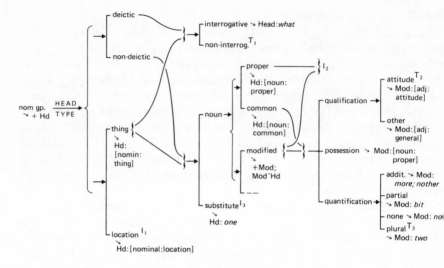

Fig. 8.3 21 to 22½ months—mathetic function: nominal group

Sample realizations: Fig. 8.3 mathetic function: nominal group

Feature specification	Example realization
[deictic/thing:interrog.]	what
[deictic/thing:non-interrog.]	that
[deictic/location:non-interrog.]	there
[non-deictic]/[location]	garden
[non-deictic]/[thing:noun:proper]	Katy
[non-deictic]/[thing:noun:proper/ modif.:qualif.:attitude]	funny Daddy
[non-deictic]/[thing:noun:common]	book
[non-deictic]/[thing:noun:common/ modif.:qualif.:attitude]	nice cheese
[non-deictic]/[thing:noun:common/ modif.:qualif.:other]	big pillow
[non-deictic]/[thing:noun:common/ modif.:possession]	Mummy glasses
[non-deictic]/[thing:noun:common/ modif.:quantif.:addit.]	nother truck
[non-deictic]/[thing:noun:common/ modif.:quantif.:partial]	bit paper

[non-deictic]/[thing:noun:common/ modif.:quantif.:none]	no clock
[non-deictic]/[thing:noun:common/ modif.:quantif.:plural]	two pen
[non-deictic]/[thing:substitute: modif.:quantif.:plural]	two one

as expressed in this network. In the discussion of the first group structures, I suggested that this choice began as one for specific pairings, and that the likelihood of a [+ qualified] choice varied from one class of entity to another. This suggests the same choice being separately made at different points in the system. By 22 months the two factors of evening out of probabilities and loosening of collocational restrictions had been achieved, so that it makes sense to see a symmetrical choice of [qualified] vs. [not qualified] as generally applying.

Even while this was occurring, other kinds of Modifier were being developed and the process was being repeated for each of these (though more rapidly). At 22½ months, asymmetries in the modification pattern included the fact that proper nouns could occur only with attitude Modifiers and no others (as in adult English) and that the substitute form *one* could occur only in a modified form. In mathetic use it was very infrequent and was always accompanied by the plural Modifier *two* (In pragmatic use—see Figure 8.9—it was always modified by *this* or *that*.)

HEAD TYPE
[location] *Here* and *there* have been treated in the description as nominals, and nominals have been distinguished as encoding either the feature [thing] or the feature [location]. Although the two categories were no longer completely differentiated as at one time (and there is thus some duplication of features and realizations at word rank), the distinction still appeared to have some validity in terms of differentiated lexis. Moreover, when nouns realized clause Location functions, they were not ever modified so far as my records show. I collected no tokens such as *sit Mummys chair* or *put in blue cup*, though this may result from a far smaller number of instances of nominal groups operating as Locations than any grammatical barrier.

Adjectival group (refer to Fig. 8.5)

This realized the feature [quality], or the function Attribute in a relational clause. In adult language there is no need to distinguish

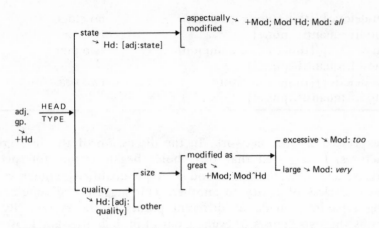

Fig. 8.4   21 to 22½ months—mathetic function: adjectival group

Sample realizations: Fig. 8.4 mathetic function, adjectival group

Feature specification	Example realization
[state]	better
[state:aspectually modified]	all clean
[quality:size]	little
[quality:size:modif. as great:excessive]	too big
[quality:size:modif. as great:large]	very big
[quality:other]	wet

[attribution] and [classification] relational clauses as is done here, and the adjectival group may be regarded as a nominal group with Epithet Head. There are three reasons why I have not taken this line from the start.

In the first place [attribution] and [classification] clauses were distinct at this stage in that the former always had a name, and not exophoric *that*, realizing the Carrier function, while the situation was reversed in [classification] clauses.

Secondly, the expanded adjectival group was the realization of the feature [quality] or the Attribute function, but never of a Modifier in a nominal group, whether or not the latter was functioning as a participant. Until there are cases such as *very big car*, it is doubtful whether *very big* should be treated as an elliptical nominal group.

A further less important consideration is that some of the realizations of Head in the adjectival group (such as *better, finished, gone*) could not occur as a nominal group Modifier.

Examples of the expanded group (Mod. + Head form) were rare as yet. One group of Heads could be modified by *all.* Other than this structure, there were only occasional examples of *too* or *very* with a size adjective such as *big.* Therefore, rather than suggesting that any Head was capable of modification, the network allows for two separate modified-or-not choices. One can predict that such a system would change in time to one with simultaneous options for selection of Head type and choice of [modified] or [not modified], as illustrated in Figure 8.5.

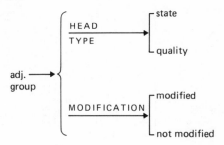

Fig. 8.5 Adjectival group—predicted later development

Prepositional phrase (refer to Figure 8.6)

As I have already outlined (see p. 174), the prepositional phrase was not yet fully developed. It realized only Location functions and features which might equally be expressed directly by a nominal group with [location] Head. Hal did not yet have a choice of a range of prepositions which could occur freely with a choice of any nominal group. At this stage, *in* could occur only with 'container' nouns and *on* only with 'surface' nouns.

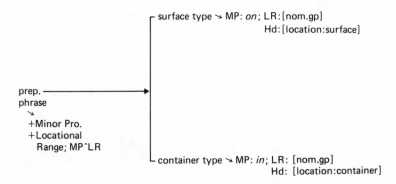

Fig. 8.6 21 to 22½ months—prepositional phrase

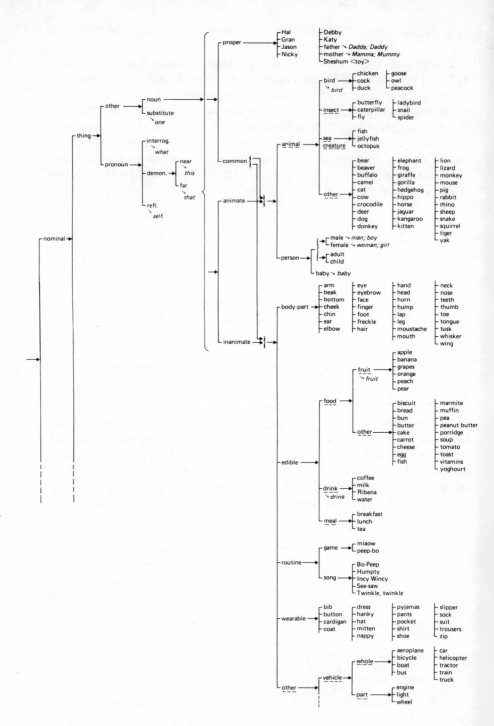

Fig. 8.7 21 to 22½ months—word rank

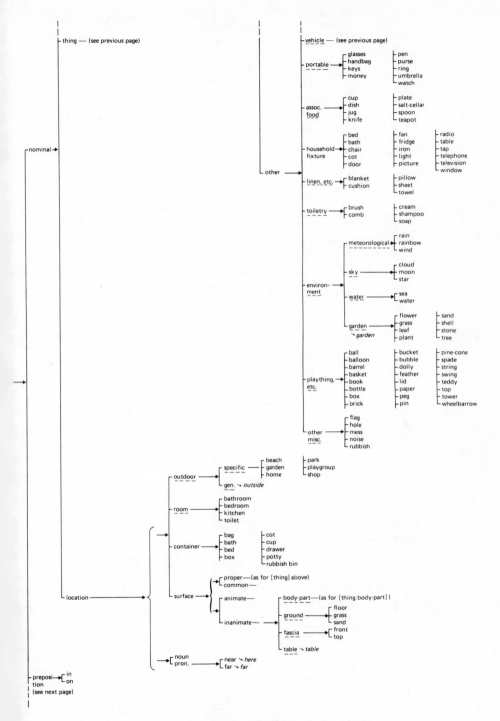

Fig. 8.7 (cont.)

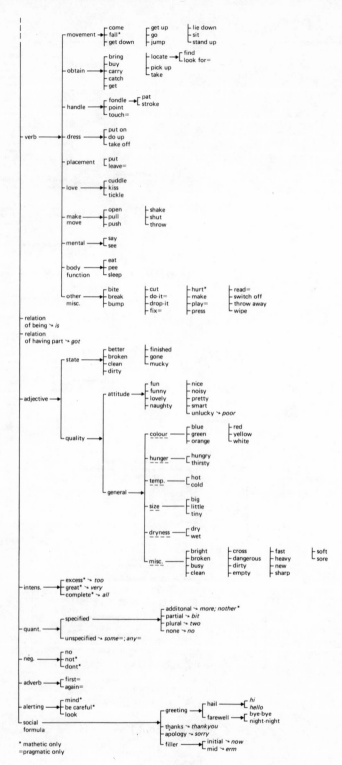

Fig. 8.7 (cont.)

Notes on mathetic potential at word rank (refer to Figure 8.7)

1. I have represented the lexicon here along the same taxonomic lines as in earlier networks, with lexical realizations corresponding to the most delicate feature names unless otherwise specified. As before, there is a certain amount of cross classification required, which has been dealt with simply by repeating lexical items in different classes. The largest area of overlap concerns the features [thing] and [location].
2. The word rank was not exclusively mathetic. By this stage there were only a handful of words not attested in both macrofunctions, so at this rank the description is not macrofunctionally specific. Those few items which were still exclusive to one macrofunction are included and marked * for mathetic only, and = for pragmatic only.
3. Most of the classifying features are required for the specification of higher rank realizations (e.g. [body part] for whole-part relational clauses, [noun: proper], [adjective: attitude] to specify realizations of Medium for different processes). Others, however (e.g. [room] as a sub-class of [location], have no intra-linguistic justification of this sort, but have been included to render the description of the lexicon more accessible. I have, however, tried to use categories (e.g. colour vs. temperature adjectives) which seem plausible with regard to collocations that occurred in discourses in which the child took part, as well as in the light of his naming and other general behaviour. In order to be clear, any such features not essential for the grammatical description have been given broken underlining.
4. Apart from the fact that the same lexicon was realizing structural functions within different macrofunctions, there was also a certain degree of differentiation between structural function and class within the one macrofunction. For example, [noun: proper], [pronoun: demon.] or [quantifier] items could function as either Head or Modifier in nominal groups; [adjective: quality] could function as clausal Attribute or as Modifier in a nominal group operating as Carrier, etc. I have therefore used class terms throughout at this rank, though any class may be sub-categorized by 'semantic' kinds of features.

Finally, for the sake of completeness, since the word rank was not macrofunctionally specific, I have included also those social formulae which did not fit into the macrofunctional framework (e.g. hi, thank you, sorry).

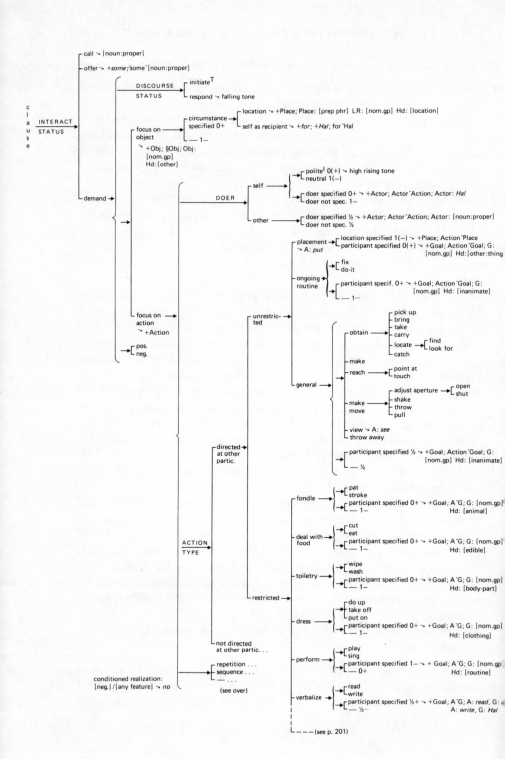

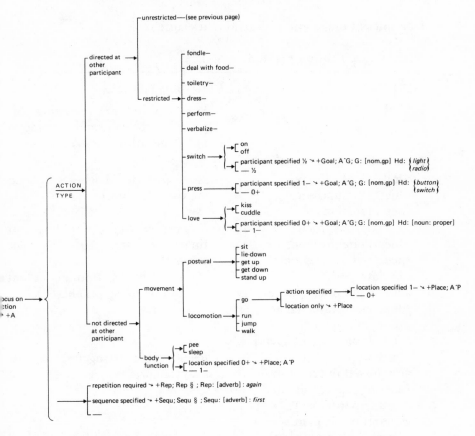

Fig. 8.8 21 to 22½ months—pragmatic function: clause rank

Examples of pragmatic realizations at clause rank

Feature specification Fig. 8.8	Text
[call] [offer]	*Da::dda* (sing-song) *Some Mummy?* (breaking off piece of biscuit and putting it in M's mouth).
[demand: initiate/pos./focus object: circumstance spec.: location]	*More leaf* (to M who is collecting them for him).
initiate/pos./focus object: circumstance spec.: self as recipient]	*Bit cream finger* (holding out finger for some of M's face cream).
initiate/pos./focus action: self doer: polite /doer spec./ directed at other participant: general: participant spec.]	*Hal carry bread?* (looking at loaf on counter being purchased).
initiate/pos./focus action: self doer: neutral /doer not spec./ directed at other participant: general: participant spec.]	*Bring chair* (struggling to lift heavy chair).
(as above): repetition]	*See Daddy again* (to be lifted to see out window).
initiate/pos./focus action: other doer: doer spec./ directed at other participant: general: participant spec.]	(i) *Mama open crocodile* (handing M toy crocodile). (ii) *Mummy get book.*
initiate/pos./focus action: other doer; doer not spec./ directed at other participant: restricted: participant specified] respond/(as above): sequence]	(i) *Write Hal* (as M picks up paper). (ii) *Eat biscuit* (gesturing to M to do so). *Play miaow first* (responding to M's suggestion of bath time).
initiate/pos./focus action: other doer: doer spec./ directed at other participant: restricted: participant not spec.]	*Daddy cut* (holding out banana).
initiate/pos./focus action:	*Go in there* (struggling against

self doer: doer not spec./ not directed at other participant: movement: locomotion: go: action spec.: location spec.]	M to enter store room in shop).
(as above): action not spec.]	*Beach; beach* (pulling M with him as he runs down path onto sand).
initiate/focus action: neg.]	*No* (as M tries to turn into garden gate after walk).
initiate/focus object/ neg.]	M: Would you like some soup? H: No

Notes on pragmatic potential at clause rank, 21 to 22½ months (refer to Figure 8.8)

INTERACTIONAL STATUS features

[call] This speech function represented a summons rather than being a more general vocative. He mimicked the adult calling tones on proper names.

[offer] Although he used the reduced form [səm] this formula was probably taken from the adult *Do you want some?*, in which case the proper noun is a Vocative. A conceivable alternative is that he was attempting something like *Some for Mummy?* (there was no second-person pronoun yet).

[demand] Although one-word utterances were much more common in this macrofunction, there was now greater specification of experiential content in H's demands, expressed by means of constituent structure.

[demand: focus on object] A demand for a thing might focus on the object itself by naming it, sometimes with the addition of *for Hal* [faɵ] as an added specification, or indicating the desired location, as with *bit cream knee, Ribena in there*, etc. Alternatively, it might be encoded as a process such as *get X; find X* (i.e. realizing the [focus on action] feature); possibly as both when demands were strung together, as in *chair for Hal; get; Mummy get.*

[demand: focus on action]

DOER features

[self doer] vs. [addressee doer]

As discussed (p. 176), Hal had begun to distinguish 'I want to' from 'I want you to ' meanings by the use of proper names, and was therefore producing Actor^Process (^Goal) structures within the pragmatic function.

ACTION TYPE features
As in mathetic language, a number of factors might influence the likelihood of a participant being specified. I have grouped the classes of [action] according to collocational restrictions on the realization of the Goal. The feature [general] indicates that there was very little restriction on the class of nominal realizing Goal, while in the [restricted] group there was much less freedom. Again, as in mathetic, there was a fairly even frequency pattern amongst the [general] group, except for a few longstanding routines occurring in highly context-dependent situations. For example, Hal would still demand *fix* or *do-it*, thrusting a recalcitrant toy or object into the addressee's hand, much more often than he would use a structure like *fix car* or *do-it [ə] car*.

There was a difference from the mathetic frequency pattern in that for some of the actions with fairly predictable Goals, the Goal might be specified with the same general probability as for a [general] action type, perhaps even with a higher probability. In some cases, this was doubtless because the context would not allow the addressee to predict the precise nature of the demand (e.g. the [performance] group), and in others because the structure was learned from the start as a whole (e.g. the [verbalize] group).

Notes on pragmatic potential of nominal group (Refer to Figure 8.9)

The Pragmatic group emerged during the previous 19½–21 month period as the original repetition request *more* being optionally concatenated with the realizations of one class of desired object (edible). The structure thus evolved initially as *more^(edible object)*. Now a few other forms occurred. Things modified by a quality, as in *clean shirt*, which was the principal group form built up in the mathetic function, were now found pragmatically too, though very rarely in comparison. Very common, though, was *this X* or *that X*, where the Head might be the name or the substitute *one*. These were built up in responses to repeated questions of the type: *Which one do you want? This one or that one?* and were not yet found in mathetic use.

Although during the previous 19½–21 month period I would not claim that pragmatic *more(^bread)* and mathetic *(blue^)shirt* were necessarily parallel structures, it seems fair now to treat *more* as a nominal group Modifier. During the period 21–22½ months, the structure *more X* did occur occasionally in mathetic contexts and I take this as evidence that Hal had by this time generalized this

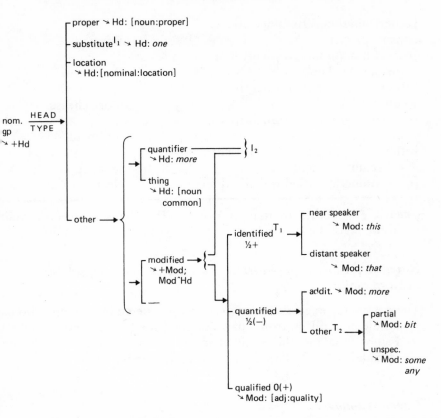

Fig. 8.9 21 to 22½ months—pragmatic function: nominal group

Sample realizations from Fig. 8.9 pragmatic nominal group

Feature specification	Example realization
[proper]	Daddy
[substitute:modified:identified:near speaker]	this one
[substitute:modified:identified:distant speaker]	that one
[other:quantifier]	more
[other:quantifier/modified:quantified:other: partial]	bit more
[other:quantifier/modified:quantified: other:unspecif.]	some more
[other:thing]	cup

[other:thing/modified:identified: near speaker]	this peg
[other:thing/modified:identified: distant speaker]	that book
[other:thing/modified:quantified: additional]	more cheese
[other:thing/modified:quantified: other:partial]	bit bread
[other:thing/modified:quantified: other:unspecified]	some apple
[other:thing/modified:qualified]	clean shirt

pragmatic structure to that of Modifier^Head which had been built up in the mathetic function.

Notes on pragmatic potential of other systems at group/phrase or word ranks

There was no pragmatic adjectival group. The embryo prepositional phase did not differ from that described for the mathetic function in Figure 8.6, and the minimal macrofunctional differentiation at word rank is indicated on Figure 8.7, as mentioned on p. 195.

General summary

This account of the 21–22½ month development of language by Hal has been a lengthy one, owing to the increasing complexity of the language. One aspect of this was the emergence of the rank scale, giving him the possibility of representing more information, and information of different 'weight' within the same clause. (Compare, for example, the status of *new* in *shoes new* and *new shoes dirty*.)

This period also saw a fascinating divergence between transitivity structures produced within the different functions. It seems that an ergative world view, where entities are inherently involved in events, was evolving when the child was 'reflecting' on reality, while the transitive view of actors doing things emerged through using language to act on reality in order to achieve something.

The development of simple group and clause structures is seen in midstream at this point. From talking about discrete entities and activities, and then discrete combinations of these, the child has begun to make sense of reality by interpreting larger classes of things and actions in a similar way.

The difference between the structures used in the two functions provides evidence that the macrofunctional distinction was still a viable one during this period, though there are also a number of reasons for recognizing that it would not be so for much longer. Another interesting and related development was the appearance of the first MOOD forms, used not to engage in genuine dialogue, but in a way which brought the two macrofunctions together (see pp. 169-70.

9 Twenty-two and a half to twenty-four months

From macrofunction to metafunction

It was during this period that the language began to settle into an essentially adult form, with the majority of utterances encoding a selection of options from simultaneous MOOD and TRANSITIVITY systems (or to be more accurate, MOOD and PROCESS TYPE systems, since there was no VOICE system at this stage—for the purposes of this book TRANSITIVITY and PROCESS TYPE may be regarded as equivalent terms.) There were also signs that SPEECH FUNCTION and MOOD should be differentiated as systems operating on different strata.

In this chapter I shall first describe the general development of an adult-like MOOD system, and then show that to continue the linguistic description in terms of distinct mathetic and pragmatic potentials has become quite untenable. In the final section I shall represent the language as metafunctionally rather than macrofunctionally organized, but this will involve a fairly lengthy introduction where the following questions are considered:

I   stratification of SPEECH FUNCTION and MOOD.
II grounds for recognizing a major clause vs. minor clause distinction;
III grounds for distinguishing elliptical major clauses from minor clauses;
IV grounds for recognizing implicit clause functions.

Evolution of MOOD system

Probably the most obvious development during this period is Hal's emerging ability to engage in dialogue by using an approximation to the adult MOOD system. By the end of the previous period, at 22½ months, Hal had developed an approximation to three adult MOOD *forms*, as we have seen. His (informative) comment form may be seen as a declarative equivalent, there was a second-person imperative distinct from this, either in the lexis used or by the presence of the negative element *dont*, and there was a very limited Wh interrogative form. By two years, all of these were used with adult speech functional meaning, and Hal had also developed a polar interrogative to express yes–no questions, which was realized by high rising tone.

Unlike the Wh interrogative, the polar form was used as a genuine information seeker from the start (at 22(28)), and was a little different in that even when he answered himself, he had to ascertain the information by exploring the environment, as in the following examples:

23 months   H has two rubber cats, only one of which squeaks. On several occasions he picks one up, saying *this one make [ə] nóise*, and then presses it to find out.

23(1)   He has various model people. He has observed that only some have eyebrows painted on the faces. He picks up one toy woman with *[ɪ s] got eyebrόws*. He looks at the face and says *no*. He then picks up another, repeating *[ɪs] got eyebrόws*, etc.

From the start, he might look to the adult to respond, as an alternative to finding out by trial and error, as here:

23 months   (H places shape over toy postbox hole).
H; Go in thére (looks at M).
M: No.
H: Go in thére (placing over next hole, looking at M).
M: No.
H: Go in thére (placing over next hole, looking at M).
M: Yes.
H: (tries it first without letting go to verify) Go in thère!

On this first occasion the adult response was an additional rather than alternative source of information perhaps, but soon he was looking principally for a linguistic response.

During this period, there were only two examples noted where he sought the kind of information actually unobtainable from personal exploration, but the first was an early example:

23(1)   (M puts heater in H's room—usually a prelude to bed.)
H: Go [nə] sléep.
M: Yes, going to sleep in a little while.
H: Nò.
M: Not now, later.
H: Làter <new word>.

The other example saw him using a polar interrogative, perhaps because he could not frame the appropriate Wh form *what colour is that?* (He was genuinely uncertain of colour names at this stage and it had become a ritual of his generally to respond *thats blue* whenever asked to identify colours.)

23(9) H: Thats blùe (pointing at blue peg).
       M: Yes, that's blue.
       H: Thats blùe (pointing at another).
       M: No.
       H: Thats blúe (pointing at orange one); thats òrange.
       M: That's orange (agreeing).
       H: Thats blúe (pointing at another peg).
       M: No.
       H: Thats blúe (pointing at blue one).
       M: Yes.
       H: Thats blúe (pointing at another).
       M: No.
       H: Thats blúe (pointing at same or another peg).
       M: No.
       H: Thats órange.
       M: Yes.
       H: Thats òrange.

Although I have said that these MOOD forms were now used in an adult-like way, they all in fact continued to be practised in self-created dialogues, even after he had begun to use them in interactive dialogue. For example:

23(12) H: (approaching kerb) Dont go on [ə] road.
       <He stops at kerb, which we may perhaps take as a non-verbal response.>
23(5) M: Which cup do you want?
       H: (continuing M's usual part) This one (pointing at first cup). This one (pointing at second cup).
       — This one (choosing).
23(5) H: What that?
       — Horse, little horse.

A striking development of this now was a move to enlist the aid of the parent in this role-play practice.

23(3) H looks intently up into M's face as he pinches himself on the leg and says *dont hurt [ə] self* <i.e. this is what you (are to) say>.
       (M does in fact repeat it and H stops pinching.)
23(12) (M has been offering things to H at meal. Each time H refuses with *nò.*)

> H: Want [ə] chéese.
> M: Oh you want some cheese (fetching it).
> H: Nò <i.e. just making suggestions for you to prolong the dialogue.>

23(26) (H had fussed earlier about not being able to find his slippers; they were found and put on. Now H takes them off, goes to M, looks intently into her face.)
> H: What happened [ə] slìppers.
> M: Oh, what happened to your slippers?
> H: (delighted) Take [ə] slippers òff!

Here one can see that he wanted to tell M something, but also wanted it to be linguistically contextualized. On such occasions, it was clear that the interrogative initially given was not any kind of private exclamation. He would look right into the addressee's face and be full of eager expectation of the other playing the part assigned.

I think that the fact that Hal did this kind of thing quite a bit during this period validates my interpretation of his earlier (and continuing) 'private' adjacency pairs as an exploration of the language's techniques for assigning and adopting roles in dialogue. I am, however, aware that precisely such an interpretation has recently been called into question by Atkinson, when discussing Hildegarde Leopold's question–answer pairs, and utterances of his own subject, Jacqueline, such as:

Whats that clock (spoken whilst looking at a 'clock' beaker). Atkinson says: 'Although one could perhaps propose an explanation in terms of the child practising dialogues, I think an alternative and fairly satisfactory explanation can be put forward.' (Atkinson 1979: 246.) This explanation is that the child perceives the function of *what's that?* as an attention-drawing one like *see* or *look*. This may well be the most plausible explanation of Jacqueline's utterances, but in Hal's case the evidence seems conclusively to point to an exploration of dialogue, especially as these practice runs continued for several further weeks, using a variety of interrogative forms (*Which one d'you want? What you got? Want some more?* etc.) And indeed he later practised longer forms of exchange, as the following examples indicate:

25(23) H: Whats that? ('reading' by himself).
> —— Tusk.
> —— That's right, tusk!

25(30) H: I'm eating a picnic; I'm eating a picnic.
> —— Are you?
> —— Yes.

For the basic two-part exchange, there was a rough progression from private role play to role play involving the adult, to dialogue proper, but all these overlapped in time. It was not the case that once he had grasped the system sufficiently to use it in an adult way, he immediately stopped the practice runs. None the less, one can say that by age 2 years the typical meaning of an imperative was a command addressed to another, the typical meaning of a Wh interrogative was a demand for information sought from the other, and the typical meaning of a high rising tone was a yes–no information demand. (Permission seekers and offers, also realized by high rising tone, were less frequent in fact, despite originating earlier.) Correspondingly, the typical way to issue a command was coming to be the adult imperative, or the use of *want* for demands involving 'Let me have/let me do' notions, but he did not immediately abandon the earlier device of encoding the names of things and actions with a high level tone.

Preliminary note on development of TRANSITIVITY

Developments in TRANSITIVITY will be discussed in some detail later but two general points should be noted here as a preliminary to the consideration of a description along the same lines as before, which will be given in Figure 9.1.

First, there were no longer two distinct experiential patterns evident. Pragmatic or command clauses now had to have a Goal element if transitive, and mathetic or information/commenting clauses might take an Agent. There was thus a general pattern of Med./Actor^Process or Agent/Actor^Process^Med./Goal.

Secondly, the possessive, relational, commenting clauses were no longer restricted to the expression of a meronymy (whole-part) relation. Also there was now an additional equative form, *thats Mummys*, etc. The first person form of this, *thats my* (also the 'minor' clause *my X*) was found not only as a classifying comment like all the other relational clauses, but also as a means of staking a claim to the possession of an object.

A macrofunctional description no longer valid

Even when specifically attempting to stress continuity, it is no longer possible to see the language as organized in terms of the basic comment vs. demand distinction of earlier days. For one thing, there is simply no evidence that information demands should be classed with other kinds of demands. If we look at the 22½–24 month language as much as possible from the point of view of earlier descriptions, then the first option is probably best seen in terms of the commodity exchanged, either goods-&-services (the domain of earlier pragmatic language) or information (developed from mathetic function).

The network provided in Figure 9.1 takes this approach, offering a general description as close to the previous one as possible. This results in a very unsatisfactory description of Hal's system as it stood by 24 months. There are four principal weaknesses.

1. The description treats the experiential content of commands (actions, locations, etc.) as unrelated to a parallel specification of content involved in information exchange. Although this has been partly true for some time, the choices involved were more clearly distinct previously (different TRANSITIVITY patterns, etc.).
2. If we are to explain the new creative productivity of the imperative, then interactionally related structures must be more clearly placed in opposition, e.g. *dont drop it* to *dropped it*. (Realizations of [goods-&-services:addressee:action specified:other inherent participant] and [information:give/other:action:process:effective] respectively—giving minimal identifying features only.)
3. Identical forms are becoming isolated in different parts of the network. For example, the following sets of features from different parts of the network could both result in the form *go in thére*. It could be a realization of either an information demand [information:demand/other:action:simple/location] or a polite first person command [goods-&-services:self:focus action:polite:action specified/location]. Similarly, two different sets of features could be realized by *thats my*. It could be either a classifying comment/ information giver [information:give/other:relation:other:possessive] or a claim [goods-&-services:self:focus object:claimed].
4. It is becoming increasingly complex to handle all the If–Then conditions.

Revision to a metafunctional analysis

The inadequacies of the network (Figure 9.1) in regard to the first two points turn on the fact that rather than being organized into a distinct linguistic potential for each of two generalized macrofunctions, the language now gave evidence of something approaching

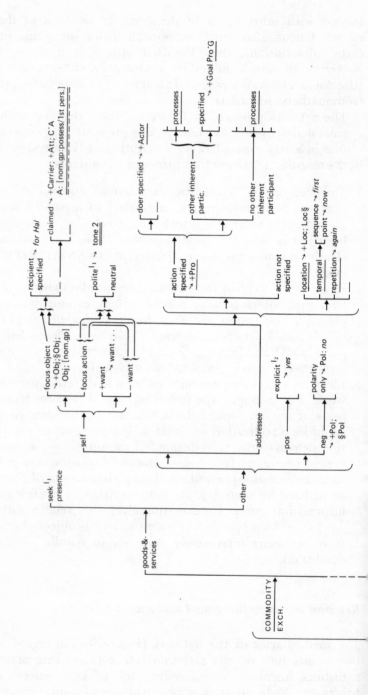

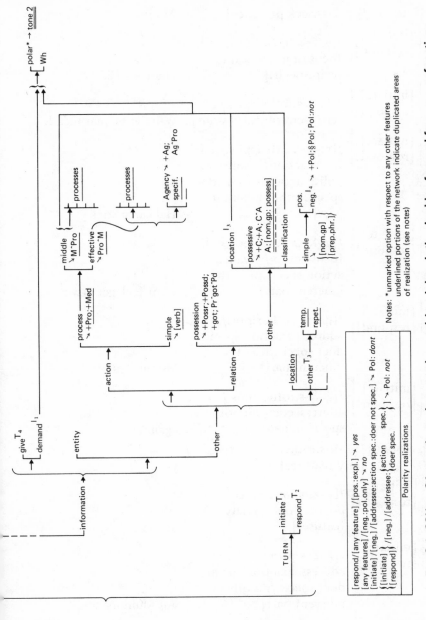

Fig. 9.1 22½ to 24 months—clause rank: provisional description looking forward from macrofunctions

Sample realizations from Figure 9.1

[initiate]/[g.-&-s.:seek presence]   Mu-mmy!

$\left\{\begin{array}{l}\text{[initiate]}\\\text{[respond]}\end{array}\right\}$ /[g.-&-s.:other:pos./self:
focus object/—want:
recip.specif.]   chair for Hal

$\left\{\begin{array}{l}\text{[initiate]}\\\text{[respond]}\end{array}\right\}$ /[g.-&-s.:other:pos./
self:focus object/+want]   want some marmalade

$\left\{\begin{array}{l}\text{[initiate]}\\\text{[respond]}\end{array}\right\}$ /[g.-&-s.:other:pos./self:
focus action/—want:
polite:action specif.:doer
specif./other inherent
part]   Hal carry stick

$\left\{\begin{array}{l}\text{[initiate]}\\\text{[respond]}\end{array}\right\}$ /[g.-&-s.:other:pos./self:
focus action/+want:
action specif.:no other
inherent part]   want [ə] get down

$\left\{\begin{array}{l}\text{[initiate]}\\\text{[respond]}\end{array}\right\}$ /[g.-&-s.:other:pos./
addressee:action specif.:
doer specif./no other
inherent part]   Mummy jump

$\left\{\begin{array}{l}\text{[initiate]}\\\text{[respond]}\end{array}\right\}$ /[g.-&-s.:other:pos./
addressee:action not
specif.:repetition]   again

[respond]/[g.-&-s.:other:pos.:explicit]/
    [any features]   yes

$\left\{\begin{array}{l}\text{[initiate]}\\\text{[respond]}\end{array}\right\}$ /[g.-&-s.:other:neg.:
polarity only]/[any
features]   no

$\left\{\begin{array}{l}\text{[initiate]}\\\text{[respond]}\end{array}\right\}$ /[g.-&-s.:other:neg./
addressee:action specif.:
doer specif./no other
inherent part]   not Mummy sing

$\left\{\begin{array}{l}\text{[initiate]}\\\text{[respond]}\end{array}\right\}$ /[info.:give/entity]   stone

$\left\{\begin{array}{l}\text{[initiate]}\\\text{[respond]}\end{array}\right\}$ /[info.:give/other:
action:simple]   sit

{[initiate] [respond]}	/[info.:give/other: temporal/action:process: middle]	Mummy sleeping now
{[initiate] [respond]}	/[info.:give/other:action process:effective:Agency specif.]	Mummy dropped [ə] paint
{[initiate] [respond]}	/[info.:give/other: relation:possession]	Hal got two ones
{[initiate] [respond]}	/[info.:give/other: relation:other:location]	drinks in [ə] room
{[initiate] [respond]}	/[info.:give/other: relation:other:possessive]	thats my
{[initiate] [respond]}	/[info.:give/other: relation:other:classif.]	thats clean bib
{[initiate] [respond]}	/[info.:give/other: relation:other:simple: pos.]	new shoes
{[initiate] [respond]}	/[info.:give/other:rela- tion:other:simple:neg.]	not wet
[initiate]/[info.:demand:polar/entity]		this one?
[initiate]/[info.:demand:polar/other: location/action:process: middle]		lid go in there?
[initiate]/[info.:demand:wh/other: action:process:middle]		whats Daddy doing?
[initiate]/[info.:demand:polar/ other:relation:possession]		Mummy got a tail?
[initiate]/[info.:demand:wh/other: relation:location]		wheres [ə] new one?
[initiate]/[info.:demand:polar/ other:relation:location]		Mummy in there?
[initiate]/info.:demand:wh/other: relation:classification]		whats that?
[initiate]/[info.:demand:polar/ other:relation:classification]		heaters very hot?

the adult metafunctional organization. The description needs therefore to be reframed to allow for parallel interpersonal and experiential systems on the lines of Figure 9.2. To do this satisfactorily in this form, however, would require isomorphism between SPEECH FUNCTION selection and MOOD form, and there are two difficulties here. One is that while all clauses were expressing an illocutionary function, not all clauses embodied a grammatical MOOD selection. The second is that for those clauses which did have a recognizable MOOD form, there were the first signs of a breakdown of isomorphism between SPEECH FUNCTION selections and MOOD realizations. Problems (3) and (4), listed earlier, in fact relate to the need to stratify discourse options from lexico-grammatical ones, and to distinguish major from moodless clauses.

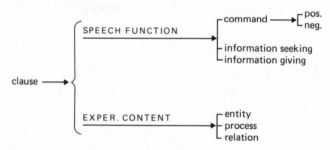

Fig. 9.2 Simplified 'metafunctional' revision of Figure 9.1

I. Stratification of SPEECH FUNCTION and MOOD systems

Incongruity of SPEECH FUNCTION and MOOD selections

1. *Want*

The first possible candidate for a mismatch between a speech act and its grammatical realization in MOOD concerns expressions like *want bread*. Such a clause could be interpreted as a command expressed as a declarative. At this stage, however, I take *want* to have been functioning almost exclusively as a first person imperative particle, and not therefore to be involved in such mismatching until later. *Want* functioned as part of a demand for an object (*want bread*) or a 'Let me' command (*want [ə] ride [ə]bike*) in almost every case, and such clauses might take level tones (often with a very narrow fall on the tonic) just as other initiations evolving from the pragmatic still did on occasion.

On the other hand, *want* did not take a preceding negative as could all other realizations of the command speech act, and in this it resembled an information-giving TRANSITIVITY process, none of which had a negative form as yet. Moreover, it was never used with rising tone for permission (thus there was *éat it* but not *want éat it*). There were not many permission-seeking tokens of any sort in the corpus, which may explain the absence of examples with *want*; however, a more probable explanation for the absence of *want* here is that Hal was already recognizing the use of *want* in offers. There were just a few occasions where he practised the form by taking on the typical adult offering role (see, e.g. 23(12) on pp. 206–7), and in the next period he began to use the form himself to offer goods. *Want* plus rising tone was therefore already reserved for a particular non-commenting use which was not permission seeking.

There were also, however, just a few occasions towards the end of this period when *want* seemed to be being used more as a statement of intention than a command, which would be evidence favouring its interpretation as a mental process rather than a first-person imperative particle. For example:

23(12) (H is nesting toy baskets together.)
    M: That's right! (as H fits two together).
    H: Want [ə] blùe one (quietly, takes it himself and tries it).

Note, however, that this is still a first-person form.

My interpretation is that *want* was definitely functioning by and large as a form of imperative, but that there were already a few hints that Hal would soon generalize the form to a process in TRANSITIVITY. During the next period, there was some overlapping of functions in this way, after which *want* could be seen to operate just like any other process, at which point its (still frequent) use as a command may be taken as an example of incongruence between SPEECH FUNCTION and MOOD selections (command realized as declarative).

2. *Rising tone*

Hal had now developed a third function for high rising tone utterances—one of demanding information. This was in addition to polite first-person commands (permission requests) and offers of edible objects. Given that the latter two developed first, it may seem perverse to suggest that now that there was also an information-demanding function the original two uses were 'incongruent'. But although rising tone was one of the varieties of non-mathetic tone employed from the start, and permission requests occurred at the very beginning in distinctively pragmatic level tone, it seems fairly clear that Hal adopted the adult tone 2 in these functions in imitation of adult interrogatives used to him and in his presence. Certainly this was the case with offers. This shows that these particular incongruent realizations have become so prominent in adult language that the child is able to learn them before he is creatively mismatching speech act and MOOD form.

3. *Claim-staking*

As well as the multiple functions of his polar interrogative form, there was one other development in the area of mismatching of SPEECH FUNCTION and MOOD selections. This concerned the staking of a claim to some object. Hal now frequently snatched things from another person, both in fun and in earnest, saying *my X, Hals X,* or *thats my, thats Hal.* This always had falling tone, and he had already developed such clauses with a more straightforward mathetic classifying function (e.g. saying *Mummys drink, Hàls drink,* as he pointed to each in turn). And now that he had a first-person possessive pronoun this might also be used in a non-challenging way in such structures.

The question is whether to treat all instances of these forms as information giving, when clearly there was a 'so hands off' command implied when staking a claim. Alternatively, one could regard these latter cases as a special category of demanding goods commands (as done in Figure 9.1). This seems unsatisfactory for two reasons. First, because he initially developed the structures in a non-pragmatic function; and secondly because he already had an established form with which to make demands for objects (*want X*). Thus the transfer of the commenting form (*thats Hals* or *my X*) to use as an implied command seems equivalent to comparable adult use: a case of genuine incongruence between the command function and the declarative realization.

I had expected that the child would first develop the adult SPEECH FUNCTION system with congruent realizations, and would only subsequently gradually develop the capacity to express meanings by an incongruent match. This is doubtless true in general terms, but it seems as if some very limited means of manipulating the system evolve almost as soon as the system has developed.

Obviously the child is exposed to certain kinds of incongruent speech act realizations throughout the early years. For example, although Hal clearly recognized that the Wh interrogative was an information-seeking form, he was also well aware that *what are you doing?* might be used as a command. For example, at 24 months, the very time when he was producing *whats [z] doing?, whats*

Mummy doing? questions, he responded on one occasion to M's
call of *Hal, what are you doing?* with *No; not what [ə] doing*,
clearly meaning 'don't say that; don't stop me'.

Another factor encouraging these particular incongruent forms
to emerge early would be the specific contexts of a child's life which
make such things as permission seeking and staking claims loom
larger than they do for an adult. Given that a metafunctional interpretation of grammatical organization implies a corresponding view
of situational contexts in terms of field and tenor (and possibly
mode) variables, the basic SPEECH FUNCTION network might be
extended for specific situations to include degrees of politeness
in commands or to allow for a *claim* category, and to predict grammatical realizations of these. One or two very general illustrations
are given below.

Example one
field: play with personal objects; exploration of notion of owner-
       ship;
tenor adult–small child; adult as teasing companion and fellow
       player;
mode face-to-face interaction.

OR
field: play with personal objects; assertion of ownership;
tenor: small child–small child; struggle for dominance and posses-
       sion of object;
mode: face-to-face interaction.

Linguistic realizations of such contexts might be along the following
lines:
field: lexical choices; TRANSITIVITY choice of identifying
       process;
tenor: 'claim' choice of SPEECH FUNCTION; first-person choice
       in nominal groups;
mode: exophoric elements; possible minor clause realization, etc.
The relevant part of the SPEECH FUNCTION network might be
extended for such contexts, as in Figure 9.3.

Example two
field: activity concerning familiar objects recognized as adult
       domain, e.g. food, furniture, personal possessions;
OR   activity concerning unfamiliar objects and environments;
tenor: small child to adult; adult as source of authority, power
       relation accepted;
mode: face-to-face; negotiation of possible action via language.

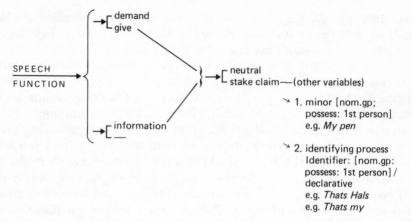

Fig. 9.3 Situationally specific extension of part of SPEECH FUNCTION network (i)

Linguistic realizations of such contexts might be as follows:

field: lexical choices; TRANSITIVITY choices;

tenor: choice of permission-seeking SPEECH FUNCTION option; interrogative MOOD and rising tone realizations.

The relevant fragment of the SPEECH FUNCTION network here might take the form shown in Figure 9.4.

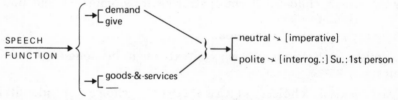

Fig. 9.4 Situationally specific extension of part of SPEECH FUNCTION network (ii)

Sample texts of this kind:

23(3) H: go on [ə] wáll (moving to wall, looking at M).

23(2) H: Hal switch off líght (looking at M as she carries him past switch).

23(29) H: Go [nə] héater (looking at M, wanting to stroke cat by forbidden radiator).

Implication in responses

It was also the case that H could increasingly make responses which were not cohesive in terms of SPEECH FUNCTION choice but which *were* cohesive in terms of some kind of implication, as well as by means of lexical and other links. Some examples are given below:

22 months M: Shall we throw the teddies to Daddy?
             H: Teddy on table <=so we can't, until we fetch it>.
22(28)   M: Oh don't bite my pillow.
             H: *Hal* pillow <=so I can>.
23(20)   M: Which book do you want Hal?
             H: (looking round) Where's [ə] new one? <=that's the one I want>.
23(26)   M: Oh you found your slippers <?=where were they?>.
             H: Slippers in [ə] cupboard.

Such cases were rare at this stage, but were a very significant development towards making the conversational interaction 'natural' and adult-like. To account for these systematically would seem to require extending the SPEECH FUNCTION network at the response feature for each of the major options, in order to provide for some kind of taxonomy of oblique responses which depend on certain kinds of causal implication being expressed. Although Halliday and Hasan (1976) and Halliday (1984a) have made a start along these lines, more precise formulations would be needed to block something like:

A: Lets put the teddies to bed.
B: Teddy is brown.

and to specify the nature of the implications involved, the understanding of which makes the response a relevant and acceptable one.

This topic will not be pursued further here; I simply make the observation that even before the adult SPEECH FUNCTION system is fully developed, the child can be seen to use both incongruent formal realizations, and responses which any conversational interactant would find acceptable and relevant, despite their non-canonical form in terms of adjacency pair structure.

Grammatical realization of SPEECH FUNCTION selections

By 24 months Hal had developed three MOOD forms. In addition, I have suggested that there were the beginnings of mismatching between these forms and SPEECH FUNCTION options. For this to be the case it must be possible to recognize the mood of an utterance independently of recognizing its status as a speech act. In other words, there must be a specific realization of the MOOD features such that the grammatical status of any clause selecting for

MOOD is evident without interpretation of the situational context. If we can only deduce the MOOD feature by means of a situational interpretation of illocutionary meaning, then clearly there is no sense in which one can talk of incongruence between SPEECH FUNCTION and MOOD systems.

In general terms, the realization of MOOD features at 24 months was as follows:

[imperative]
— Process realized by base form of verb;
— First-person imperative by presence of *want* (falling or level tone);
— Second-person negative imperative—Polarity element expressed as *dont*.
    examples: *want [ə] ride [ə] bike.*
         (dont) eat it!

[indicative]   polarity option not shared by this class

[indic.:declarative]
— verbal group might have *gonna* as auxiliary;
— both -ing and past tense forms possible as well as base form of verb;
— negative potential element *cant* might be present.
    examples: *doggy drinking [ə] milk.*
         lion cant get out.

[indic.:interrog.:polar]
— realized by high rising tone.

[indic.:interrog.:Wh]
— presence of Wh form.

Indeterminacies

(i) In certain cases there would be no formal differentiation between a declarative and an imperative. For example, *put book on [ə] table* might be a first person declarative or a second-person imperative.

(ii) Interrogatives, as defined, were not yet restricted to any possible definition of major clause.

(iii) Processes of the relational type did not share the [declarative] realization in terms of verbal group flexibility, but did not yet occur as imperatives anyway.

II. Major vs. minor clauses

Even if there were no grounds for placing SPEECH FUNCTION and MOOD systems on different strata, it would still be necessary to distinguish between mood-choosing and moodless forms, in order to show the oppositions between the different MOOD forms.

The network in Figure 9.1 specifies all the options for any speech act, thus placing in opposition to one another the following commands on the one hand:

bread; want some bread; Hal get ball; Mummy get ball; get ball again; again; go in the garden; in the garden, etc.

and the following statements on the other:

bread, thats bread, on the chair, sit(ting) on the chair, Daddy sit(ting) on the chair.

But there is no way of usefully taking account of Hal's beginning mastery of the MOOD system without placing the different MOOD structures in direct opposition to each other, and therefore in joint opposition to those utterances which cannot be seen to select for MOOD. Furthermore, any advantage of the Figure 9.1 description, in displaying the range of realizations for any illocutionary function even at the cost of relating grammatical forms, may well be obscuring the fact that there was now a functional distinction between major and minor clauses.

In the most general terms, the major/minor distinction seems to be related to the necessity for linguistic explicitness. In adult language, it is involved in the congruent realization of the SPEECH FUNCTION system in the following way:

information exchange	: initiating	↘	major (full)
	: responding	↘	major (elliptical)
goods-&-services exchange	: initiating	↘	major
		↘	minor
	: responding	↘	minor
calls, greetings, exclamations, confirmations,			
	etc. ↘		minor

(see Halliday 1984a; Martin 1981a).

Thus, an initiating information clause is most likely to be fully explicit, and a responding language-as-action clause most likely to be minor. The likelihood of a congruent realization is itself conditioned by situational factors, such as distance between interlocutors (not very relevant in the case of the young child, where virtually all speech is face-to-face), and distance of speaker to what he is talking about (e.g. report of past event vs. ongoing commentary).

There are not enough recorded instances of any one pair of related/ major/minor forms (such as *want bread; bread*) to demonstrate conclusively that the fuller form would be favoured in situations where greater explicitness was contextually warranted. Nevertheless, the following observations on Hal's language by 24 months seem to point to the major/minor distinction being a genuinely functional one by this time. (I shall discuss the question of distinguishing elliptical from minor clauses later on pp. 273–4.)

1. Where reflective language was concerned, almost all single adjectives and many non-elliptical utterances expressed as nominal groups could be recognized from voice quality and tone as exclamations, rather than information givers. For example, *bŭ::::g! twò ones!!*

2. Although information giving proper was not invariably expressed by means of major clauses, a far higher proportion of reports and narratives of this kind were realized by major clauses than was the case in ongoing running commentary. Hal had over the past months frequently failed to get his message across at first when trying to convey information in single-word utterances, the adult addressee having to sort out and verify possible interpretations by further questioning. This had presumably motivated him to pay greater attention to the needs of the addressee. (Though for months, even years, to come difficulties would still arise from failure to be sufficiently explicit.)

3. Where language-as-action is concerned, we would expect explicitness to be less crucial, and it is true that Hal did still frequently initiate demands with such utterances as *more!* or *drink!* However, an examination of occasions when there was a failure on the addressee's part to respond, or to respond appropriately, shows that he then would switch to a fuller form. For example,

23(17) (H takes off bib in mid-meal.)
    H: (calls emphatically) Bìb!
    M: (having observed his action) All right; you don't have to wear it.
    H: (since M has misunderstood his initial command). Want thàt bib (pointing to another, hanging up). Want cleàn bib.
23(22) H: (apparently tugging at his bib) Bĩb.

      M: OK (removes it, assuming he was pulling it off deliberately).

      H: (irritated) Want [ə] put [ə] bib *òn* <i.e. H had been trying to stop it coming off, not to remove it.>

23(5) H: (pulling at M's handbag) Bag.

      M: (deliberately 'misunderstanding') Yes, that's my bag.

      H: Carry bag; want [ə] carry bag.

4. Overall, responding utterances were less likely to be full forms than initiating ones were, though in many cases they might be elliptical rather than minor.

III. Ellipsis

Just as the examination of the differentiation of SPEECH FUNCTION and MOOD systems requires a consideration of formal expression of MOOD features, the latter requires consideration of what counts as a major clause. I have therefore discussed above the grounds for seeing [major] and [minor] as valid features in the language. However, in order to assign certain clauses one or other of these features, it is first necessary to distinguish elliptical major clauses from minor ones.

For an utterance to be regarded as elliptical in adult speech, the preceding text must supply the ellipsed part of the clause (see Halliday and Hasan 1976: Chap. 4), but in a developmental grammar we must also be clear that the child has previously provided evidence of having the full structure in his productive repertoire. From a very early date, exchanges like the following were common:

Adult: How does the doggie go?
Child: Woof, woof.

Adult: Where's the pen?
Child: On table.

Adult: What have you got there?
Child: Hat.

But although we may conjecture that such *de facto* ellipsis may help the child in learning the fuller forms, it seems to make no sense to regard them as formally elliptical, since even to specify the conditions of the ellipsis option, one would need to credit the child with a mastery of MOOD structures that he had never produced. There can hardly be a system

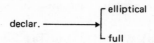

until both apparently elliptical and full forms are possible (allowing at least the possibility of exploring the conditions under which one or other choice is favoured).

This will never be a straightforward issue, though, since the 'elliptical' form will usually match a developmentally prior one. So, for example, it will always be debatable in the following cases whether Hal's (b) responses are immature realizations 'left over' from the earlier system, or are genuinely dependent on the preceding text.

(a) M: What colour's this one?
    H: Thats blue.
(b) M: What colour's this one?
    H: Orange.
(a) M: And what's the antelope got?
    H: Its got horns.
(b) M: These are the birdies. And what have the birdies got?
    H: Beaks.
(a) M: What's the bear eating?
    H: Bear eating [ə] fish.
(a) M: What's she doing?
    H: Eating [ə] bread.
(b) M: What's the boy doing?
    H: Sleeping.
(a) M: You want this jug?
    H: Want this jug.
(b) M: D'you want slippers?
    H: No. Shoes.

It is not possible to prove that the (b) forms were examples of ellipsis rather than persisting immature forms, but it is possible to show by the (a) examples from the same time that in these cases the fuller form was equally available to the child. It therefore seems quite proper to allow for ellipsis of all elements except that required by the probe (i.e. Complement here). There were no examples at this stage of Residue ellipsis.

IV. Implicit elements

So far, then, I have suggested that there are some minimal grounds for stratifying SPEECH FUNCTION and MOOD systems, that there are reasonable formal grounds for assigning major clauses different MOOD features, and that it is possible to distinguish endophorically elliptical major clauses from minor ones. The next question that must be addressed concerns the possibility of exophoric ellipsis or 'implicit' clause functions.

1. Implicit Process element

All Hal's MOOD structures, with the exception of the polar interrogative, depend on the presence of a Process element, and in general terms the formal realization of any TRANSITIVITY option has to be the presence of a Process, since it is only in terms of a Process that participants can be defined. One exception is the process *be*. In a relational process the presence of the Process element is obviously not necessary for the roles of the participants being related to be unequivocally interpretable. I am therefore allowing clauses such as *glasses on table* or *Mummy too big* to count as major relational clauses alongside examples like *this is wet pants* or *thats [dæs] clean bib*. (There are also examples like *too big* and *not Daddys* to be considered, where the item being classified in some way receives no linguistic expression either. I will return to these later.)

A more important case of an unexpressed Process element in Hal's language occurs in first-person imperatives which constituted a demand for goods. I have explained (see pp. 214–15) that I wish to treat *want* at this stage as a MOOD element (i.e. an imperative marker). While demands such as *want [ə] carry bag* present no difficulty in these terms, a demand such as *want [ə] drink* is more problematic. In a metafunctional analysis, MOOD and TRANSITIVITY features must be simultaneously selected, yet in this case there is no TRANSITIVITY Process element encoded. I propose here to allow the TRANSITIVITY feature [possession] to be selected, although in first-person imperatives it will not be realized lexically. The occasional second-person imperative which selects [possession] has it explicitly encoded, as in *have it* or *don't have ticket*.

2. Implicit participants: (i) relational clauses

There were four kinds of [intensive] clause:

(a) [possessive], e.g. *That's Daddys.*
(b) [attributive], e.g. *Porridge hot.*
(c) [classificational], e.g. *That's kangaroo.*
(d) [locative], e.g. *Pussy's in [ə] garden.*

For all these there were related utterances such as:

(a_1) *Daddy's* (identifying object as belonging to F).
(b_1) *Broken now* (retrieving piece of cheese from tray of bib).
(c_1) *Bear* (pointing at picture in book).
(d_1) *On the table* (pointing at picture of basket in book).
<this type was rare>

There were also negative forms for all of these where *not* preceded in each case.

There are various ways these latter can be treated. One is to regard them as minor clauses along with:

(e) *Mess!* (= I've made a lovely mess! What a mess! etc.)
(f) *Daddy* (= Daddy went out. I saw Daddy go, etc., etc.)
(g) *Bread* (= Give me bread. I'm putting bread there. Cut the bread too. He gave me/someone bread, etc.)

In these cases, no TRANSITIVITY function can be assigned, although SPEECH FUNCTION selections can be interpreted from context.

However, it is also possible to argue that in the case of utterances contextually recognizable as classificatory kinds of clauses, there is not the same ambiguity as to TRANSITIVITY role, and that given that (a_1) to (d_1) above are clearly related to a specific class of major clause, there are grounds for treating these too as relational clauses but with an implicit, unrealized Carrier function. Attributive relational clauses in systemic grammar are assigned the structural functions of Carrier and Attribute, as in the following examples:

John	is	a teacher
The tree	is	spindly
Carrier		Attribute

If we consider the child's clauses *thats Daddys* and *Daddys* to be closely related in this way, then a negative form *not Daddys* can also be seen as part of the same paradigm, instead of being grouped with other minor clauses, such as (e)–(g) above. This seems especially desirable since full negative forms were produced soon after 24 months; for example, *Daddy not hungry, 'snot too hot*, while there was nothing equivalent to *Daddy didn't go* or *he didn't give me bread*, etc.

While it would be missing a grammatical generalization to fail to note that just those non-imperative clauses which appear to have an Attribute function (and no others) have a negative form, I do not wish to be interpreted as adopting the kind of criteria used by Greenfield and Smith (1976) for assigning TRANSITIVITY functions to single-word utterances. Although we might agree in this particular case on the function to be assigned, it would not be because I take their view that situations are 'structured like sentences', and that the TRANSITIVITY role of any utterance can be deduced from situational context. In a systemic grammar, exophoric ellipsis, like endophoric, involves the selection of a systemic feature (or set of features) which does not get encoded as lexis or structure. Analyses such as that by Greenfield and Smith are unconstrained by any notion of system, of linguistic opposition. Thus they see the child's utterance as an impoverished version of an adult structure. Consequently, any aspect of an action, event or description that an adult interprets by means of a particular TRANSITIVITY function, but which the child does not, is treated as 'absent' or 'implicit' in the child's structure. However, my proposal for regarding *thats Daddys* and *Daddys* as sharing the same systemic features in the child's grammar is in order to capture a formal generalization about the *child's* language (i.e. the opposition between the positive and negative forms discussed above). That is to say, the unmistakable relationship between *thats Daddys* and *not Daddys*, or between *thats hot* and *not hot*, will be lost from the description if *thats Daddys* and *Daddys, thats hot* and *hot* are not treated as comparable kinds of relational clause. It is therefore the wish to interpret the child's system most accurately in its own terms that motivates a systemic description using the notion of implicit structural functions. The two-element form *not^Attribute* clearly represents a precursor of the Carrier^*not*^Attribute structure found after 24 months. Including the former as relational clauses at 22½–24 months allows this ontogenesis of polarity in indicative clauses to be most clearly represented.

Perhaps I should again stress here, though, that not every non-demanding utterance expressed solely as a group or phrase will be interpreted as an Attribute (encoding feature [intensive] see Figure 9.8). No TRANSITIVITY function can (or should) be assigned to the following, for example:

24(2) H enters house from outing with F, and says to M *stick*: his first attempt at telling her about being given a lollipop on a stick at the shops.

23(9) *two ones!!* Overheard from H, exclaiming triumphantly at adding another to the pen he has already misappropriated from M's desk drawer.

23(11) *up there* said by H to himself, placing an object in a high place.

Implicit participants: (ii) material process clauses

From 18 months, the development of TRANSITIVITY within the mathetic macrofunction has been presented in terms of some kind of [action] feature being encoded, initially simply as a lexical item. As the child comes to interpret the world from the adult perspective of things affected by or involved in actions, these are expressed in terms of a process having an inherent participant.

However, sometimes even now, non-imperative clauses occurred with no participant expressed at all; for example:

Go in thére? (seeking permission).
Write on [ə] bóok? (seeking permission).
Fell off [ə] chàir (after doing so).
Been outside (returning).

There are various ways to look at these. One possibility is to note that there was usually a Circumstantial element present, and for a case like *go* this might well be an inherent participant. Therefore these may only be a special case in that the obligatory participant is a Location element rather than a Medium. However, processes like *write* and *fall(off)* are not very convincingly handled in this way.

Alternatively, we can note that there were not many tokens of this sort, and these can perhaps be ignored or counted as a special class of minor clause. Whether in fact this proves the easiest solution may, however, depend on the approach taken to non-middle (two-participant) clauses which lack one participant, invariably the Agent, so I will discuss these next.

'Effective' clauses without an Agent

It is during this period that for the first time information or comment clauses which earlier had the form Process^Med (^Loc) began to appear also with a preceding Agent. For example:

23(2)   H: Hal stroke Katy (doing so).
23(1)   H: Daddy putting [ə] hanky in [ə] pocket (observing).
23(11) H: Mummy carry drink (observing).

This development then allows for the possibility of treating cases like the following as elliptical:

23(25) M: What are you doing now?
          H: Switch off light.
23(15) F: What did you bump?
          H: Bump [ə] finger.

In the same way, the following middle (one-participant) clause could be elliptical:

23(9) M: What's the boy doing?
H: Sleeping.

These all seem respectable cases for ellipsis since Hal could and did produce equivalent clauses with all constituents present.

However, it is not possible to analyse all material process clauses as either [effective] or [middle], with 'missing' elements accounted for by endophoric ellipsis. There were also examples of responses comparable to those given above that were not strictly elliptical. For example:

23(26) F: What's the matter?
H: Bump [ə] finger.

Then, even more seriously, there were innumerable cases of initiating, and therefore not endophorically elliptical, utterances, such as the following:

wipe [ə] table
draw birdie
shut [ə] Daddy's book
pull pants up
gonna find [ə] moon
gonna get [ə] spoon
put [ə] soft teddy on [ə] table

These, of course, are typical of clauses from the previous months, and at first it seemed best to treat them as less mature forms, as is done in Figure 9.5 (ignoring processes without any participants for the moment).

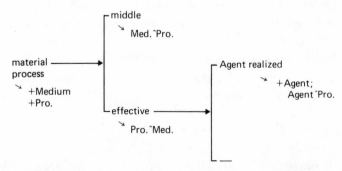

Fig. 9.5 One treatment of variation in structures, 22½–24 months

Whether actions were at first distinguished into classes, depending on whether there was an inherent Agent or not, or whether the Pro.ˆMed./Med.ˆPro. distinction was simply an imitated word order pattern is unknowable, but by 24 months the child was making an explicit distinction—only some clauses were being produced with Agents. The interpretation implied in Figure 9.5 assumes that the variability of this realization resulted from the child being in the midst of forming a generalization which interprets certain events in terms of an Agent and a Medium. Thus, the move from a Pro.ˆMed. structure to an AgentˆMed.ˆPro. one, is seen as parallel to the earlier development from Pro. to Pro.ˆMed.

This is the most obvious possibility. However, I shall be suggesting that given the greater speed of changes now and the reorganization of the system that was taking place at this time, this particular variation can be linked to the development of a Subject function. In order to explicate this, it is necessary to discuss first certain other developments which took place in Hal's language, and these will be outlined below.

Implicit participants: (iii) polar interrogatives

When we look at data also in the coming weeks, i.e. after 24 months, it becomes clear that if indicative non-elliptical middle processes are to be recognized as having an obligatory Medium and optional Agent, as in Figure 9.5, then some special account will have to be given for certain interrogatives, especially those realizing offers and requests for permission. This is because these clauses almost invariably omitted what was in effect the Subject/Actor element, whether the clause was middle *or* effective. Thus, in interrogative mood it was not necessarily the Agent which was the optional structural function.

Taking examples from this and the next period (24–25½ months), the pattern is as follows:

Interrogative *want* examples from 24–25½ months:

Offers of things	Want some more paper?	Addressee Subject omitted

Other interrogative examples from 22½–25½ months:

Permission requests	Play those?	Speaker Subject omitted
	Sit up here?	
	See letter?	
	Put cars in there?	

Interrogative *see* examples from 24–25½ months:

Information requests	See, Mummy?	Addressee Subject omitted
	See meat?	

Note with regard to the last group that information requests from 22½–25½ months with a third-person Subject never omitted the Subject element (e.g. *door shut?*, *heater's very hot?*, *lid go in there?*).

General interpretation of implicit participants in non-relational clauses: emergence of the Subject function

Where the interrogative pattern, described above, links with the declarative clause pattern for material processes, discussed earlier, is that soon after 23 months it was only ever the speech roles (I, you) which remained unexpressed in declaratives. One cannot make too much of this, because the great majority of declaratives were still accounts of the child's own doings, so the majority of Agents (expressed or not) would be first-person forms. None the less, it is quite striking that although third-person Subjects might be absent in elliptical responses, as here:

22(28) M: What's she doing?
        H: Eating [ə] bread.

yet there were no 'missing' third-person Subjects in initiating utterances of the kind listed on p. 229.

Given these data, it seems that the realization or not of 'participant' elements in the non-relational clause was gaining a functional pattern, which suggests that it was the speech roles which were at stake, and that rather than being a maturation of a TRANSITIVITY structure, it may be the development of the interpersonal Subject function which is apparent here.

According to Halliday (1984b), the unmarked Subject, which therefore tends to be omitted in face-to-face interaction, is the first person in a 'giving' clause of offer or statement, the latter typically expressed as a declarative; and the second person in a 'demanding' clause of command or question, canonically expressed as an imperative and interrogative respectively. Thus the Agentless effective clauses, the Mediumless middle clauses and the *see?* interrogatives would all fit into the predicted adult pattern.

Offers and permission requests are more complicated. As in adult English, Hal's *want X?* offers of the next period omitted a second-person Subject rather than a first-person one, and in adult language this is doubtless because they are encoded as interrogatives. This may be the explanation in Hal's case too. There are anyway innumerable examples of such *want X?* clauses spoken by adults in the data set, and being a stereotyped case, Hal's *want X?* offers do not require too much general explanation.

When it comes to considering polite first-person commands, which I have interpreted as permission requests, it is true that some tokens could be interpreted instead as 'Shall I?' suggestions or offers of service, which would make the absent first-person Subject congruent with the adult pattern. However, the majority do appear more convincingly taken as permission seekers (and *Can I?* developed before *Shall I?* or *I'll*—). These permission requests do not have an equivalent minus Subject form in adult, and being commands and interrogatives, the unmarked and therefore most readily omissible Subject should be *you*. However, these had developed from Hal's first-person demands, and were therefore negotiating about the speaker's fulfilment of a role, and this evolution may explain his temporary adoption of a form not consistent with adult use.

Summary of considerations relevant to a metafunctional description of Hal's language, 22½–24 months

Before going any further, I will attempt to sum up the points made so far in this chapter, as the discussion has been an involved one. At the beginning of the chapter, the developing system of MOOD was discussed. It was pointed out that the presence of claimstaking speech acts, expressed by possessive relational clauses which already had a canonical descriptive, commenting function, provided some grounds for distinguishing between SPEECH FUNCTION and MOOD options. Moreover, there were hints in the way that *want* was just beginning to be used in non-demanding contexts, that there would be further grounds for such a distinction a little later on. The varied uses of the rising tone also pointed in the direction of distinguishing SPEECH FUNCTION and MOOD systems.

Following this, there was a discussion of the formal and functional grounds for distinguishing between those clauses embodying a MOOD feature from the other minor (moodless) clauses. In order to assign the features [major] or [minor] in certain cases, it was found necessary to reach decisions concerning apparently incomplete clauses. Two kinds of clauses were considered. The first type were relational clauses, and the notion of an implied Carrier function was argued for, on the grounds that this treatment best captured the oppositions apparent among the linguistic forms.

The discussion on material process clauses was more complicated. First, it was observed that where only a Pro.·Med. structure had been observed in the mathetic function up to 22½ months, the pattern for commenting or information-giving clauses at 2 years was

(Ag.ˆ)Pro.·Med. Further data were then presented to show that the presence or otherwise of the Agent function did not appear to be random, as we might expect from an immature structure. On the contrary the presence of the Agent in a potentially Ag.ˆPro.ˆMed. (and indeed the presence of a medium in a Pro.·Med. structure) was conditioned by interpersonal rather than experiential factors.

By looking at clauses occurring in speech acts other than information-giving or moods other than declarative, it could be seen that the presence or otherwise of these TRANSITIVITY roles was conditioned by the variable need to express an interpersonal Subject function. Where a first- or second-person Subject could be left implicit because of the dynamics of conversational interaction, then the Agent (or even the Medium in intransitive clauses) with which the Subject would be conflated, did not appear in the structure. Since only Agent or Medium elements expressing a first- or second-person Subject were left unexpressed (except in the case of true endophoric ellipsis), an explanation in terms of the Subject function proves more revealing than the original hypothesis that (Ag.ˆ)Pro.·Med. structures were variable because in mid-development.

Metafunctional analysis, 22½–24 months

A number of the issues relevant to the formal analysis of Hal's language from 22½ to 24 months have now been dealt with. Most of the rest of this chapter will therefore constitute the formal description for this period, looking at the SPEECH FUNCTION system at the discourse or semantic stratum, and at clause rank only at the lexico-grammatical stratum.

SPEECH FUNCTION

Up till now, the system has been described in terms of [give] + [information] or [demand] + [goods-&-services], the latter option occurring both as an initiating and responding move (marked initially by tone differences).

The principal change at 24 months was that [information] utterances had gained a [demand] option, and [goods-&-services] utterances had in a marginal way produced a [give] form.

Thus, we have a system as represented in Figure 9.6.

Goods-&-services exchanges

In adult speech there are certain linguistic markers which help to clarify SPEECH FUNCTION choices on the goods-&-services side.

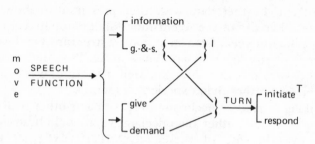

Fig. 9.6 Provisional SPEECH FUNCTION network for 22½–24 months

For example:

(i)   demand goods-&-services;   *please* tag
(ii) demand goods-&-services in response/   *thank you*
      receive (offers of) goods-&-services;
(iii) give goods-&-services in response/compliant   *OK, all right*
      response to demand for goods-&-services.

Hal had not yet developed any of these, but there is no question of his longstanding ability to express a demand ((i) above), and he could also accept or refuse adult offers ((ii) above). Although the tonal distinction between spontaneous initiating demands and those made in response to an offer received no longer applied, since all took falling tone, the following texts illustrate his ability to accept or refuse offers linguistically.

22(22) M: Shall I draw a birdie?
        H: Mummy draw birdie.
22(24) M: Shall I take the plaster off?
        H: No! Leave it on.
23(21) M: Shall I put it in the washing up?
        H: *Hal* [pɒn ə] washing up.

Thus, demanding goods-&-services, whether as an initiating or responding move, was clearly part of Hal's linguistic resources. What is more questionable, though, is whether he had any systematic response to a demand to supply goods-&-services (i.e. giving in response, (iii) above). It will be remembered that responses to instructions at an earlier stage were often made not to the addressee but to himself, as a mathetic aid to successfully carrying out the task. This was no longer prominent, but no addressee-oriented positive response had yet emerged, and a positive response was usually simply a non-verbal compliance. None the less, he could certainly respond with *no* if he chose not to comply.

Information exchanges

On the information side, Hal now gave and demanded information, as provided for in Figure 9.6, and the arguable question is whether he had an initiate/respond distinction also. This is not allowed for in the Figure 9.6 description as there had been no formal development like the tonal choice which differentiated moves for pragmatic utterances. It is of course true that he had been supplying information in response to adult prompts virtually from the start of mother-tongue speech, as in:

M: What' you got there?
H: Hat.

However, at that time the success of an adult initiating move depended to a considerable extent upon whether Hal was disposed to make his 'responding' utterance anyway (i.e. regardless of the occurrence of the adult first pair part).

None the less, I feel that the Figure 9.6 description is too conservative, and that the TURN system did in fact apply to informational utterances by 24 months. Evidence for this lies in the relative infrequency at 2 years of turn-taking violations (ignoring of questions put to him) which were quite frequent before. This, together with the development of elliptical responses, suggests that there was now a genuine initiate vs. respond system for information giving.

Hal also showed from the start that he could receive information, in the sense of assimilating it (initially new names but gradually more than this). However, his linguistic 'responses' demonstrating this were again not really verbal acknowledgements to the addressee, but mathetic comments initiated for his own benefit to help him process the information given him. For this reason it seemed misleading to treat them as dialogue responses, orientated to the conversational partner, as in an adult system.

By 24 months, however, verbal responses to information received might be justifiably viewed as acknowledgements to the addressee. But it is difficult to pinpoint when such a change occurred. It was presumably taking place gradually along with the change from commenting to information giving, which was never linguistically marked. By 2 years, he had still not developed any of the adult markers of information received, such as *oh, yeah*, or the elliptical tags *is it?, did he?*, etc., which would have provided quite strong evidence, but he had certainly learnt the appropriateness of a follow-up comment to a response to his own questions, as in the following example from a little later:

24(20) H: What's that? (pointing in book).
    M: Bag of wool.
    H: Man got [ə] big bag of wool.

Based on the above discussions, there would appear to be some grounds for expanding the provisional SPEECH FUNCTION network of Figure 9.6 to that of Figure 9.7.

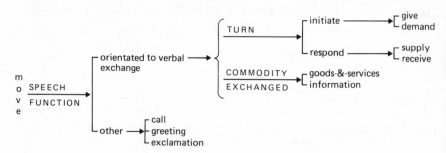

Fig. 9.7   22½–24 months—semantic stratum: revised SPEECH FUNCTION system

Sample realizations in text of SPEECH FUNCTION network, Figure 9.7

To help clarify the network further, some text examples are given below.

_____

[*orientated to verbal exchange:*
initiate:give/goods-&-services]

22(25) H: Some Mummy? (holding up biscuit).
    M: Thank you, darling.
23(10) H: Put on Daddy? (removing necklace from own neck).
    F: (laughs and tosses H into air . . .)

initiate:demand/goods-&-services]
23(5) H: Mummy fix car (thrusting toy car in her hands).
    M: All right, I'll have a go.
23(16) H: Dont eat [ə] toys (to cat).
23(8) H: Want [ə] go on [ə] beach.
    M: No, love. It's too cold today.

respond:supply/goods-&-services]
22(26) M: Put it in the drawer, will you?
    H: No.

respond:receive/goods-&-services]
22(25) M: Shall I do it for you?
          H: *Hal* do it.

initiate:give/information]
23(1) H: Little girl crying.
          M: Yes, she must have hurt herself.

initiate:demand/information]
23(2) H: Where's [ə] lid?
          M: Don't know, love.
23(25) H: Heater's very hot?
          F: Yes, it is.

respond:supply/information]
22(29) M: And what have the birdies got?
          H: Beaks.
23(20) M: What did you do today?
          H: Throw frisbee.

respond:receive information]
22(26) H: Whats this?
          M: It's a beaver.
          H: Beaver.
23(18) M: You are a baby, Hal.
          H: *Not* baby; that's Hal (pointing at self).

[*other:*
  call]
  H: Ka::ty! (running through house).
  H: Mu:::my! (to summon M in morning).

  greeting]
  H: Hi!
  H: Daddy.

  exclamation]
  H: What a mess!
  H: Ooh!

Notes on revised SPEECH FUNCTION network (refer to Figure 9.7)
[orientated to verbal exchange] vs. [other]

Although calls and greetings typically occur in adjacency pairs in adult dialogue, Hal did not look for or acknowledge a verbal response to his calls and greetings. It was no good responding *yes* to a summons, and irrelevant to respond *hello* to a greeting, as far as he was concerned. Moreover, he did not respond verbally to his own name being called, nor to a greeting offered. It is true that paired moves like the following were quite common:

H: Hi!
Shopkeeper: Hi!
H: Daddy!
F: Hello, Hal.
H: Mu-mmy.
M: Just a minute.

However, it was the adult system which was chiefly responsible for creating the pair structures. Equally common were exchanges like the following:

23(19) F: Hello (entering).
      H: Car in there (holding up shoebox of toys he has been playing with).
23(22) Shopkeeper: Hi!
      H: (silence)
      Shopkeeper: Not talking today.
23(10) Babysitter: Bye-bye.
      (H exits in silence.)
      M: Say 'bye-bye', Hal.

As can be seen from the adult follow-ups, a complete lack of verbal response where a second pair part is expected always made the adults present feel slightly uncomfortable, though this was certainly not Hal's intention.

[*orientated to verbal exchange: initiate: give/goods-&-services*]
I have already discussed the rather marginal nature of Hal's giving of goods-&-services in response, [respond: supply] in this network. It may also be questionable whether an [initiate: give: goods-&-services] option had been sufficiently developed to warrant allowing this feature combination, since initiating offers were very limited in nature and infrequent. It is probably best to see this as a highly marked option at this stage rather than to exclude it completely.

Notes on lexico-grammatical clause network (refer to Figure 9.8)

Experiential roles
One point which obviously requires comment is the disappearance from my description of the Actor-Goal TRANSITIVITY functions which I suggested were built up in the pragmatic clause up to 22½

months, and which (following Halliday 1984b) will be required in the description of mature language. Two sets of functions are unnecessary at this point, since there were no longer two distinct experiential patterns serving the two macrofunctions. The experiential patterns for material processes could be described at this point using either ergative or transitive terminology.

I am maintaining the ergative terms here, which were required in the earlier mathetic analysis, but it should be understood that this is not in order to make the same generalizations as would apply in adult language (i.e. to link functions across clause types). The language is not yet sophisticated enough to provide grounds for doing this. I take it that at some point in the future the description of the grammar will be facilitated by distinguishing for all clauses both PROCESS TYPE (mental, material, etc.) and clause VOICE (middle vs. effective). It will then be necessary to use both sets of functions in the description. However, this case study has not been taken far enough to pinpoint how or when this occurs. It is not surprising that the child does not manipulate a system of this complexity the moment he adopts a metafunctional linguistic organization, although presumably the transition development of dual transitivity patterns lays the foundations for such a development at a later stage.

PROCESS TYPE

[mental]
As mental (including verbal) processes were earlier distinguished from the others on the grounds that they did not follow the mathetic Pro.˜Med. generalization, and as this is a distinct class in the adult system, the feature [mental] has been maintained. Moreover, in the next period it proved to be the first class to have a negative declarative form, and was already distinct from materials in having no indicative -*ing* form.

[possession]
These clauses were those using *have* or *got*. During 21 to 22½ months, *got* had been used in such clauses as *deer got antler*, to express a meronymy relationship only. By 24 months, it was used to encode the current possession of any kind of object, as in *Daddy's got boiled egg*. (As in this example, third-person subjects frequently took an [s/z] element before the *got*.)

In addition, Hal began producing *have* for the first time, usually in immediate response to adult use. For example:

23(22) M: Do you want to have an apple or a pear?
        H: Have [ə] pear.

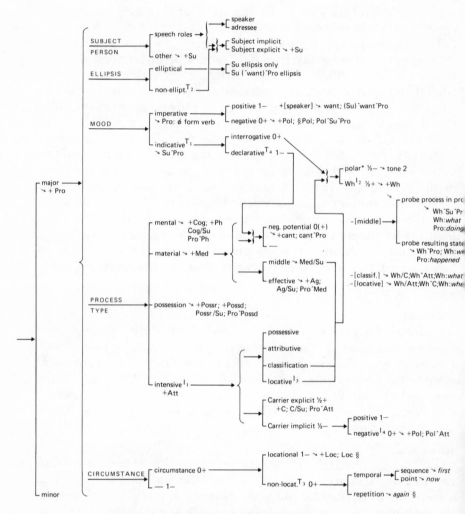

Fig. 9.8 22½-24 months—metafunctionally-based description. Lexico-grammatical stratum; clause rank; major clause

22(27) M: Do you want that toast or shall Mummy have it?
       H: Mummy have it.

But there were also a few spontaneous second-person imperatives such as *(Mummy) have it; dont have it*, etc.

Rather than being related to *get*, meaning 'go and fetch', which he used in indicative and imperative moods, *got* appears to have been most closely associated in meaning with *have*. However, the two were used in different moods; *got* only in the indicative, and *have* in the imperative.

This [possession] type of clause was distinguishable from the [intensive] relationals, not only in having a different structural form, but also in being free to select imperative mood, which they could not. (*Be careful* was possible, but as a stereotype phrase with no indicative equivalent.)

[intensive]
These clauses were of four kinds:

[intensive:possessive] These had a possessive nominal group as Attribute, as in *that's Katy's*.

[intensive:attributive] These had an adjective functioning as Attribute, as in *Mummy's busy*, and could now also take a Deictic Carrier, as in *That's blue*.

[intensive:classification] These are distinct from the [attributive] in having a noun Attribute, and in still being restricted to a Deictic Carrier. Thus there was *That's [ə] man*, but not *Daddy's [ə] man*.

[intensive:locative] These had a prepositional phrase or adverbial group as Attribute, as in *pussy's in the garden*.

Realization statements

As the language is not being formally described below clause rank, realization statements have been limited to specifying the insertion, position and conflation of functions or occasionally to specifying lexical items directly, where there is no function/class distinction. While the grammar is undoubtedly easier to read when realizations are given in the network for each appropriate feature, the following points should be noted here:

1. I have given the realization of [major] as +Process, and of [Subject person:other] and [Subject explicit] as +Subject. This covers the facts in general terms, but the possibility of an implicit Process for first-person [imperative/possession] clauses and some [intensive] clauses requires that for a thoroughly generative

account, the introduction of the Process element be delayed and separately inserted for different feature combinations.

2. Similarly, the insertion of the Subject function is in fact dependent on the [non-elliptical] or [elliptical:Su ellipsis only] options. Rather than complicating the account with numbers of conditioned realization rules, I have allowed these inaccuracies to stand so that the general picture can be most readily perceived.

3. The convention of conflating an experiential function with an interpersonal one which may itself fail to be realized allows us to have non-realized experiential functions, without suggesting that ELLIPSIS, for example, is a system itself directly dependent on experiential choices.

Probabilities

I have wished to make the point in this network that interpersonal and experiential systems were operating simultaneously, and this is a very important aspect of the grammar. However, with five systems available for simultaneous feature selections it becomes difficult to give indications of frequency patterns in the choices. Within any one system, the difficulty is simply the empirical one with the larger grammar of having enough data for each system to work out even rough and ready frequencies. Where this seems possible, approximate weightings have been given as before, but the greatest imbalances probably concern simultaneous selections, and these cannot be so readily noted on the network itself. The most glaring of these are the following: [intensive]/[circumstance], [mental]/[circumstance] and [mental]/[imperative] combinations, all of which were very rare, as might be predicted from the grammar of the previous period.

By this stage, it is not always easy to know of course when absence of a text example for a particular feature combination relates to a failure to collect sufficient data to turn up the structure in question, or is a genuine restriction in the child's language. For example, there were certainly not attested examples of every material process occurring with the features [interrogative:polar], which is being regarded as an option available for all material processes. However, since there is no obvious semantic or functional pattern to link those individual processes which were recorded in this form, and since polar interrogatives were a small minority of clauses, it is doubtful whether there was any grammatical limitation which would have blocked the non-attested cases. On the other hand, there was no single recorded example of an [intensive] clause taking imperative mood, and since this restriction applied to a well-defined experiential meaning area with a specific structural form, it has been created as a genuine *grammatical* restriction.

Interrelationships in network

For a small grammar, the network may appear to require rather a lot of If-Then marking conditions, but these represent 'holes' in the paradigmatic system, which are only to be expected in a rapidly developing grammar. Most of those shown here were temporary asymmetries in the language: in time all kinds of elliptical interrogatives were produced; relational clauses also gained an imperative mood, etc.

A related aspect of this network is that at one point in particular, the interpersonal and experiential systems are more interdependent than might be expected from the definition of a metafunction as a relatively independent set of dependent systems. This too is a developmental phenomenon. At 24 months, Hal could not form Wh interrogatives for every kind of clause for which he used a declarative form. It is consequently impossible at this stage to specify the interrogative system independently of PROCESS TYPE features, as can be done for adult.

Textual developments

One striking difference between the grammar I have described for Hal at 24 months and any adult description of English lies in the absence from the former of any systems relating to the textual metafunction. Although I have ignored this area in order to limit the scope of the study, a few brief notes are provided below to fill out the picture of the linguistic potential thus far described.

THEME and INFORMATION

At clause rank, the systems relating to the textual metafunction in adult are those of THEME and INFORMATION. I have very little to say concerning the former, since up to 2 years Hal did not produce monologues of any length which might provide data for considering Thematic choice in text development (see Fries, 1983). Nor were his structures long enough or complex enough on the whole to allow for different orderings of elements which might be attributable to marked vs. unmarked Theme selection. There were a very few cases of variably ordered structures, such as:

(i) Not baby; thats Hal.
   Thats Hals porridge; not Daddys porridge.
or (ii) 'S broken now.
   Now its broken.

However, it would be difficult to demonstrate that such occasional variations were systematic realizations of Thematic choice.

There was, however, clearly a system of INFORMATION established by 24 months. Even before this, there were some examples of the information Focus being placed away from the unmarked final position. For example:

21(17) *Mŭmmy* drink, *Hàl* drink (pointing in turn at drinks).
21(24) *thàt* one (choosing something).
   twò one (indicating).

During the period 22½–24 months there were many more examples.

22(18) M: That's *Màtthew's* big man, isn't it?
   H: *Hàl* big man.
22(26) M: That's Daddy's little *brùsh.*
   H: Thats *Hàl* brush.
22(22) M: Where's *Dàddy?*
   H: *Thères* Daddy.
22(27) H: (to F) Some *mòre!*
   M: *No;* Daddy's a bit *tìred nŏw.*
   H: *Mùmmy* do it.
23(13) H: Put [ə] bib *òn.*
   M: (out of sight) Put *whát* on?
   H: Put [ə] *bìb* on.
23(13) F: Put the drink down *thère* (indicating table).
   H: Put it on *nèw* table (takes it to other, new table).
23(14) M: Mummy do it if . . .
   H: *Hàl* do it. (He succeeds) Hal *dò:* it!

It is much easier to observe the operation of Given and New choices in dialogue than to establish the development of Thematic ones, but perhaps it may anyway prove typical for the former to develop first. The question will not be considered in any further detail, since my purpose here is simply to present informally some 'loose ends' of data which may be of interest.

Cohesion

Certain of the 'circumstantial' elements in Hal's system were in fact cohesive in nature: namely *first, again.* In addition, there was the system of ELLIPSIS already discussed. This can be specified as a clause system, but it is cohesive in its effect. The joint creation of adjacency pair structures and lexical expectancies were further text-creating features of the language. Here I wish to mention briefly anaphora and conjunction in order to fill out the picture thus far offered.

Anaphora

Hal's language now contained a number of elements which could serve as reference items, namely:

pronouns	(1st person : I, my)
	3rd person : [i] [ɪ] [ɪt]
	demonstratives : this; that
adverbs	here; there
determiner	another

And the noun substitute *one* was a phoric element now well established.

These were still used exophorically on the whole, as in the following examples:

23(1)   Mummy cooking it (watching M at stove).
23(12) Want nother pussy <i.e. as well as picture I have now>.

But during 22½–24 months there were also a few anaphoric examples.

23(22) Want nother spoon. Not that one. Want nother one.
22(27) M: What colour's Mummy's pen?
       H: That's blue.

Very often these may be interpretable both exo- and anaphorically.

Conjunctive relations

Hal had not yet built up a system of relations realized by the conjunctions *and, but, so,* etc. His only conjunction at 2 years was *and,* which had only been used so far to link minor clauses, as in *Mummys glasses and Daddys glasses.* However, he now produced the element *too,* which may also be interpreted as an additive one, and this occurred anaphorically as well as exophorically:

22(19) M: I'm going inside.
       H: Hal go inside *too.*

Moreover, it was during this period that Hal began to produce sequences of clauses much more often, which the hearer could interpret as related, very often in a causal fashion.

23(9) H: Mummy open it. Cant <= I can't> open it.
23(5) H: Mummy fix it. S'broken.
22(27) M: No Daddy's a bit tired now.
H: Mummy do it.
23(27) (H removes food from mouth. M grimaces.)
H: Don't like it. Put it in rubbish.

Martin (forthcoming) treats such clauses in adult English as being in an implicit conjunctive relation. Taking this view, Hal at 24 months had a very simple system of conjunctive relations, which lacked on the whole any formal realizational markers. This illustrates what seems to be a typical developmental pattern. This is for the child first to place linguistic items in juxtaposition as a means of implying a relationship between them, and later to develop an explicit relational signal. An earlier example of this would be the placing of single words together in strings prior to the development of formal structures. Similarly, the labelling of objects by turn could at 2 years be explicitly linked by the conjunction *and*, as described above. Or, a little later, comparisons which had earlier been implied by successive utterances, as in the following text, could be made explicit with *like*, as illustrated.

21(25) H: (patting soft-haired dog) Pussy <= feels like cat>.
(stands back and points at dog) Doggy <= it is dog>.
24(14) M: That's a wolf.
H: Wolf. Like a big dog.

Summary

Specific changes in the language that occurred during the period 22½–24 months included the development of constituency and a rank scale, the beginning development of the first non-congruent SPEECH FUNCTION realizations and the accompanying establishment of TRANSITIVITY and MOOD structures. Other developments noted in passing, but which need much fuller examination, include the development of dialogue and monologue skills to provide cohesion by inferring or implying conjunctive or other relations between clauses.

All these developments relate to the move towards a linguistic system organized on a metafunctional basis. Throughout the transition period, Hal's language has been described in terms of two semi-autonomous grammars, operating in two distinct functional contexts. This picture was most accurate for the very early transition stages, and most idealized for the later ones. This is because mathetic and pragmatic systems gradually came to share their lexico-grammatical realizations, and as time went on these were not always assigned to one or other function by intonation. Simultaneously, the two functional contexts began to overlap, so that there were pragmatic elements observable in mathetic occasions of language, and mathetic aspects to pragmatic uses.

During the period 22½–24 months, the overlapping at both contextual and formal levels had reached a point where little is gained and much is lost if the language is viewed in terms of two systems. This chapter has sought to demonstrate that contexts for language use were becoming complex, with both field and tenor aspects to be taken into account for any utterance, and that substantial grounds existed for seeing simultaneous MOOD and TRANSITIVITY systems operating in the grammar on the adult model.

10 Concluding summary

This case study has sought to explore the development of one child's resources for language, from the protolinguistic stage to the basic mastery of the mother tongue. That is to say, it traces language development from idiosyncratic baby sounds, interpretable in terms of observational judgements as to what the infant achieves by any utterance, to the stage where the child not only uses some of the same linguistic expressions as those around him, but has the same capacity for encoding two or more kinds of meanings simultaneously. Halliday's study of his son Nigel suggested one possible route by which a prelinguistic child might become a recognizable language user, and this study has been an attempt to see how far another child, developing language in the normal way within the family, might or might not follow a similar path.

I have, in addition, attempted throughout to provide descriptions of Hal's language which are 'generative'—i.e. as explicit and complete as possible, within certain limits. This was in order that all my interpretations and general claims could be supported with reference to the data, and also in order to try to demonstrate, or at least illustrate, some of the developments of the transition, described by Halliday (1975a) in more general terms. These explicit descriptions were further intended to illustrate the nature of a language system in flux, and also served as a working strategy to make sure that all aspects of the developing language were taken account of. (At times, of course, the data presented problems not adequately coped with by my descriptive techniques, and I have noted these areas at various points throughout the book.)

Development from Phase I to Phase III

I have already discussed in some detail the extent to which Hal's protolinguistic development—in terms of the nature and range of the signs, and the development of the functions—corresponded to that of Nigel, and I shall not go over this ground again here (see pp. 90-9. I would say that this study contributes to a growing body of evidence for the contention that infants in their second six months of life do evolve vocal (or vocal-gestural) symbol systems, which have a fairly predictable range of uses. What is not so clear is whether as extensive and clearly demarcated a set of functions as Halliday has proposed will prove the most generally applicable framework, and in what way we will need to interpret apparent overlaps of expressions between different functions (see pp. 98–9).

During the protolanguage stage an infant may be observed to vocalize with reference to an object, behaviour, emotional feeling, etc., and may also be observed to intend or achieve something by the uttering of the sound. However, as Dore (1978: 97) has accurately observed, such sounds 'are not detachable from their uses.' This means that an experiential content such as 'nice taste' will not be expressing 'Give me something with a nice taste' on one occasion, and 'This has a nice taste' on another, until the child has some means of separating the experiential contents of messages from their possible interpersonal statuses, and of combining and re-combining the two kinds of meaning freely. Still less will a protolinguistic utterance be expressing anything like 'Tell me, has this got a nice taste?', because the communicative role of seeker (or giver) of information is one created by and dependent on language itself, unlike the social roles involved in strictly protolinguistic contexts.

An exploration of the transition period therefore involves tracing the child's strategies for developing modes of meaning which are re-combinable in different ways, and for developing information exchange as the most important function of language, a function which the protolanguage cannot fulfil and which the child does not require of language in the earliest stages.

The most striking similarity between Nigel and Hal in their language development strategies is the distinction each made, with the learning of mother-tongue vocabulary, between the two fundamental functions of language as either an instrument for understanding the world (mathetic function) or a tool for getting things done (pragmatic function). These two transition functions resembled proto-language functions at first by each having a linguistic potential (systems and realizations) largely exclusive to itself. Thus, the move from protolanguage to transition language may be characterized as in Figure 10.1. However, the boundary between the two transition grammars is never in fact as absolute as this useful idealization suggests, and becomes less so all the time.

As time passes, instead of being *either* mathetic *or* pragmatic, a context for an utterance may have aspects relating to both—that is to say a component of 'things talked about' *and* one of inter-active relations, though at first one of these will be foregrounded.

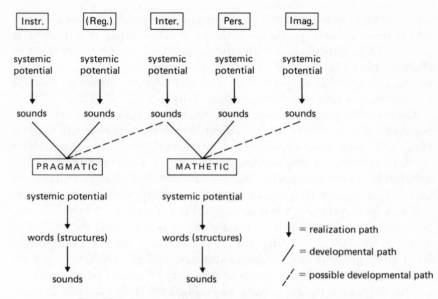

Fig. 10.1 Development from protolanguage to transition

One reflex of this is that the linguistic potential becomes less exclusively reserved for one context. At the simplest level, once there is *chēese* in contrast with *chèese*, we can distinguish two aspects to the realization: the lexical item *cheese* relating to the field (*what is being talked about*), and the tone, expressing its speaker–hearer relations.

In this case study, I hope to have shown how mathetic contexts become less exclusively associated with the reflective interpretation of the world, as speaker–hearer relations become more prominent with the development of the concept of information; and how pragmatic contexts become more orientated to experiential content, developing TRANSITIVITY options, quantifying groups and so on, as well as focusing on social, including communicative, roles.

Another side to all this is that utterances are becoming speech acts in a more genuine sense than protolinguistic utterances can be said to be. Pragmatic utterances of the transition, unlike the protolinguistic ones from which they evolved, come to look for and accept responses in terms of language, rather than solely in terms of material or emotional satisfaction. Meanwhile, with the move on the mathetic side towards information exchange comes the development of those speech acts which are intrinsic to language itself, such as statement, answer or question.

The development of a metafunctionally based language is not therefore to be seen simply as a case of the mathetic function building up an experiential grammar and the pragmatic one building up an interpersonal grammar, which then get put together, though this is not entirely a false picture. It is certainly true that experiential systems are first and most extensively developed within mathetic contexts, while the pragmatic function lays the foundation for the development in particular of the imperative mood system. However, a detailed examination of Hal's developing language suggests that the bringing together of the two grammars is accomplished when the mathetic language has come to be concerned also with addressor-addressee relations, building up its own SPEECH FUNCTION options (exclamation, comment → information giving), and pragmatic language has come to be concerned also with experiential content, (building up a TRANSITIVITY system, or making use of experiential systems such as that of the nominal group, originally built up within mathetic).

Gradually there comes to be more and more overlap between the experiential potential (and realizations) on each side, while the SPEECH FUNCTION-MOOD options built up within each function come to form an integrated potential available for any utterance, simultaneously with the joint experiential potential. Eventually, therefore, any utterance will be serving both reflective and active functions, and rather than selecting from one of two mutually exclusive grammars, a text will embody simultaneous choices from a single grammar, with different sets of options relating to different aspects (experiential and interpersonal) of any one semiotic context.

Comparison with Nigel

When it comes to comparing Hal's transition language with that of Halliday's Nigel, the similarities are probably more striking than the divergences, although the two individuals do not favour exactly the same strategies in their route from macrofunction to meta-function, nor would their systemic potential be identical at the point when metafunctional organization may be said to be achieved.

Obviously the most noticeable similarities lie in the way both adopt—soon after the first words are produced—a grouping of protolinguistic functions into a two-way opposition between language as reflection and language as a means of action, and in making this explicit by means of intonation. In these terms, both children's developments may fairly be characterized. Even their use of tone contrast is similar in being basically a falling vs. non-falling dichotomy, with the reflective mode signalled by falling tone. However, Hal used both level and rising tones in the pragmatic function, and maintained throughout a more exclamative rise–fall contour as a variety of mathetic. Moreover, where Nigel's tone system was suddenly created at 19 months and maintained consistently for about six months (Halliday 1975a: 87-8), Hal evolved his more gradually from the later protolanguage, and had already begun to adapt it by about 20 months, when pragmatic responses began to take falling tone.

The nature of the functional division itself is very similar, but not identical. The 'response not required' vs. 'response required' characterization, which Halliday gives to Nigel's mathetic vs. pragmatic choice, is not entirely apt for Hal. One reason is that Hal developed an informative use earlier, which therefore made some demands on the addressee within the mathetic function. Also at the beginning, when *verbal* pragmatic responses were not looked for, the requirement that any particular addressee respond (even physically) could be subordinate to the requirement that some particular effect on the material world be achieved (see p. 123).

Hal's more rapid development of information giving is of course another difference between the two, although this should not be overstressed, since at first he could (or would) only give 'unshared' information that he felt very strongly about and wished to convey. He did not impart just any information which happened to be sought by the addressee. There is a genuine dissimilarity in development here though, since Nigel made grammatically explicit the distinction between giving shared and unshared information (Halliday 1975a: 105-6), while Hal did not. However, when Hal wished to make explicit the fact that a particular utterance was an information giver, he did so by introducing it with an interrogative form (or cue-ing someone else to do so). There is thus some similarity in their strategies: Nigel systematically encoded all true information givers as interrogatives, while Hal used the interrogative quite frequently for a time to mark the information-giving status of a following utterance.

The children differed in the extent to which they made use of the mathetic/pragmatic distinction as an organizing principle, and Hal was less thoroughgoing than Nigel here. I say this because in Nigel's case all kinds of utterances, including greetings and routine exchanges, were clearly assigned to one or other function, which is not so obviously true in Hal's case (see p. 130). Moreover, Nigel generalized the response-demanded criterion on the pragmatic function eventually to the development of an information-demanding

speech function, whereas Hal had already abandoned the macrofunctions as a basis for his language by the time he came to develop
genuine systematic information demands.

Finally, although we do not have detailed accounts of Nigel's
systemic potential during the transition period, Halliday speaks of
the mathetic function as being 'the main impetus for the learning
of vocabulary' and as providing 'the context for ideational systems
such as those of transitivity (the grammar of processes), time and
place, qualifying, quantifying, and so on' (Halliday 1975a: 57).
This macrofunction also leads in his account to the development of
the narrative genre. Then, when pointing out that 'each function
carries with it a strong sub-motif of the other' (Halliday 1975a:
108), he also adds that the more interpersonal 'intensification
and evaluation' involved in *very old tree, loud noise, too X*, etc.,
were also developed first in mathetic contexts.

The pragmatic function, on the other hand, is described for Nigel
as providing the context for systems such as 'mood, modality,
person, attitude and the like' (Halliday 1975a: 57), and as giving the
main impetus for the development of dialogue.

Hal's developmental path corresponds to such a description in
general terms, but does not of course match it in all details. For him,
too, the mathetic function appeared to motivate vocabulary learning,
the initial development of process structures and qualifying nominal
groups, as well as the kinds of intensifying and evaluative elements
described for Nigel. In addition, though, the exclamative tone,
Attitudinal Epithets and the speech function of information giving
were further interpersonal aspects, or elements of the 'pragmatic
sub-motif', developed within the mathetic context by Hal.

Although it is true that information giving does lead to the
development of the narrative genre, another difference between
the two children lies in the fact that Hal did not in fact develop the
narrative mode to any great extent during this period. Talking
of past or future events, or even relating news, were new possibilities
exploited to a small extent, but he never perfected and repeated his
own accounts of events witnessed or experienced as Nigel did (see
Halliday 1975a: 112). Hal used the mathetic mode much more to
simply classify and record ongoing observations, or to help process
information or instructions received, or even to practise and perfect
casting information into a dialogue rather than monologue format.

As far as the pragmatic macrofunction is concerned, it contributed
for Hal to the development of the command speech function and
imperative mood (though not elaborated to Nigel's three-person
system), to the person system and the initiate+respond structure of

dialogue adjacency pairs. Unlike Nigel, Hal had no modality system at this stage. Where Nigel's 'mathetic sub-motif' concerned the talking of things and relations within pragmatic contexts too, and possibly the development of the causative element in processes (see Halliday 1975: 108), Hal evolved on the pragmatic side the following experiential elements: the Actor^Process^Goal TRANSITIVITY pattern, quantifiers (*some, more, bit*) and Deictic determiners (*this one, that one*). The latter two evolved here doubtless because they expressed kinds of attitudinal choices in effect, while Attitudinal Epithets were expressed first as mathetic realizations, probably because these involved more the learning of socially standard evaluations.

Where Hal differs most from Nigel is in the area of information demanding, which after a few pragmatic attempts at requesting a name (see p. 154) did not in the end emerge as a pragmatic development, but awaited the mastery of the adult interrogative mood, by which time the mathetic/pragmatic dichotomy was being abandoned as an organizing strategy.

From the above comparative summary, drawing on this study and Halliday's *Learning How to Mean* (1975a), we gain a picture of individual differences and preferences, against a common background of development, which allows us to accept the broad generalizations which emerge from Halliday's account. These are that development to the mother tongue can be characterized in terms of a three-phase development (protolanguage—transition—mother tongue), with a corresponding move from microfunctions to macrofunctions to metafunctions. Microfunctions are the observed infant uses of language, each with its own possible choices and realizations; macrofunctions are the linguistically defined, more general alternative functions of reflection-learning and action, each having a partly distinct grammar; and metafunctions are sets of simultaneously available paradigmatic systems within a single integrated grammar.

At the same time, we may expect that individual children may vary in the number and kinds of choices they make within microfunctional contexts, may show some variation as to exactly how the transition functions are interpreted or made explicit (if they always are, which remains unknown), and finally may adopt different strategies or priorities for 'bringing the two macrofunctions together' —in other words, for moving from a macrofunctional to a metafunctional manner of linguistic organization.

Appendix
Selected developments, twenty-four to twenty-seven months

Although I have argued that by 2 years of age Hal had passed from a transitional to a metafunctional linguistic system, it was not until about 27 months that MOOD, POLARITY and VOCATION systems were truly simultaneous with all TRANSITIVITY options, and a clear Finite element had emerged as a MOOD function. I shall not attempt to describe Hal's post-transition language in any detail here, but it may be of interest to indicate the path along which inter-personal systems developed over the next couple of months, as these systems in particular were either more restricted than in adult lan-guage or had non-adult realizations at 24 months.

1. POLARITY

It will be remembered that at 24 months, *yes* and *no* were very restricted in application. *No* could be a goods-&-services refusal, or else was used to comment on a failure to find a sought item in a particular location. *Yes* was a very rare contradictory response to an adult negative in a goods-&-services context.

e.g. 23(26) (H wants to go to shop.)
        F: We don't want anything at the shop.
        H: Yes; Yes; Yes.

During 24 to 25½ months, *yes* and *no* were freely used as responses to both goods-&-services and information clauses.

Examples of *no*

Naming
    24(6) M: Is it yellow? (pointing at red jumper).
          H: No.

24(7) M: There's a big gorilla (teasing, pointing at dog).
       H: No.
24(9) M: Have you got wet pants?
       H: No, dry.
24(16) H: See [ə] butterfly? (holding up piece of fish).
       M: That's a butterfly, is it?
       H: No, fish.

Reporting

24(26) M: Did June give you a lolly?
       H: No.
24(27) M: Oh, did you ride a horsie at the shops?
       H: No.
24(27) M: Did the giraffe pull it <poster> down? (teasing).
       H: No. Hal pull it down.

There appeared to be a progression, then, from *no* = not there, to *no* in response to relationals (he already had *not wet*, etc.), to *no* also used in response to material process clauses.

Examples of *yes*

At about 25 months, *yes* was used for both positive reponses to information-seeking interrogatives and for acceptances of offers.

Positive response to interrogative question

24(26)   M: Did you play in the garden?
            H: Yes.
24(28)   (M has been misnaming for fun, H saying *no*.)
            M: Is it an elephant? <right name>.
            H: Yes.
24(29)   M: Was Daddy cross with you?
            H: Yees.
25 months M: Did you put the horsie in there?
            H: Yes.

Accept offer

24(30) M: Do you want tea?
       H: Yes.
24(30) M: Shall we sing a song?
       H: Yes.
25(2) F: Do you want me to help?
       H: Yes.

Positive response to command

These came a little later; the first case is given below.

25(12) M   M: Will you shut the door for me darling?
           H: Yes (does so).

Negation within clause structure

Declarative

Within the mathetic function, the negative element had been found only in categorizing types, such as *not soup*; *not Daddy's*. After 24 months, these continued in full clauses such as, *Daddy's not hungry*, as well as in minor or elliptical types, especially in an argumentative context. Examples of the latter follow.

24 months H: Whats that?
           M: That's a woman.
           H: Man. Not [ə] woman. *There's* [ə] woman (pointing at another figure).
24(25)   (H has labelled a picture as a 'star'.)
           M: Actually I think that's a flower.
           H: Not flower, star.
25(5)   H: Whats that?
           M: Vultures.
           H: Not vultures; birdies.
25(5)   F: Have some fish.
           H: (bossily) Sardines, not fish.

Mental reaction processes were the next to occur in a negative form, with *don't want* and *don't like* being produced soon after 24 months, but only in first-person clauses at first. It was a few weeks later that the first negative material processes were produced—e.g. *Mummys not crying*—and these were relatively infrequent for some time.

The first negative interrogative, however, was not recorded until 28(3) with *why it doesn't go round?*, and these remained rarities for several months to come.

2. VOCATION

Up to two years, Vocatives were restricted to greetings (*bye-bye Daddy*), calls (*Mummy*), offers (*some, Mummy?*) and very occasional apologies (*sorry, Mummy*). After this, they were used very frequently with second-person imperative commands:

24(16) H: Stop that Daddy.
24(16) H: Sit there Mummy.

The first example recorded in an interrogative structure was also arguably a command in illocutionary function.

24(19) (H holds up salt and addresses each parent in turn.)
      H: See, Mummy?
         See, Daddy?
         See?
         Salt.

Other early non-imperative examples included the following:

25(14) H: What are these? (pointing at bedposts on four-poster bed in picture.)
      (M hesitates, pondering appropriate label.)
      H: What are these, Mummy?
24(16) (M is about to enter bathroom.)
      H: Stop Mummy. *I'm* going [ə] bathroom, Mummy.
25(2) (M takes Hal's hand in street, on seeing car pulling into driveway ahead.)
      H: I'm running Mummy, I'm running.

What is noticeable here is that these occasions were either information *demanding*, or else were declaratives which may be construed as commands, or at least as causally linked to an explicit or implicit command.

It was not in fact until after 25½ months that Vocatives were used simply to mark information as open to acknowledgement, rather as question tags may do, as in the following examples.

25(23) H: I found another one, Mummy.
26(7) H: Mummy, I'm eating yoghourt.
26(11) H: I got [ə] peg, Daddy.

Until this point, it is probably fair to see the restrictedness of this grammatical feature and its tendency to turn indicatives into commands as evidence for the fact that the macrofunctional bias was only gradually eliminated.

Imperatives

First person

For about 8 weeks after his second birthday, Hal continued to use *I want to X* as the principal realization of a first-person imperative. However, during this time two developments were taking place.

1. *Want* was gradually coming to be used more often than before in contexts which were not directly demanding goods-&-services of another. For example:

   25(6) H: Want [ə] *blue* pen (rummaging in pencil case.)

2. Hal began to develop alternative first-person imperative forms, which were *let me* [ami] and *lets* [ʼɛs]. However, up till about 25 months, these were restricted to a few stereotyped expressions, namely: *let me see, let me do it* and *lets go.*

The next step after 26 months was that *want* began to function like other processes: it was used in the third person (*Mummy doesn't want it*), and later in the past tense (*I didn't want milk*). At the same time, the *let* forms of exclusive and inclusive imperative expanded to become clearly productive forms. *Want* was still of course used to express a command very often, but by this stage it can be regarded as a process in declarative mood realizing this speech act incongruently, rather than as an imperative mood form.

Second person

After 24 months, the *Mummy do it* form, which had stress on *Mummy* only if contrastive, began to give way to the adult imperative, sometimes with an added Vocative tail, e.g. *sit down, Mummy*, though there were plenty of contrastive occasions when the Subject was fronted as here:

M: Going to get your little chair?
H: *Mummy* get your chair.

Polar interrogatives and tags

Polite commands

During the period 24–25½ months, polar interrogatives (realized by high rising tone on a 'declarative' structure) were used for an additional function. As well as for information demands, offers and permission requests, Hal began to use the form for polite requests of the addressee. For example:

24(1)   H: Play those? (= will you?)

During this period, permission requests were also alternatively realized as a falling tone declarative plus high-rising tag, such as *all right?*, *OK, hm?* For example:

25(12) H: I put [ə] cars in thère, all ri'ght.

By 27 months, polite commands were of three kinds, all expressed by means of a modal auxiliary and explicit subject:

Can I . . .? permission seeking, i.e. polite first-person exclusive.
Shall we . . .? suggestion, i.e. polite first-person inclusive.
Will you . . .? polite second person.

Tags

However, the first possible productions of a Subject^Finite structure occurred before this, in the form of tags on first-person declaratives, such as the following:

25(5) H: I'm writing, [an] I.
25(6) H: I'm making [ə] people, [an] I.
25(7) H: I'm stand up, [an] I.
25(11) H: I'm sit in Daddy's seat, [an] I.

(At this stage, both *I* and *I'm* occurred with both ϕ and *-ing* forms of verb; but it can be seen that all *tagged* main clauses had the Finite element). Probably at this point [an] would best be treated as a tag formula rather than a negative Finite, but after 25½ months there were all kinds of different Finites and Subjects involved.

25(16) H: Daddy took [ə] wood off, didn't he?
25(23) H: We gonna see Sue, aren't we?
25(24) H: They're helping, aren't they?
26(10) H: I got big cupboard, haven't I?
26(24) H: He got slippers, hasn't he?
26(27) H: I saw aeroplanes, didn't I?

Further evidence not only for the development of the Mood element (Subject + Finite), but for its adult role in making a proposition arguable, can perhaps be seen from dialogues where some disagreement occurs. One new development here was of responses where the Residue was ellipsed. For example:

26(10) M: You've been in the sand all day.
   H: No, I haven't.

Another is Hal's idiosyncratic preference for repeating the Mood element twice for contradictory emphasis.

26(24)   M: Try your toast now. It's not too hot now.
            H: It *is*; its too hot.
27 months M: It <= dog> isn't playing peep-bo, I don't think
                darling.
            H: *Tis*; its playing peep-bo.

Obviously there is a lot to say about the development of discourse features after 24 months, about the appearance of fresh
TRANSITIVITY patterns (e.g. causative middle clauses such as
I made him go), the development of the tense system, etc. However,
as this study is limited to an account of the protolanguage and transition periods, I have simply selected for brief mention in these final
notes a few areas of the grammar where the move to parallel interpersonal and experiential systems can be seen to continue. Thus, at
27 months, with MOOD, POLARITY and VOCATION systems
available to all TRANSITIVITY clause selections, and the emergence
of the two principal functions of the MOOD system: Mood (Subject
+ Finite) and Residue, Hal's lexicogrammar had evolved to a form
very much closer to that of the adults with whom he chiefly interacted.

Bibliography

Atkinson, Martin (1979), 'Prerequisites for Reference' in E. Ochs and B. B. Schieffelin (eds) *Developmental pragmatics*, New York, Academic Press (1979: 229-49).

Austin, John (1962), *How to do things with words*, New York, Oxford University Press.

Bailey, Charles James (1973), *Variation and linguistic theory*, Arlington, Va., Centre for Applied Linguistics.

Bates, Elizabeth (1976), *Language and context: the acquisition of pragmatics*, New York, Academic Press.

Bates, Elizabeth *et al.* (1979a), 'The acquisition of performatives prior to speech' in E. Ochs and B. B. Schieffelin (eds) *Developmental pragmatics*, New York, Academic Press (1979: 111-29).

Bates, Elizabeth *et al.* (1979b), *The emergence of symbols*, New York, Academic Press.

Bates, Elizabeth and Brian MacWhinney (1979), 'A functionalist approach to the acquisition of grammar' in E. Ochs and B. B. Schieffelin (eds) *Developmental pragmatics*, New York, Academic Press (1979: 167-211).

Benedict, Helen E. (1976), *Language comprehension in 10-16 month old infants*, Doctoral dissertation, Yale University.

Bloom, Lois (1970), *Language development: form and function in emerging grammars*, Cambridge, Mass, M.I.T. Press.

Bloom, Lois (1973), *One word at a time*, The Hague, Mouton.

Bloom, Lois (1974), 'Talking, understanding and thinking' in R. L. Schiefelbusch and L. L. Lloyd (eds) *Language Perspectives*, Baltimore, University Press, 285-311.

Bloom, Lois (1978), 'Developmental change in the use of single word utterances' in her *Readings in language development*, New York, Wiley (1978: 161-5).

Bowerman, Melissa (1973), *Early syntactic development*, Cambridge, Cambridge University Press.

Bowerman, Melissa (1978), 'Structural relationships in children's utterances: syntactic or semantic?' in L. Bloom (ed.) *Readings in language development*, New York, Wiley (1978: 217-30).

Braine, Martin D. S. (1963), 'The ontogeny of English phrase structure: the first phase', *Language* 39, 1--13. Also in L. Bloom (ed.) *Readings in language development*, New York, Wiley (1978: 60-73).

Braunwald, Susan R. and Richard W. Brislin (1979), 'The diary method updated' in E. Ochs and B. B. Schieffelin (eds) *Developmental pragmatics*, New York, Academic Press (1979: 21-42).

Brown, Roger and Ursula Bellugi (1964), 'Three processes in the child's acquisition of syntax', *Harvard Educational Review* 34, 133-51.

Bruner, J. S. (1975a), 'From communication to language—a psychological

BIBLIOGRAPHY 263

perspective', *Cognition* 3, 255-87, reprinted in I. Markova (ed.) *The social context of language*, Chichester, Wiley (1978: 17-48).

Bruner, J. S. (1975b), 'The ontogenesis of speech acts', *Journal of child language* 2, 1-19.

Bullowa, Margaret (ed.) (1979), *Before speech: the beginning of interpersonal communication*, Cambridge, Cambridge University Press.

Butler, C. S. (1976), 'Some important aspects of the interpersonal function', University of Nottingham, Mimeo.

Carter, A. L. (1978), 'The development of systematic vocalizations prior to words: a case study' in N. Waterson and C. Snow (eds) *The development of communication*, Chichester, Wiley (1978: 127-38).

Carter, A. L. (1979), 'Prespeech meaning relations in P. Fletcher and M. Garman (eds) *Language acquisition*, Cambridge, Cambridge University Press, 71-92.

Chafe, Wallace L. (1970), *Meaning and the structure of language*, Chicago, Univ. of Chicago Press.

Chafe, Wallace L. (1976), 'Givenness, contrastiveness, definiteness, subjects, topics and points of view' in Charles N. Li (ed.) *Subject and topic*, New York, Academic Press (1976: 25-55).

Chomsky, Noam (1957), *Syntactic structures*, The Hague, Mouton.

Chomsky, Noam (1965), *Aspects of the theory of syntax*, Cambridge, Mass., MIT Press.

Dixon, R. M. W. (1979), 'Ergativity', *Language* 55, 59-138.

Dore, John (1973), *The development of speech acts*, Doctoral dissertation, City University of New York.

Dore, John (1975), 'Holophrases, speech acts and language universals', *Journal of child language* 2, 21-40.

Dore, John (1978), 'Conditions for the acquisition of speech acts' in I. Markova (ed.) *Language and social context*, Chichester, Wiley (1978: 87-111).

Dore, John (1979), 'Conversation and preschool language development' in P. Fletcher and M. Garman (eds) *Language acquisition*, Cambridge, Cambridge University Press (1979: 337-61).

Edwards, Derek (1978), 'Social relations and early language' in A. Lock (ed.) *Action, gesture and symbol*, London, Academic Press (1978: 449-69).

Fawcett, Robin P. (1980), *Cognitive linguistics and social interaction*, Heidelberg, J. Groos and Exeter Univ. (Exeter Linguistics Studies 3).

Ferrier, Linda (1978), 'Word, context and imitation' in Andrew Lock (ed.) *Action, gesture and symbol*, London, Academic Press (1978: 471-83).

Fillmore, Charles J. (1968), 'The case for case' in E. Bach and R. T. Harms (eds) *Universals of linguistic theory*, New York, Holt, Rinehart and Winston (1968: 1-88).

Fillmore, Charles J. (1970), 'The grammar of "hitting" and "breaking" ' in R. A. Jacobs and P. S. Rosenbaum (eds) *Readings in English transformational grammar*, Waltham, Mass., Ginn (1970: 120-33).

Fillmore, Charles J. (1977), 'The case for case reopened', *Syntax and Semantics* 8, 59-81.

Firth, J. R. (1957), *Papers in linguistics 1934-1951*, London, Oxford University Press.

Fries, Peter (1983) 'On the status of theme in English' in J. S. Petofi and E. Sozer (eds) *Micro and macro connexity of texts*, Hamburg, Buske (1983: 116-152) (Papiere zur Textlinguistik Bd. 45).

Greenfield, P. M. (1978), 'Informativeness, presupposition and semantic choice in single word utterances' in N. Waterson and C. Snow (eds) *The development of communication*, New York, Wiley (1978: 443-52).

Greenfield, P. M. and J. H. Smith (1976), *The structure of communication in early language development*, New York, Academic Press.

Grieve, Robert and Robert Hoogenraad (1979), 'First words' in P. Fletcher and M. Garman (eds) *Language acquisition*, Cambridge, Cambridge University Press (1979: 93-104).

Griffiths, Patrick (1979), 'Speech acts and early sentences' in P. Fletcher and M. Garman (eds) *Language acquisition*, Cambridge, Cambridge University Press (1979: 105-20).

Gruber, J. S. (1975), 'Performative—constative transition in child language development', *Foundations of Language* 12, 513-27.

Halliday, M. A. K. (1956), 'Grammatical categories in modern Chinese', *Transactions of the Philological Society*, 177-224. Extract reprinted in his *System and function in language* (ed.) G. Kress, London, Oxford University Press (1976: 36-57).

Halliday, M. A. K. (1968), 'Notes on transitivity and theme in English: Part 3', *Journal of Linguistics* 4.2, 179-215.

Halliday, M. A. K. (1970), 'Language structure and language function' in J. Lyons (ed.) *New horizons in linguistics*, Harmondsworth, Penguin (1970: 140-65).

Halliday, M. A. K. (1973), *Explorations in the functions of language*, London, Arnold (Explorations in Language Study).

Halliday, M. A. K. (1975a), *Learning how to mean: explorations in the development of language*, London, Arnold (Explorations in Language Study).

Halliday, M. A. K. (1975b), 'Sociological aspects of semantic change' in L. Heilmann (ed.) *Proceedings of the 11th International Congress of Linguists*, Bologna, Il Mulino (1975: 853-79).

Halliday, M. A. K. (1976), *System & function in language: selected papers* (ed.) G. R. Kress, London, Oxford University Press.

Halliday, M. A. K. (1977a), 'Language as a social semiotic: towards a general sociolinguistic theory' in A. Makkai, V. Becker Makkai and L. Heilman (eds) *Linguistics at the crossroads*, Lake Bluff, Ill., Jupiter Press (1977: 13-41). First pub. in A. Makkai and V. Becker Makkai (eds) *The First Lacus Forum*, Columbia, Sth. Carolina, Hornbeam Press (1975: 17-46).

Halliday, M. A. K. (1977b), 'Text as semantic choice in social contexts' in T. A. van Dijk and J. Petofi (eds) *Grammars and descriptions*, Berlin, de Gruyter (Research in Text Theory 1) (1977: 176-225).

Halliday, M. A. K. (1978a), *Language as a social semiotic: the social interpretation of language and meaning*, London, Arnold.

Halliday, M. A. K. (1978b), 'Meaning and the construction of reality in early childhood' in H. L. Pick and E. Saltzman (eds) *Modes of perceiving and processing of information*, Hillsdale, New Jersey, Lawrence Erlbaum Associates (1978: 67-96).

Halliday, M. A. K. (1979), 'One child's protolanguage' in M. Bullowa (ed.) *Before speech*, Cambridge, Cambridge University Press (1979: 171-90).

Halliday, M. A. K. (1984), 'Language as code and language as behaviour: a systemic-functional interpretation of the nature and ontogenesis of dialogue' in Robin Fawcett et al. (eds) *The semiotics of culture and language*, London, Frances Pinter (1984).

Halliday, M. A. K. (in press), *A short introduction to functional grammar*, London, Arnold.

Halliday, M. A. K. and Ruqaiya Hasan (1976), *Cohesion in English*, Cambridge, Cambridge University Press.
Halliday, M. A. K. and J. R. Martin (eds) (1981), *Readings in systemic linguistics*, London, Batsford.
Huddleston, R. D. (1981), 'A fragment of a systemic description of English' in M. A. K. Halliday and J. R. Martin (eds) *Readings in systemic linguistics*, London, Batsford (1981: 222-36).
Hudson, R. (1971), *English complex sentences: an introduction to systemic grammar*, Amsterdam, North-Holland.
Ingram, David (1971), 'Transitivity in child language', *Language* 47, 888-910.
Labov, William and T. Labov (1978), 'Learning the syntax of questions' in R. Campbell and P. T. Smith (eds) *Recent advances in the psychology of language B*, (NATO Conference Series III, Vol. 4B) New York, Plenum Press (1978: 1-44).
Lewis, M. M. (1936), *Infant speech: a study of the beginnings of language*, London, Routledge and Kegan Paul, 2nd enlarged edn. (1951).
Lock, Andrew (ed.) (1978), *Action, gesture and symbol: the emergence of language*, London, Academic Press.
McNeill, David (1971), 'The capacity for the ontogenesis of grammar' in D. I. Slobin (ed.) *The ontogenesis of grammar*, New York, Academic Press (1971: 17-40).
Macrae, Alison (1979), 'Combining meanings in early language' in P. Fletcher and M. Garman (eds) *Language acquisition*, Cambridge, Cambridge University Press, (1979: 161-75).
McShane, John (1980), *Learning to talk*, Cambridge, Cambridge University Press.
Martin, J. R. (1981a), 'How many speech acts?' *UEA Papers in Linguistics* 14-15, 52-77.
Martin, J. R. (1981b), 'Register and metafunction, Department of Linguistics, University of Sydney, mimeo.
Martin, J. R. (forthcoming) *English text: system and structure*.
Menn, Lise (1978), *Pattern, control and contrast in beginning speech*, Bloomington, Indiana University Linguistics Club.
Miller, Wick and S. Ervin (1964), 'The development of grammar in child language' in U. Bellugi and R. Brown (eds), *The acquisition of language* (Monograph no. 29 of the Society for Research in Child Development), Chicago, Ill., Society for Research in Child Development (1964: 9-34).
Moerk, Ernst L. (1977), *Pragmatic and semantic aspects of early language development*, Baltimore, University Park Press.
Myers, Terry (ed.) (1979), *The development of conversation and discourse*, Edinburgh, Edinburgh University Press.
Nelson, Katherine (1973), *Structure and strategy in learning how to talk*. (Monograph no. 149 of the Society for Research in Child Development.), Chicago, Ill., Society for Research in Child Development (1973).
Newson, John (1978), 'Dialogue and development' in A. Lock (ed.) *Action, gesture and symbol*, London, Academic Press (1978: 31-42).
Ochs, Elinor and B. B. Schieffelin (eds) (1979), *Developmental pragmatics*, New York, Academic Press.
Richards, M. P. M. (1978), 'The biological and the social' in A. Lock (ed.) *Action, gesture and symbol*, London, Academic Press (1978: 21-30).

Rodgon, Maris M. (1976), *Single word usage: cognitive development and the beginnings of combinatorial speech*, Cambridge, Cambridge University Press.

Schaffer, H. R. (ed.) (1977), *Studies in mother infant interaction*, New York, Academic Press.

Schlesinger, I. M. (1971), 'Learning grammar: from pivot to realisation rule' in R. Huxley and E. Ingram (eds) *Language acquisition*, London, Academic Press (1971: 79-89).

Schlesinger, I. M. (1974), 'Relational concepts underlying language' in R. L. Schiefelbusch and L. L. Lloyd (eds) *Language perspectives*, Baltimore, University Park Press (1974: 129-51).

Scollon, Ronald (1976), *Conversations with a one year old*, Honolulu, University of Hawaii Press.

Searle, J. R. (1975), 'Indirect speech acts', *Syntax and Semantics* 3, 59-82.

Shotter, John (1978), 'The cultural context of communication studies: theoretical and methodological issues' in A. Lock (ed.) *Action, gesture and symbol*, London, Academic Press (1978: 43-78).

Sylvester-Bradley, B. and C. Trevarthen (1978), 'Baby talk as an adaptation to the infant's communication' in N. Waterson and C. Snow (eds) *The development of communication*, Chichester, Wiley (1978: 75-92).

Trevarthen, Colwyn (1977), 'Descriptive analyses of infant communicative behaviour' in H. R. Schaffer (ed.) *Studies in mother-infant interaction*, New York, Academic Press (1977: 227-70).

Trevarthen, Colwyn and Patricia Hubley (1978), 'Secondary intersubjectivity: confidence, confiding and acts of meaning in the first year' in A. Lock (ed.) *Action, gesture and symbol*, London, Academic Press, pp. 183-229.

Waterson, N. and C. Snow (eds) (1978), *The development of communication*, New York, Wiley.

Wells, Gordon *et al.* (1978), 'Discourse and the development of language'. Paper given at 4th International Congress of Applied Linguistics, Montreal.

Werner, Heinz and B. Kaplan (1963), *Symbol formation*, New York, Wiley.

Index

antecedents of informative function 133-6 (*see also* personal/interactional continuum)
interpersonal meaning 13, 24, 28, 32-4, 126, 169, 176, 251, 255
interrogative 14, 19, 43-4, 154, 169, 205-8 (*see also* MOOD)
interrogative, polar 205-7, 228, 259-61
interrogative, Wh 169, 187, 207-8, 216
intersubjective approach 38, 48-51
intonation 10, 40, 49, 131 (*see also* tone)

Jacob 97, 131 (*see also* Menn, L.)
jokes 135

labelling *see* classificatory utterance
Labov, W. and Labov, T. 43-4
learning 82, 84, 117, 120-2, 127; through pragmatic function 152; 155
lexical classes 110-11, 137-8, 160-1
LEXICAL COHESION 24
lexical increase 121, 132, 253
lexicogrammar 16, 20, 24, 27, 32-6 (*see also* strata, linguistic)
lexis 9, 29, 36, 156 (*see also* first words)
Location 183, 189, 191, 228
logical structure 187

McNeill, D. 4, 6
McShane, I. 53, 94, 131-2
major/minor clause 204, 221-3, 226-7
Martin, J. R. M. 17, 22, 34
material process 22, 228-33
mathetic macrofunction 55, 84, 89, 91 evolution of 114-23, 127-32 evidence from other studies 129-32, 134 in single-word strings 145, 147-50, 166, 169, 171, 173, 180-95
mathetic/pragmatic dichotomy 155-61, 167-8, 170, 172-3, 203, 208-10, 247, 251-4
mean length of utterance 5, 29, 31
meaning 21 of Subject 25, 30, 31-2, 34, 39, 49
Medium 145, 175-7, 178, 183-6, 230, 232-3

Menn, L. 95, 97, 131
mental process 175, 183, 215, 239
meronymy 138, 186, 208
metafunction 24-5, 30-1, 32-4, 47 compared with macrofunction 127-9; 132, 232-3, 253-4 (*see also* experiential; interpersonal; textual)
microfunction *see* function, protolinguistic
middle clause 22, 230, 239
modality 6, 10, 24, 130, 253
mode 27-8, 31-3, 46, 217
Modifier 8, 156, 161, 187, 191, 200
monologue 142
MOOD 13, 15, 20, 21, 23, 24, 28, 31, 33-4, 126, 169-71, 187, 204-8, 214-23, 225, 232, 254
motivation for child to learn mother tongue 133
motivation of categories 17-18, 21, 44, 48, 52, 122-3, 156, 165, 182
multiple determination of clause functions 23, 24-5

names, naming 9, 10, 47, 54, 63-4, 75, 82, 83-4, 88, 94-6, 102-3, 110, 137 request 138
narrative 31, 145, 222, 253
naturalistic study 41-2
negative 97, 103, 106-7, 123, 142, 169, 174 first mathetic 186, 205, 214, 239, 254-8
Newson, J. 38, 49
Nigel 1, 48, 50, 55, 89 comparison with Hal's protolanguage 90-91 move to Phase II 129-31, 133, 163, 187, 251-4
nominal group 156-7, 166, 173, 174, 187-9, 200-2
non-arbitrary grammar 23-4
non-bi-uniqueness of form and function 161
nonverbal cues 40
nonverbal request 138
nonverbal responses 57, 59, 64, 74